WITHDRAWN

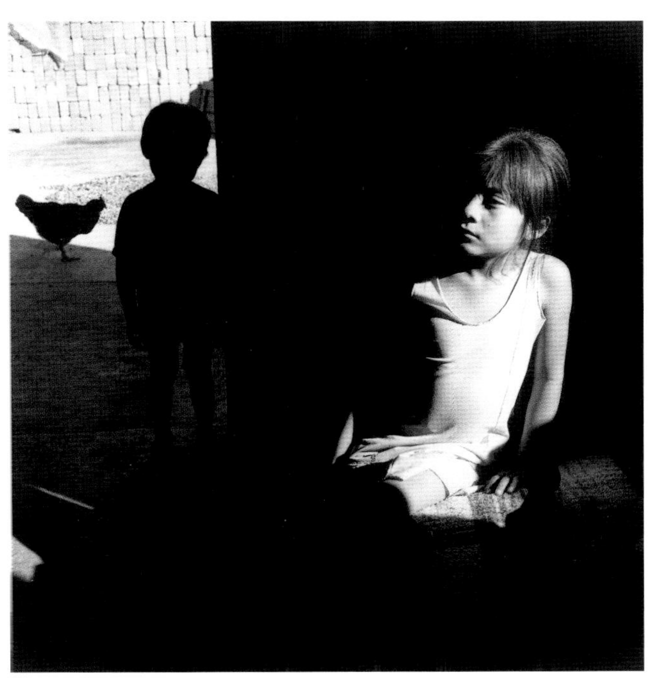

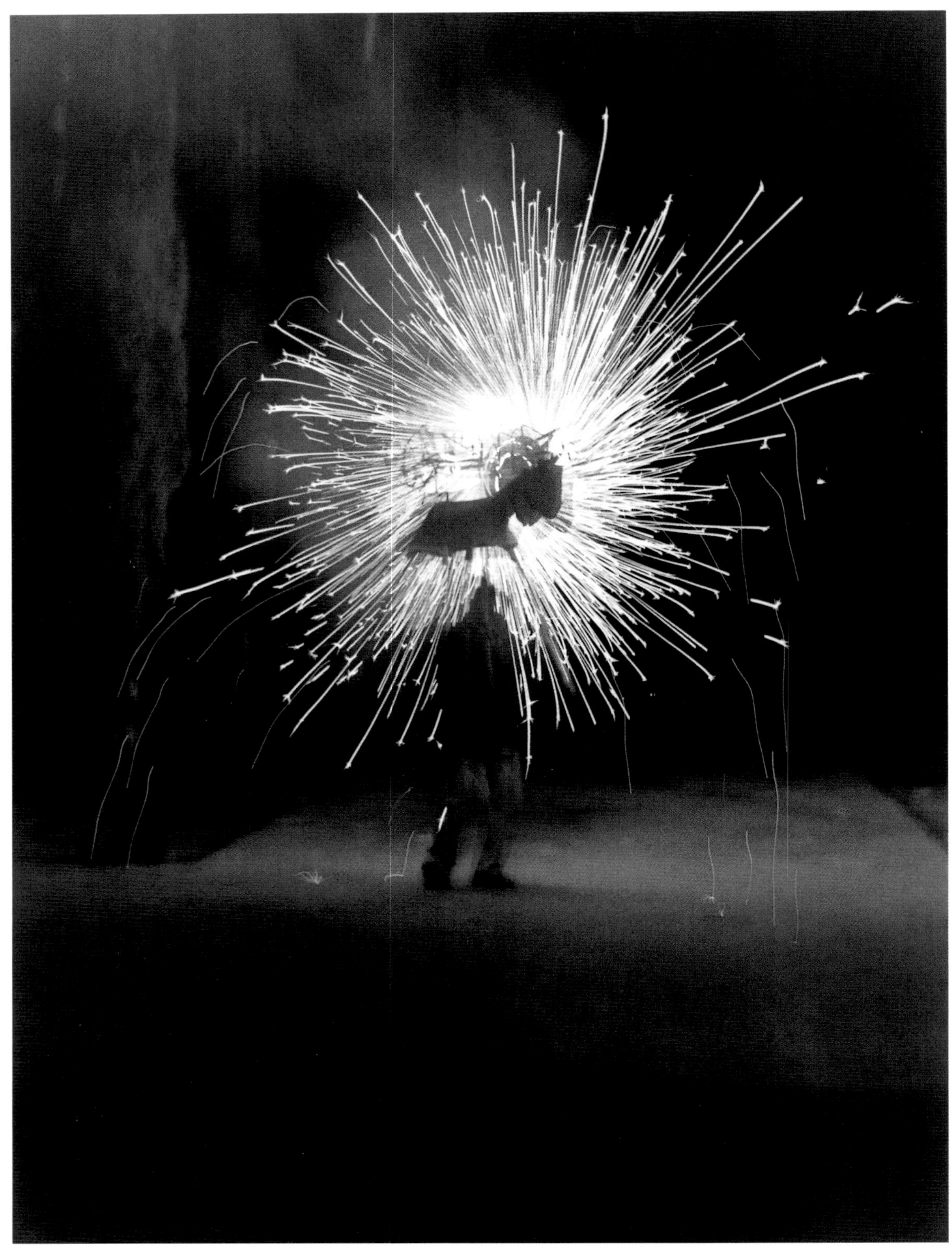

ChangingDreams

A Generation of Oaxaca's Woodcarvers

Photographs by Vicki Ragan
Text by Shepard Barbash

Museum of New Mexico Press
Santa Fe

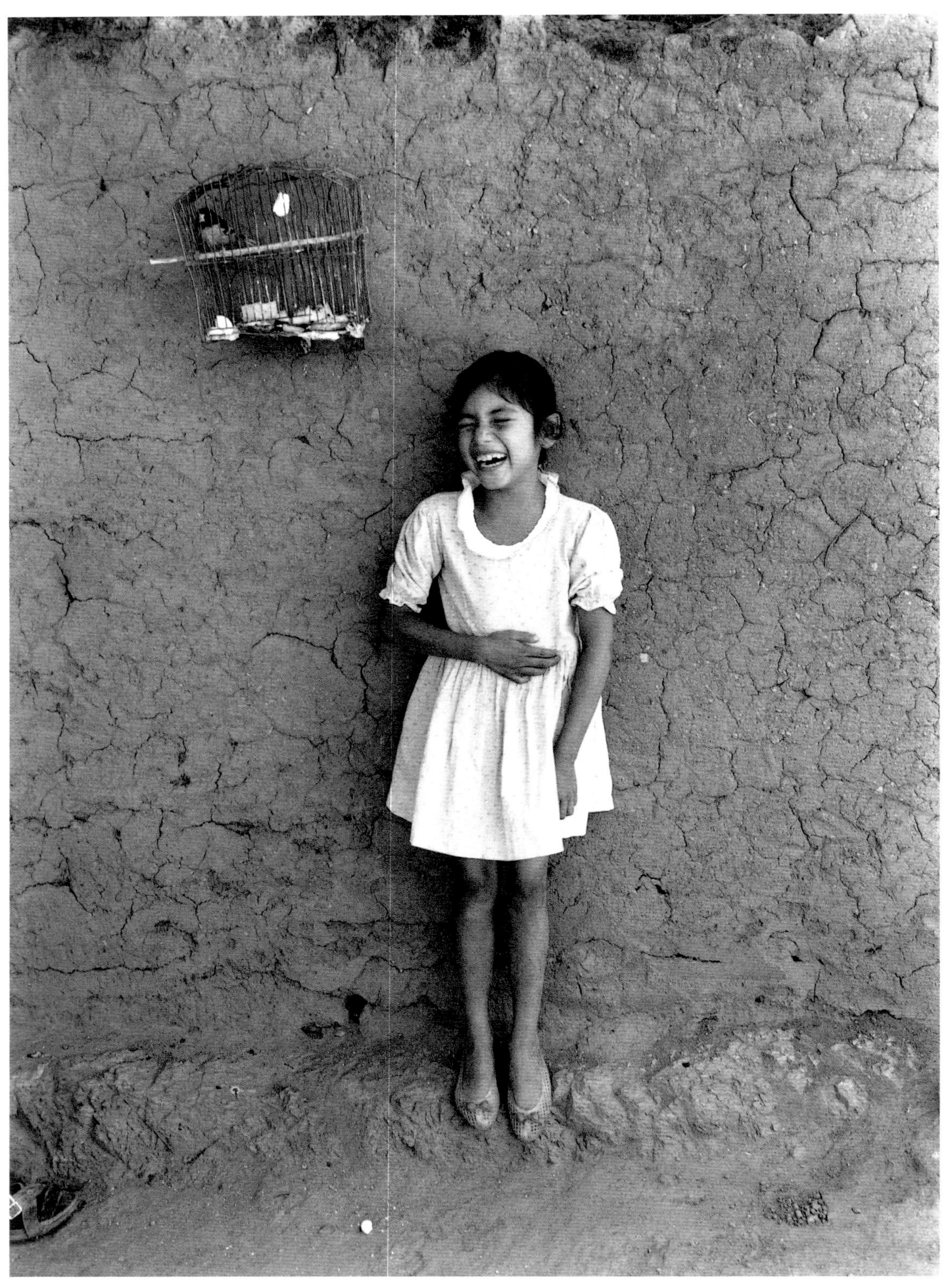

Preface

THIS BOOK IS THE PRODUCT OF OUR OWN CHANGING DREAMS. In the spring of 1986, after five years in Manhattan, I decided I wanted to be a foreign correspondent in China. My wife, Vicki, agreed on the condition that we go someplace less daunting, so on Halloween we loaded up the car and set out for Mexico City. For the next year I freelanced where I could, mostly for the financial press, before landing a dream job with the *Houston Chronicle*.

I lasted about a year. Daily journalism, even when it isn't pretending to cover entire countries, is a game for faster minds than mine, where energy spent on spouses, children, and life's other dreams is best kept to a minimum. By February 1989, when our son, Eddie, was born, we wanted to get out of the capital, a smoggy, congested city, and I wanted to get out of journalism and write a book. At Vicki's suggestion, we moved to Oaxaca, our favorite place in Mexico, and did a book on the valley's woodcarvers. After that, in late 1990, we changed dreams again and moved to Atlanta.

Oaxacan Wood Carving: The Magic in the Trees took us two years to research, during which we each got hepatitis, Eddie got amoebas and paratyphoid fever, and our beloved young terrier died of parvo. So I can't say I was thrilled when Vicki decided out of the blue a few years ago that it was time to move back to Oaxaca and do the sequel. I thought she was nuts. Weren't we getting a little old for that sort of thing? Had I not written every last word there was to write about the carvers? But in the end, vanity and restlessness prevailed over my fears, and in September 2004, we returned for a three-month visit to take up an old thread and reconnect with our friends. We have been back every year since.

Changing Dreams began as a series of diptychs, each comprising portraits of the same subject taken fifteen years apart. Anchored by the photos, the text came later. Vicki did not follow my pen; I followed her eye. We work better that way. Neither of us likes photo illustrations. Why take a picture if it can't stand alone?

The carvers made it easy for us—welcoming us back with the same smiles, soda pop, and chairs drawn hastily into semicircles as if we'd never left; digging out their photo albums to show us snapshots of ourselves in younger days; helping us to identify and track down the children in Vicki's old portraits, now grown to adults. And of course sharing their dreams and stories. A generation of change hadn't altered their readiness to answer my questions for hours on end. Only a fool could come up empty on such an assignment.

I was also lucky that the most lucid, fair-minded source in Oaxaca, the city's former mayor, Alfonso "Poncho" Gómez Sandoval, was serving his city well while I was doing my research there. Like the carvers, Poncho and his wife, Nancy Mayagoitia—who have since moved to Mexico City—gave us so much of their time that we quite naturally became friends.

Readers of *Oaxacan Woodcarving* may know that we thanked Henry Wangeman and Davis Mather for their help on that book. Henry, who runs Amate Books, the best bookstore in Oaxaca, has informed the spirit of *Changing Dreams* as well. Davis, who has been going to Oaxaca far longer and knows it much better than we do, lifted our spirits when we were gloomy and hooked us up with every person he could think of—including our wonderful agent, Joanna Hurley, who found us an equally wonderful publisher just when we thought there weren't any.

Without merchants, there would be no carving tradition in Oaxaca. Jerry Boyd, who sells more carvings than anyone, and Rosa Blum, Henry's wife, who loves the carvers more than anyone, were generous with their information about who was doing what in the market. Collector Gary McClure and dealer John Murray shared their favorites. Friends helped move the project forward in various ways. Photographer Graciela Iturbide was an early inspiration and guide. In the midst of Oaxaca's political troubles, the U.S. consul there, Mark Leyes, found time to make the chaos less inscrutable. Many thanks to Susan Evans of Design Per Se; Linda Craighead, director of the Palo Alto Art Center; poet Blake Leland; author Christine Mather; designer Robert Rostick; and printer Teresa Engle.

Of course the talented crew at Museum of New Mexico Press gave us their all. Editor Mary Wachs saw the big picture, designer David Skolkin helped give it form, and Karla Eoff, my copyeditor, did her best to make me look good and keep me from embarrassing myself.

Finally, our son, Eddie, who insists his parents can no longer embarrass him, deserves a gold star for enduring our wanderlust and for braving the lonely months cooped up with us, far away from his friends, in a land where you can't drink the water. He has always made parenting easy—easier than writing books.

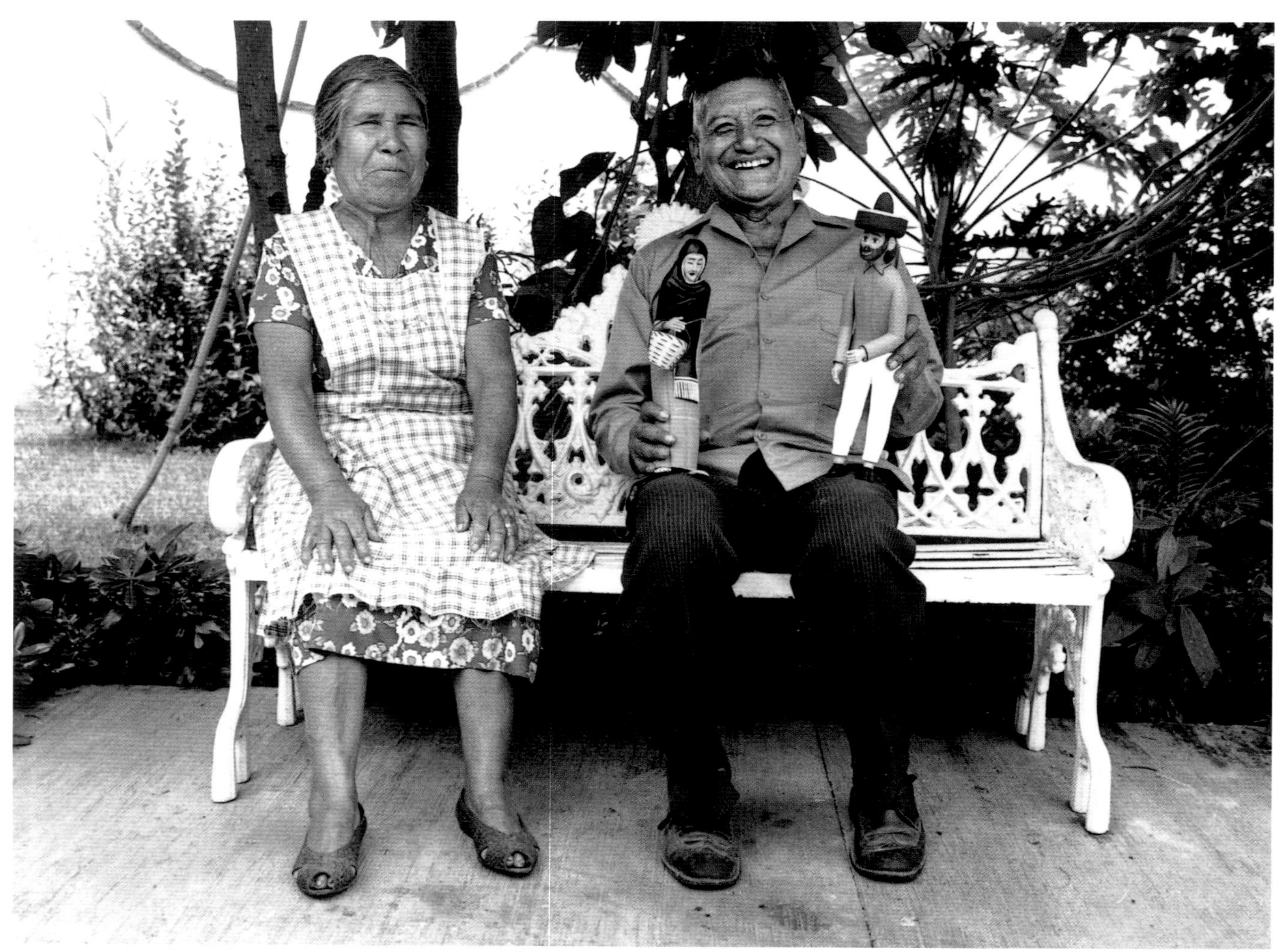

Manuel Jiménez and his wife, Viviana Hernández. Arrazola. 1989.

Introduction

Prologue

A THOUSAND MILES SOUTH OF THE BORDER—and north of it, too—the woodcarvers of Oaxaca are pursuing the American dream. From their dusty villages in the desert sun to the orchards of Oregon and kitchens of Chicago, the carvers have joined millions of Mexicans who, unable to find good work at home, are pulling their country unevenly toward prosperity by making a space for themselves in the United States.

The carvers work for Americans. They make whimsical figures for tourists and merchants who come to their homes. When that fails, they sneak off to the States to do all the less glamorous things Americans feel ambivalent letting them do. They are the embodiment of bilateralism, a fancy term to denote divided souls. When at home they are part of what the guidebooks say makes Mexico exotic. Indeed their omnipresent, brightly colored craft has come to symbolize Oaxaca, a scenic valley rich with pageantry, music, and handmade wonders. The very names of their villages—Arrazola, San Martín Tilcajete, La Unión Tejalapan—add to that magical strangeness tourists love. Once across the border, the carvers seem decidedly less exotic but no less foreign to their new neighbors and employers.

But the truth is, the carvers are becoming more like Americans. A taste of wealth and liberty has inflamed their ambitions, estranging them from their wearisome state even as more Americans fall in love with its charms. As attractions in a tourist town and emigrants fleeing its limits, they have found more roads to happiness and more unmet desires along the way. They are dreamers: artisans and aliens who cling to their fiestas but who wish they could work at something else.

Prices of the carvings have soared in recent years even as supply has risen, a sign that the carvers have grown more assertive and aware of America's wealth but are still unaware how markets work. In some ways they haven't changed at all. They remain remarkably creative and eager to please. What the high prices reflect and what this book hopes to convey are the growing aspirations and changing dreams of a people struggling to catch up without leaving too much behind, whose creations we enjoy but whose lives we barely understand even as they move closer to our own.

More of Everything

To have grown up in Oaxaca's artisan villages near the end of the millennium is to have had one's expectations destroyed and replaced with new ones. This is perhaps true of growing up anywhere. Expectations are like the horizon, inescapable and unreachable, changing with every movement. But the forces besieging Oaxaca's solitude seem especially unsettling and hard to predict.

Not long ago, before picture-taking cell phones and the Internet, a visitor walking through the carving villages of Arrazola and San Martín Tilcajete could still find campesinos whose days and nights were tyrannized by the most elementary, isolating chores of survival. Most families grew their own food, built their own shelter, and fought the diseases they died of on their own. They lived in one-room huts with leaking roofs. They had no plumbing or telephones. They traveled little. Cars were unaffordable and bus service infrequent. Even the most prosperous artisans seemed cut off and lonely on the days when tourists weren't around. Public gathering spaces—central squares, soccer fields, basketball courts—were few and underused. Fiestas brought neighbors together, but ceremoniously. Living the same hard life, people had little to say and said little. Solitude and bad government cut off prospects and smothered ambition. The prevailing expectation in these "traditional societies" (as changeless rural poverty is sometimes quaintly called) was that the future would not be much different from the past.

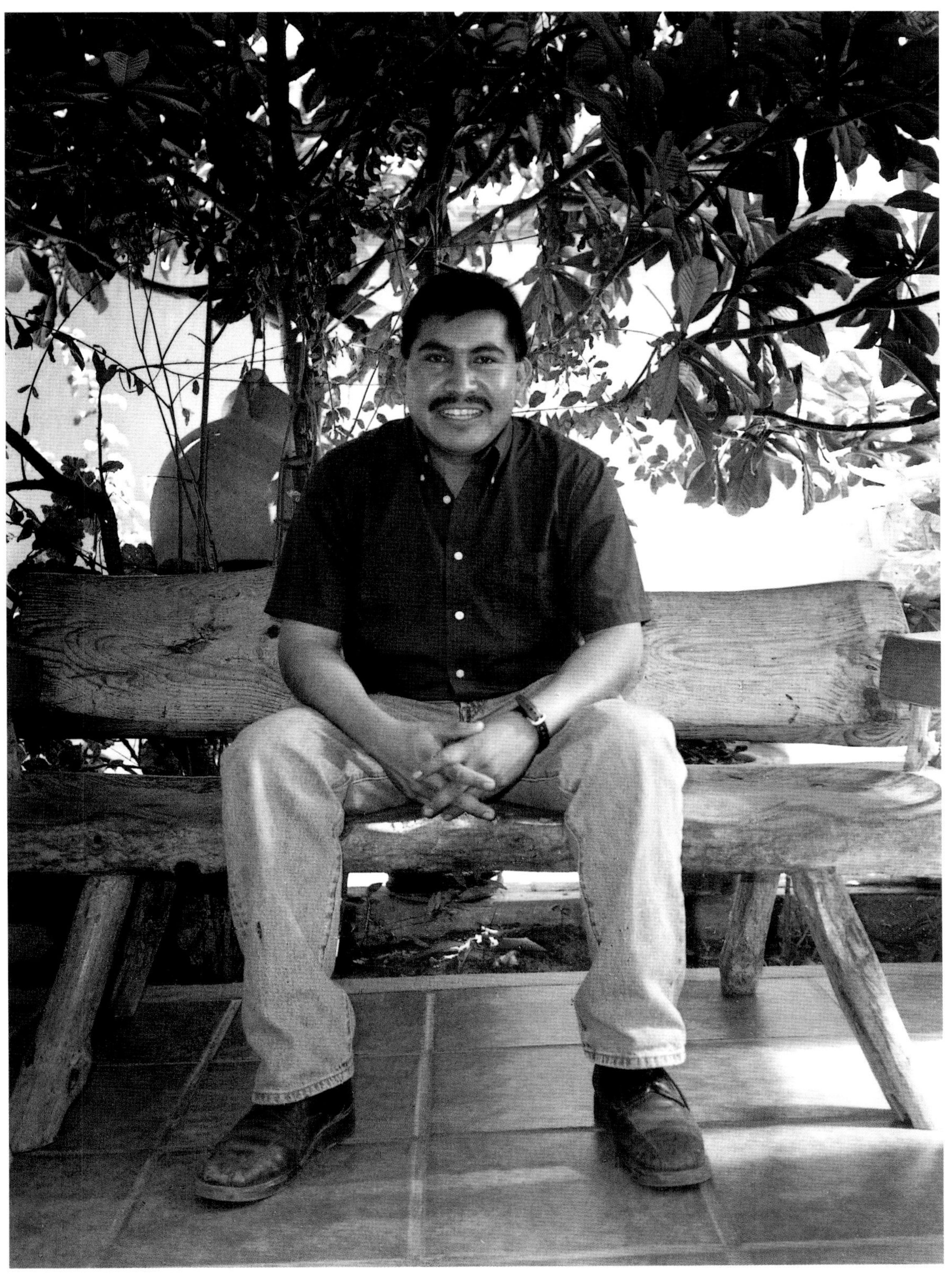

Jacobo Ángeles. San Martín Tilcajete. 2006.

A changing world would have it otherwise. Money has been the great accelerator of change in the Oaxaca valley: money from the state, money from the tourist industry, and money from the *mojado*, the illegal worker in the States.

After monopolizing public spending for decades, in the 1990s the federal government in Mexico City began to give municipalities funds with which to manage more of their own affairs. Villages that had long subsisted on voluntarism and bartering now are expected to create their own budgets, pay salaries, collect taxes, and deliver a range of services. This they have struggled to do, but the money has bought the carving villages some basic things, such as health clinics, running water, and junior high schools. Other federal programs are giving cash and food directly to the elderly and the poor.

The state has also spent more to improve roads, public transit, and telecommunications. Nearly everyone in San Martín and Arrazola now has a phone and a listed number. Taxi and bus service to and from both villages is frequent and affordable. The drive to the tiny carving village of La Unión Tejalapan, which used to take an hour over dirt roads and riverbeds (impassable during the rainy season), now takes twenty minutes, on pavement the whole way. The drive to Oaxaca from Mexico City now takes five hours instead of ten.

Buoyed by their government's spending and money from abroad, the carving villages have grown steadily wealthier. Most of the artisans have replaced their adobe and bamboo huts with four-room houses of concrete and brick. Many now have cars. Settlement patterns resemble what one saw a generation ago in U.S. cities, as young families move up into the hills or out to the edge of town. Subsistence farming is disappearing as more villagers commute to Oaxaca or leave the state entirely for better jobs, and as more land gets taken over by housing.

Horizons are expanding in other ways as well. More youths attend high school and college in Oaxaca. More women are working outside the home. Friendship and courtship are less restricted. More girls and women now ride bicycles—a big boost to their mobility—because more of them now wear pants. Many of the streets they pedal on are newly paved. Contact with other villages is routine, and marrying "outside the village" is no longer uncommon. (There are even some Gringo spouses.) Family planning and prenatal care have improved.

Signs of social capital—a by-product of plain old capital—are everywhere. Public squares have been beautified with plantings and gazebos, and are in constant use. In San Martín, the village church, built in the eighteenth century and damaged by earthquakes, has been restored. A hardy band of women sells figures in the zócalo, which has been covered, and a small market sets up there on weekends. In the fall of 2005, the municipal authority sponsored its first-ever carving competition, with cash prizes, and spent a small fortune to put up a huge road sign at the entrance to the village advertising its status as a carving town. Old people assemble in the zócalo on Seniors Day to have their blood pressure checked and get screened for diabetes. Young people gather at taco stands or browse the stalls that sell pirated DVDs on weekends. Arrazola has an Internet café.

It is hard to imagine more sweeping prosperity descending upon a society in less time. Oaxaca may be falling behind the rest of Mexico economically, and Mexico behind the United States, but the changes in the carving villages seem no less great for that laggardness to the campesinos living through them.

Modernity has meant more of everything: more people moving to the capital, more cars on the roads (twice as many since 1990), more political competition (Mexico's system of one-party rule ended in 2000), more religious competition (three Protestant sects have opened new churches within a three-mile radius of one another inside the city). NAFTA has brought more trade and investment (McDonald's and Sam's Club have arrived). Government subsidies to mechanize agriculture have increased crop yields (San Martín had one tractor in 1990, now it has ten). Electoral reform has brought more money into campaigns and more corruption into government. (Radio station owners manipulated their control of airtime a few years ago to help elect one of their own as mayor of Oaxaca.) There is more freedom of expression and more concern for human rights (the state's new human rights commission receives thousands of complaints every year). There are more political protests throughout the state because the state's municipalities now have more money and power and the nation has more parties strong enough to compete for them. More planes are bringing in more visitors from more places (Continental now flies direct between Oaxaca and Houston). More pyramids have been unearthed at the ruins of Monte Albán outside the city. More foreigners live in the city (including four thousand Americans). There are more hotels and good restaurants, more movie theaters and museums, more concerts in the zócalo, more craft shops all over. There is more smog and sprawl and graffiti. There may be more drug trafficking. There are definitely more fiestas.

There is more life: average life expectancy in the state has increased from forty years in 1950 to seventy-two years in 2000.

More cash is circulating in the economy, although because most of it is outside the banking system and beyond the reach of the state, no one knows how much more. The thousands of artisans for which Oaxaca is famous—carvers, ceramists, rug weavers, blouse embroiderers, fireworks makers, tinsmiths, and so on—may as well not exist as far as the Finance Ministry is concerned. Like most Oaxacans, they generally report no income, pay no taxes, and receive no social security. Like most Oaxacans, they are also actors in the most dynamic part of the state's economy—ungovernable, immeasurable, and everywhere visible.

Fifty Years of Novelty

Commerce, that implacable engine of change, gave birth to Oaxaca's wood-carving tradition fifty years ago, and commerce has changed almost everything about it, including its name. In 1957 a peasant from Arrazola walked ten miles into the city of Oaxaca with a sack of carved tree branches and found an American curio merchant willing to take his wares for cash up front. The merchant, Arthur Train, ran a small curio shop that catered to both souvenir-hunting tourists and serious collectors like Nelson Rockefeller and Alexander Girard. The campesino Manuel Jiménez had struggled for years through a series of jobs and had only recently begun to carve. Train, who deserves great credit for promoting artisans whose poverty and isolation might otherwise have left their talents stillborn, saw in Jiménez's figures an expressiveness that set them apart from the small handmade toys of the day. As he did for many others, Train launched Jiménez on a career that brought him world renown as a folk artist, wealth on a scale astonishing to his village, and a measure of immortality for having, as Jiménez put it, "robbed my destiny" and invented a tradition. "Jiménez will never die," Manuel liked to say.

By the time Jiménez did die, in March of 2005, the craft he had started and tried so hard to hide from his neighbors had spread to a hundred other families in Arrazola and to half a dozen other villages in the Oaxaca valley and the mountains beyond. Hundreds of merchants in Oaxaca and around the world have succeeded Train, building an audience for the carvings that has grown bigger than even Rockefeller (who bought his folk art by the jet-load) might have imagined. Carvers have become merchants themselves, buying sacks of unpainted figures from neighbors and villages not on the tourist path and painting and reselling them to their clients in Oaxaca and abroad.

Whether through carelessness or careful marketing, the figures have acquired a more exotic name. They are now commonly referred to as *alebrijes*, a made-up word originally used to describe a class of antenna-filled monsters made by a papier-mâché artist in Mexico City, Pedro Linares, who coined the term. The creatures made their way into the carvers' oeuvre in the late 1980s courtesy of a Oaxacan folk-art dealer who was looking to extend his product line, much the way Train extended his by asking Jiménez to carve devils or the Three Kings.

With the death of Jiménez, the *alebrijes* also have a new generation of standard-bearers more reflective of the times. Unlike Jiménez, who worked alone, disdained other carvers, and traveled reluctantly, the most ambitious and successful carver of recent years, Jacobo Ángeles of San Martín, employs twenty people in his workshop (including fourteen nephews and nieces who paint figures and three aunts who sand them), buys carvings from more than eighty families in six villages, and leads a hectic bilateral life. An emblem of the region's changing mores, Jacobo manages everything in partnership with his wife, María, who shares top billing on their business card. The couple have built the nicest home in San Martín and filled it with Mexican art. They have also opened the town's first restaurant and crafts gallery, where they sell Oaxacan cuisine made by Jacobo's aunt and figures made by their fellow villagers.

"My dream is to make San Martín known around the world for carvings the way Teotitlán is known for rugs," Jacobo says, referring to the most famous and wealthiest of Oaxaca's many crafts villages.

He gets plenty of help from the competition. Directly across from the restaurant, Jacobo's ponytailed, English-speaking rival, Zenén "Zeny" Fuentes, keeps up a busy

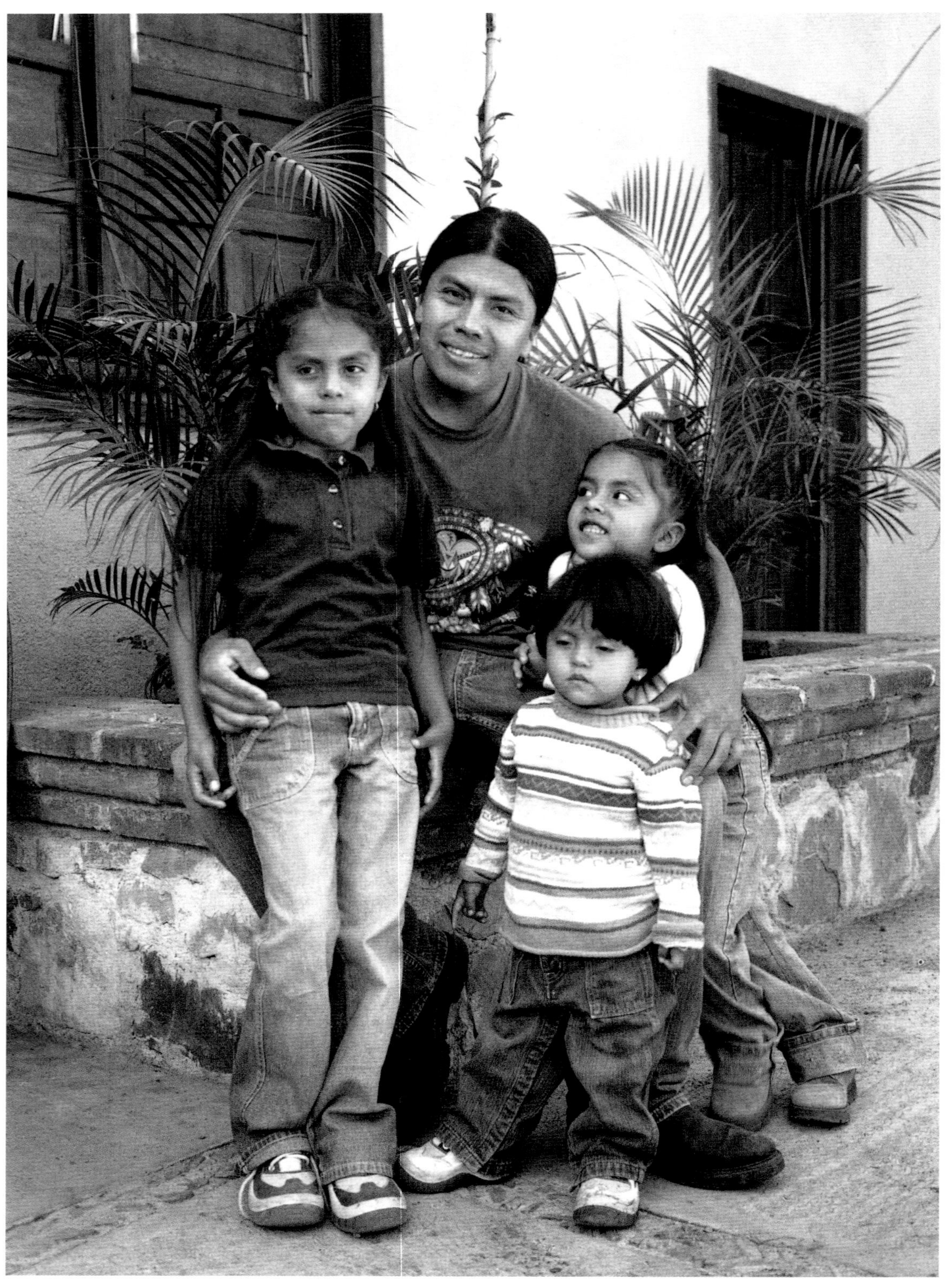

Zenén Fuentes Jr. San Martín. 2006.

transnational schedule catering to the multicultural tastes of the billion-dollar U.S. education industry. The oldest of nine siblings and father of four, Zeny sells carvings and does "hands-on" workshops for school districts and universities coast to coast through CRIZMAC Art and Cultural Education Materials, a small private company based in Tucson, Arizona. If schoolchildren who don't know their U.S. presidents know anything about Oaxacan wood carving, chances are they learned it through him. "I once taught sixty art professors and nine hundred art teachers at a conference in Battle Creek, Michigan," Zeny says proudly.

CRIZMAC also offers a fifteen-minute video, *Oaxacan Woodcarving: Innovation Meets Tradition* ($39.95 with teacher's guide, suitable for grades four through twelve), and sells a representative sampling of Zeny's work online, including the Elegant Elephant ("great for the classroom or your own personal collection"), the Happy Hippopotamus ("you'll fall in love . . . colors vary"), and the Howling Wolf ("wonderfully expressive . . . highly collectable!"). It's never been clear who innovates faster—the carvers or their marketers. What *is* clear is that Zeny has built two nice houses, one at the entrance to the village and the other high on a hilltop near where his grandfather and namesake used to farm.

Zenén Sr. also carves, but it was the old man's son Epifanio—Zeny Jr.'s dad—who first beat the path into the United States that made the family's fortunes possible. In 1980 Epifanio Fuentes was a wetback harvesting oranges in Corona, California. Ten years later, he was an esteemed visiting artist demonstrating his craft at the Heard Museum in Phoenix, Arizona. Ten years after that, he was a gracious host staging parties—with fireworks, dancing, and talks on Oaxacan culture—for U.S. tour groups bused to his home. He went from not knowing how to use a bathtub to designing a tiled bathroom of his own; from getting jailed as an illegal at the border to getting frequent-flyer miles for visiting his granddaughters in Miami; from helping his dad grow corn in the rain-fed Oaxacan countryside to watching his son teach teachers in the well-watered U.S. classroom. At this writing, he has a steady gig with the Education Outreach Program of Margaritas Mexican Restaurant and Watering Hole (locations in Connecticut, Massachusetts, New Hampshire, and Maine).

Epifanio was one of the first, but stories of farmhands in the desert turned guests of honor in the northern snow are not so rare. At least a dozen campesinos who lived in adobe huts in the 1980s have gone on to become big attractions boosting traffic at museums, schools, stores, and restaurants throughout the United States. These in turn comprise but a fraction of the carvers' presence in the U.S. market. A Google search of "Oaxacan wood carving" in 2006 yielded eighteen thousand hits. These included dozens of online stores; thirty carvings for sale on eBay; lesson plans posted by elementary-school teachers (presumably trained by Zeny); descriptions of past and future museum visits; a call for donations to support a "multifaceted media project" fostering cultural exchange between San Martín carvers and the children of Cambridge, Massachusetts; an offer to place volunteers to teach English to the carvers and help market their work; and much more. Online shoppers could buy unsigned "aliens" for $22.95; a foot-high, sax-playing cat painted by Epifanio's daughter Rubí, for $225; an exquisite Jacobo Ángeles beaver "with just the right touch of turquoise to give it pizzazz!" for $795; and hundreds of other carvings.

Arthur Train understood fifty years ago that novelty was good for sales, an eternal truth that explains why the carvers remain aesthetically rudderless—destined to crowd store shelves with strange and gaudy inventions, all screaming for attention. The carver who once thought it daring to carve Satan dancing with the Virgin of Guadalupe now makes crucified devils with erections. Manuel Jiménez applied his aniline paints with an old cloth; his heirs today shoot out their acrylic points with hypodermic needles (although some do use cactus spines). Dealers boast of figures with "thousands of hairs." If the carvers could charge a dime a dot, they would be millionaires.

Has commerce eaten its young and wrecked the art? The question has been asked, and answered in the affirmative, for at least thirty years. Dealers and collectors invariably date the carvers' "golden age" back to the year they first discovered them. Anthropologists as a rule have *never* liked the carvings, fretting that their success has crowded out other more indigenous and (in the scholars' view) meaningful expressions of rural society. Indeed to anyone leery of global capitalism—defined here as foreign salesmen making money off Mexican peasants and Mexican peasants making money (but not enough money) serving foreign tastes—the carvings and the forces that popularize them are not good things, and the people who make (and buy) *alebrijes* should be doing something better.

But, alas, some of us just can't help ourselves. My wife and I own more than three hundred carvings from Oaxaca, purchased over three decades. Before one of our last trips there, we vowed not to buy any more. By the end of the week, we had purchased the following:

2 sets of wedding couples, by Ventura Fabián

1 pregnant nun, by Avelino Pérez

1 devil musician trio (sax, guitar, upright bass), by Eloy Santiago

1 green-headed bird clarinetist, by Antonio Fabián

1 gray skeleton with pink-dyed, cactus-fiber hair, by Blanca Cruz

1 screaming head, unpainted, by Isidoro Cruz (Blanca's dad)

1 Virgin of Guadalupe in floral dress, by María Jiménez

1 purple pig with flowers, by Arón Jiménez (María's brother)

1 striped cat balancing on a soccer ball, by Margarito Melchor

1 small white goat, by Ventura Fabián

1 skeleton napkin holder, black on purple, by Pablo Vásquez

1 eight-card poker hand (full house: twos over fours), by Inocencio Vásquez (Pablo's dad)

We saw a Virgin carved into an ear of corn that we really wanted, by Gabino Reyes of La Unión, but it was already sold, and my wife wanted a few miniatures from the Xuana family in San Martín, but we already have a lot of those so I talked her out of it. (We didn't even make it to the third carving village, Arrazola, where our collecting began.) Our favorite pieces of all, commissioned by a bookstore owner around the theme of books and reading, were fortunately not for sale. As it was, we filled an extra suitcase—all in all a normal trip. Some vows are not worth keeping.

Migrating Antonios

By far the greatest source of wealth in Oaxaca has been not the state's clumsy federalism nor the campesino's facile artistry but the U.S. economy's unending dynamism, which, like Zeus commanding from afar, has drawn millions of Mexicans away from their homes, communities, and country with dreams of prosperity. An estimated twenty million Mexicans now live in the United States, and these send tens of billions of dollars back to their families each year—more dollars than are spent or invested in Mexico by all the tourists and all the foreign companies combined. Repatriated earnings from illegal aliens have become the prime source of wealth not only for thousands of poor villages throughout Mexico but also for the handful of prosperous aberrations we inaptly call "carving villages"—as if wood carving and not the mass migration of men (and increasingly women) were really what mattered most in these places.

Faced with a glut of carvings on the market, declining sales abroad, and an unsteady supply of tourists at home, an increasing number of carvers have put aside their craft to become wetbacks (*mojados*, as they call themselves). Women in San Martín and La Unión estimate that 40 percent of their men are in the United States. "One more year" is a beloved's common refrain: he's staying one more year so we can finish the house, one more year so we can put the kids through school, one more year to pay the doctors, buy a car, start a business. Teenage boys will stay for months or years at a time (until past their teens), return home to enjoy a fiesta, build a house, find a bride—then go back to the States again, or not.

So many people from San Martín have settled in Santa Cruz, California, or make it their second home that businesses have sprung up in both places to cater to their bilateral lifestyle. Every month a woman from nearby San Pedro Guegorexe leaves Oaxaca with bundled orders of salted grasshoppers, mescal, *tasajo*, and other regional specialties, and returns like the Wells Fargo wagon with clothes, electronics, and other bargains from the States. Phone companies compete for the surging electronic traffic, as loved ones half a continent apart call each other on their cell phones—even as their aging fathers continue to herd goats and cattle, cut off from communication on the hills nearby.

There's no telling where a carver will wind up. In 1990 Antonio Aragón was living up the hill from Manuel Jiménez. He made lithe, delicate animals that were full of movement, tastefully painted by his wife, Beatríz, and reasonably priced. His five brothers also carved, but Antonio stood out. He was the first in his family to attract a steady U.S. patron and the first in Arrazola to be deployed as a foreign buyer's local agent, a delicate responsibility in a small village. The patron trusted him to handle large amounts of money in a cash-poor economy, and the other artisans trusted him as a go-between who would not copy and undersell them.

As a successful and sociable broker-artisan, Antonio seemed a counterpoint to the solitary Manuel Jiménez. Heir to the tradition Manuel started and an embodiment of its transformation, Antonio was featured in an anthropologist's study as the archetype for the commercially successful, export-focused, Third World artisan. Possessor of the two most valuable things such an artisan can have—a U.S. visa and a U.S. patron—he went to the States six times, bringing his copal tree branches with him and staying for as long as supplies lasted. Back home, he began building a house for his wife and four children.

But Antonio never commanded high prices for his carvings, nor did he build a broad following of dealers and collectors. He rose and fell with his patron. When the latter's sales dropped and Antonio's visa was not renewed—he was judged a risk because he didn't have a Mexican bank account—he got out of the carving business and drove a taxi. When that proved a bust, he went with his son to Hermosillo and (after three tries) sneaked into California. At the time of Jiménez's death, Antonio and his son were sorting materials in a recycling plant in Los Angeles. "He wants to spend one more year there so he can start a business when he comes home," Beatríz said at the time. He finally did come home two years later, on December 17, 2006, three weeks after riots convulsed the capital, prompting Beatríz to wonder whether he ought to have stayed away just a little bit longer.

In San Martín, Antonio Fabián resisted becoming a *mojado* for years. Even after 9/11, when tourism collapsed and his son, teenage daughter, and son-in-law—carvers all—gave up and headed north, he stayed home, built a new house with the dollars they earned, and persevered as a carver. Like Aragón and his son, Fabián's daughter Rosario and her husband got caught three times before making it across the border, at Agua Prieta. "Soon I will be laughing at you as you are laughing at me!" Rosi shouted at her captors. Ten days later, she was working as a waitress outside Chicago.

Teenage peasants in Chicago winters, thousands of miles from home! What can stop this flow of human millions into the States? Perhaps only a huge depression. For now, evidence of at least one employer's gratitude can be seen as far away as San Martín, where the Fabiáns have hung a plaque from Outback Steakhouse honoring

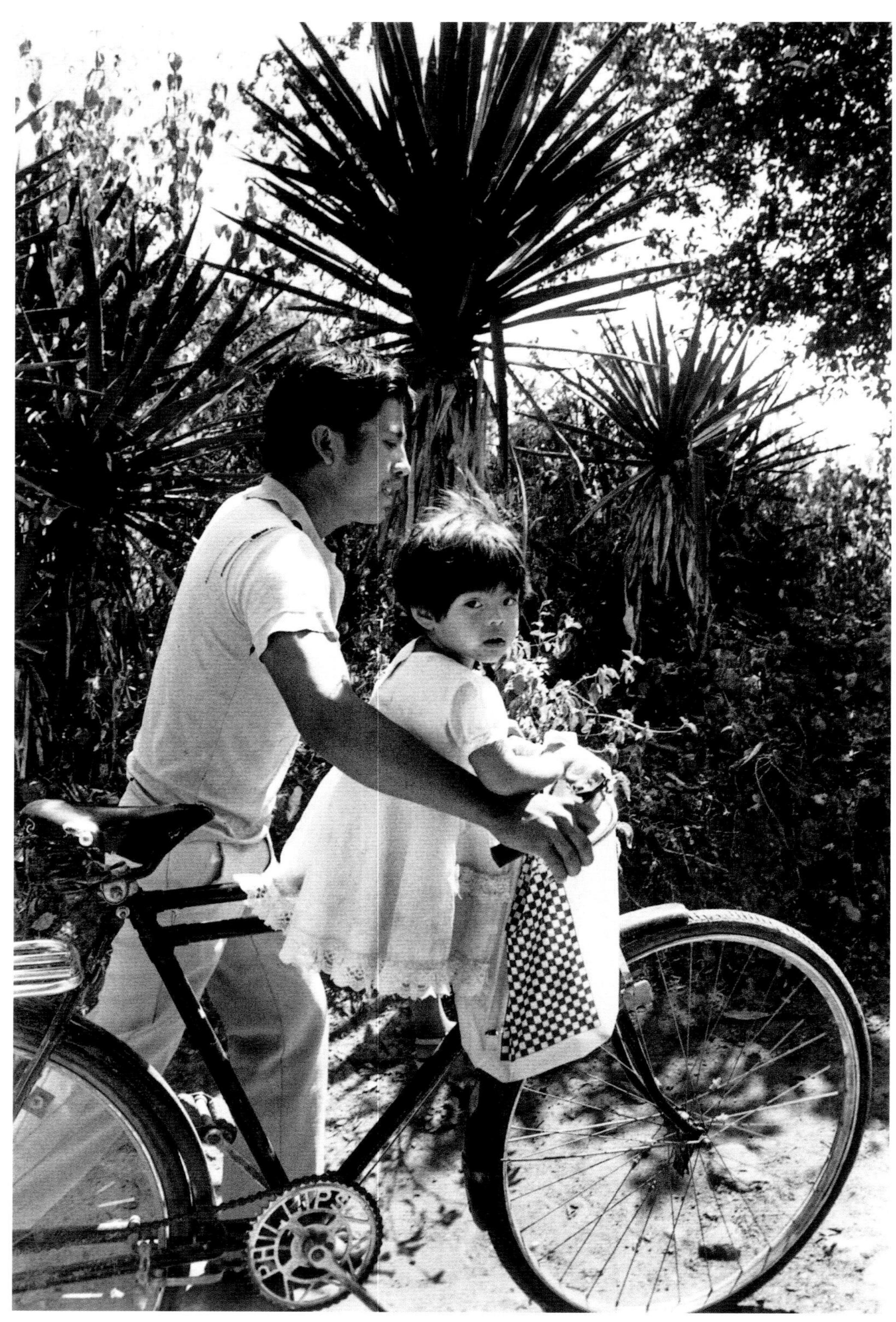

Antonio Fabián with daughter Rosario. San Martín. 1989.

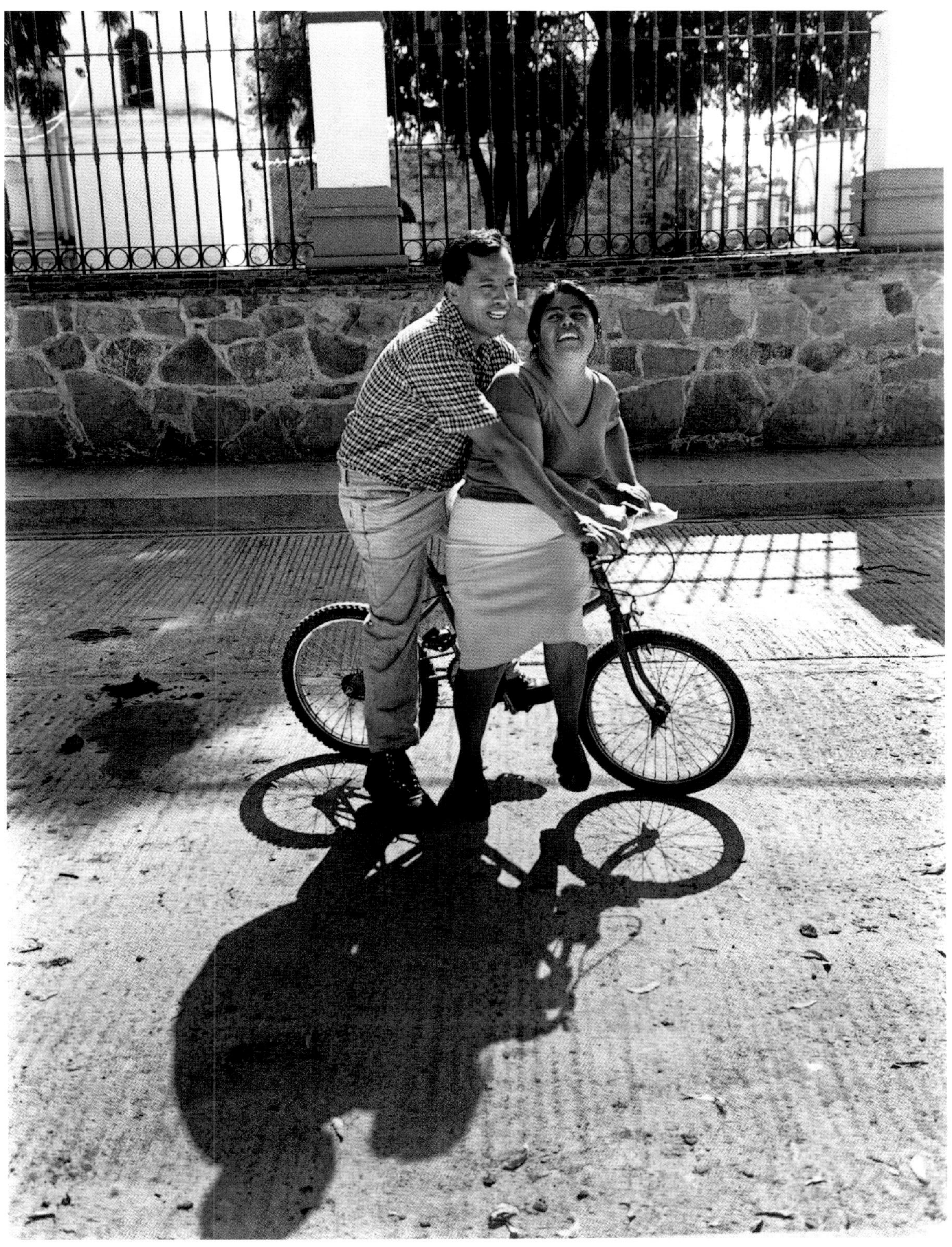

Antonio Fabián with wife, Emilia Calvo. San Martín. 2004.

their son, Eduardo, who earned $10 per hour as a cook and was named "Outback of the Month" for November 2002. Four years later, as of this writing, the Fabián household—the house that Outback built—is empty of men: worn down by the unrest in Oaxaca, which hurt carving sales badly, Antonio has joined his children in Chicago.

On a hill overlooking the Fabiáns, the house of still another "*mojado* Antonio" is under construction. Married at eighteen, the gifted carver Antonio Xuana took off for Santa Cruz sixteen years later, by which time he and his wife had produced thousands of carvings and four children but no home of their own. "The Mexican spends, he doesn't save," Antonio says, explaining himself. He crossed the Arizona desert in four days and stayed in Santa Cruz for two years. With five brothers-in-law and several hundred others from San Martín already there, he had no difficulty finding work and a place to live. A brother-in-law got him a job in construction—first pouring concrete, then doing roofing on a crew with three other Mexicans. He earned as much as $700 per week, twice what his *mojado* friends were making in restaurants, ten times what his dad, Abad, earns as one of the better carvers in San Martín, and more than twenty times the minimum wage in Mexico.

Xuana returned home with money to build his house and with lasting impressions of the differences between the two countries. He marvels at the efficiency of the U.S. economy and is mystified by Americans' purchasing power. How can it be that blue jeans and computers and televisions cost so much less in the States than in Mexico, even though American wages are so much higher? He contrasts the ease with which he put up houses in Santa Cruz with the tedium of building his own house in San Martín. "Here you mix the concrete, shovel it, cut it into blocks—everything by hand. There no—everything arrives already made. Here it took eight days to build the roof. There it takes me two."

Straddling the debate about immigration, he agrees that Mexicans contribute to the productivity he marvels at by working harder for less, but he also accepts as true the complaints Americans make against them: that they vandalize property crossing the border, drive without insurance, burden school systems and hospitals, and add to crime rates where they concentrate in large numbers.

"It's not ignorance, it's that the Mexican is *desmadroso*," he says, using a word that can be translated to mean either "fun-loving" or a "fuck-up" or, as in Antonio's case (so he describes himself), a little of both. "Americans want everything to be perfect," he says.

To hear the three Antonios and other *mojados* describe it, the most perfect part of Mexico's *desmadroso* economy is the ever-innovating system by which millions of Mexicans have managed to escape it. A vast network of smugglers, family, and friends—millions of them already in the States—has grown up over the years, offering to still more and younger millions a full menu of travel options, priced according to the prospects for risk and reward and the extent of amenities (meals, change of clothes, bus tickets) supplied along the way.

The journey, though perilous, gets easier with practice, partly because a *mojado* learns the ropes but also because, thanks to his first visit, he now has more money to finance the trip and more contacts in the States to secure it. Xuana's first trip, by auto and on foot, took him two weeks. His second, by plane to Tijuana and auto the rest of the way, took four days and included stops at the border and in a safe house in Los Angeles to bathe and eat. When we last saw him, he had returned from Santa Cruz the month before and was already contemplating a third trip (which he ultimately took). "I have friends in both places," he says.

Back Home

When a carver who has been a *mojado* returns home, he typically tries to make a go at carving again. He may have cooked steaks for Outback, pressed uniforms for the U.S. Army, cleaned stores for Macy's or dorm rooms for a university; picked lettuce in Nevada or strawberries in Oregon; worked for Salvadorans, South Koreans, or other Mexicans; laid down fine wood floors, washed cars, waited tables, cut grass—all things carvers tell us they've done. He may come home with a ponytail, wearing an earring, and cursing in English—that is the caricature Oaxacans have of him. But whatever he's done and whatever he's become, when he comes back to his village he sees few better options than to pick up his machete and resume his old craft for the Americans he left behind.

This he finds no easier to do than it was before he left. *Alebrije*-making by any name has always been a high-turnover, seasonal enterprise. Few merchants from the

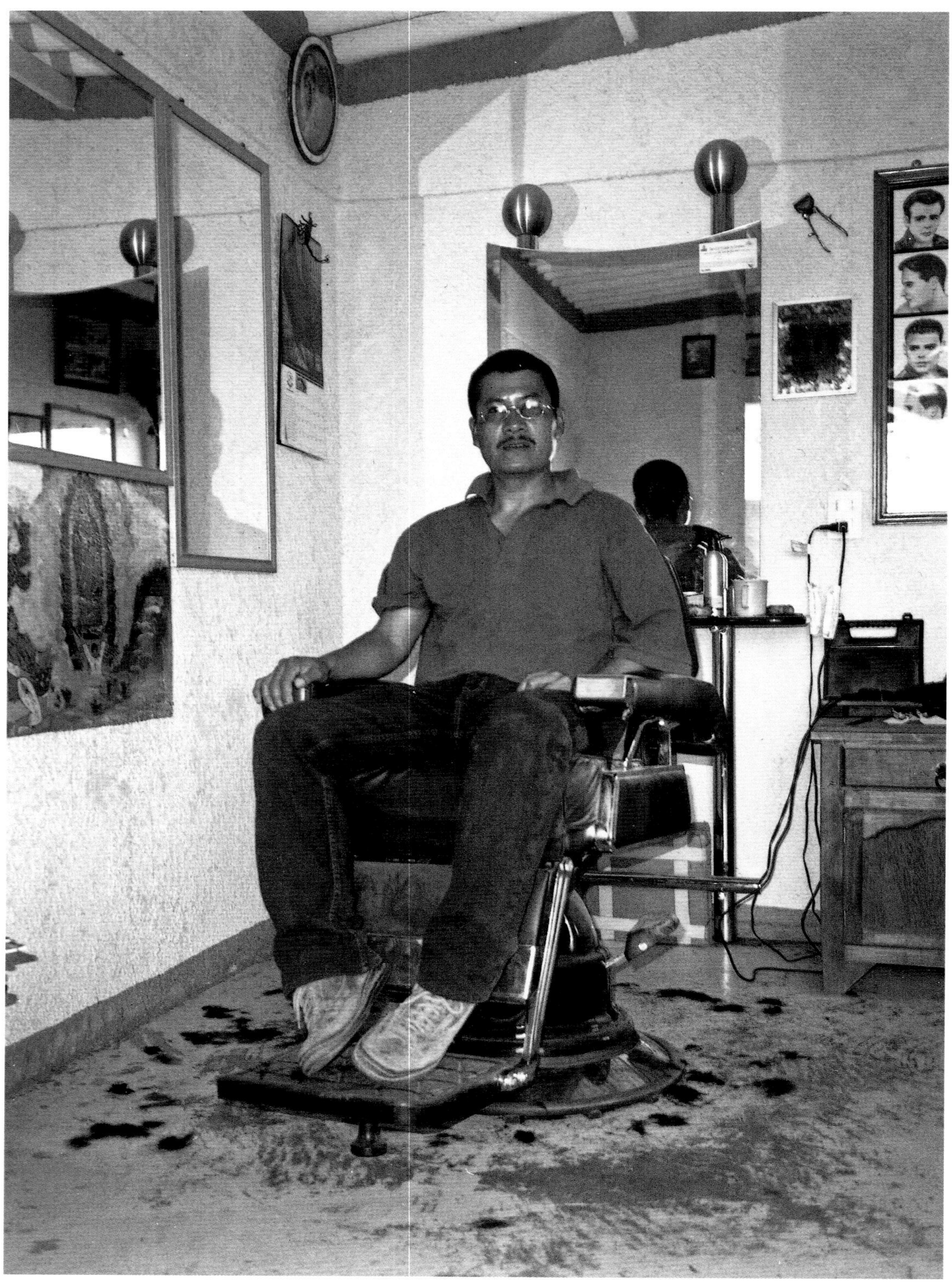

Miguel Santiago. Arrazola. 2006.

1980s still sell carvings, and more than a few carvers from that era—including roughly one of every four featured in *Oaxacan Wood Carving*, the book that supposedly helped them all so much—have moved on to other things. Most continue to patch their livelihoods together out of an ever-shifting combination of low-paying jobs in a slow-growing economy that remains dominated by tourism and the state. Epifanio Fuentes was an aberration from a poor place twenty years ago, and he is still an aberration today, even as the carvings he and others make have grown ubiquitous. Hundreds of figures gathering dust at 40 percent off in downtown Santa Fe testify eloquently to the misplaced hopes, dreams, and creative urges on both sides of the border.

Even carvers who have "robbed their destinies" are discovering that prosperity does not conquer restlessness, and that being an aberration carries a price.

Miguel Santiago, seventh of thirteen siblings and once among the most esteemed artisans in Oaxaca, admits to feeling down and distracted sometimes, even in his success. "It doesn't signify anything that you were in a book or museum—it doesn't fill the emptiness inside you," he says, sounding not very much like a campesino. He has started a rock band, tried his hand at painting and pottery, and opened a hair salon. A full-size bus for his band looms incongruously on the dirt road by his house. "You are seven offices and fourteen necessities," Manuel Jiménez once chided him, watching him cut Manuel's son's hair.

Which is worse—to be a slave to poverty or to one's aspirations, chained to a plow or to a phantom?

Manuela Melchor is the daughter of Martín Melchor, a campesino turned carver with political connections and a comedic touch. Manuela is studying to be a detective but dreams of becoming a historian. She would be the first in San Martín to become either. "I can't say whether children are happier now," she says. "Maybe before they were more tranquil. But they were also trapped."

As a young girl, Epifanio Fuentes's wife, Laurencia, used to thrill at the fuzzy sound of the loudspeaker announcing the movie that was to be shown that weekend (on a makeshift cloth screen) in the village church. Such were the highlights of a narrow childhood. Her daughters' favorite outing now is to browse the jewelry shops in Oaxaca.

"We *never* went to Oaxaca," Laurencia says. Girls were lucky if they went to school. So great is the change that not only may her daughters now go to school but they may decide *not* to and still have thriving careers. "They don't want to study, they want to be artisans like their dad," Laurencia says. And if their dreams should prove foolish and they come to regret their choice? "At least they were free to choose."

Worse for the restless than a mistaken dream is no dream at all. Or so the dreamer says.

ChangingDreams

Vicente García
La Unión Tejalapan

AFTER A DECADE TRAVELING BACK AND FORTH between Oaxaca and the Pacific Northwest, Vicente García has forgotten how to carve. Evidently it is no great loss. Like a lot of peasants who tried making a go of it as artisans, Vicente found that he could make more money as a *mojado*. He chose the Northwest because its tranquillity reminded him of home. He has made the trip four times (as of this writing). He finds work by going to stores that sell fresh produce. He harvests apples, strawberries, and mushrooms. When the season ends in March, he goes home to work his own land in La Unión—a journey of three thousand miles.

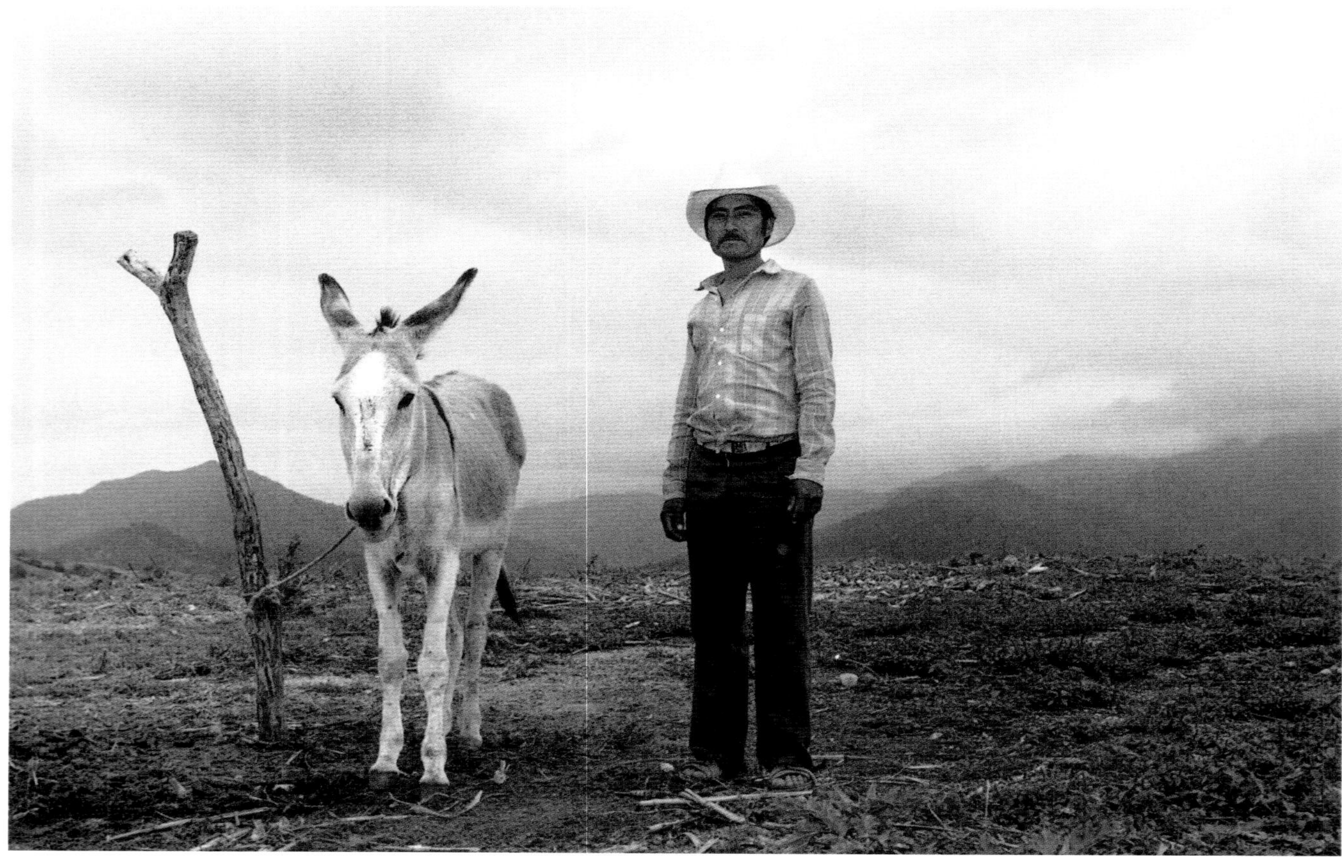

Vicente García. La Unión Tejalapan. 1989.

The life sounds bleak but it really isn't so bad. The García family is close and hopeful. Their goals are clear. Vicente works illegally in the States so that his daughter Almadelia won't have to. The wages he earns are putting her through college. Determined to break the chain of illiterate, innumerate ancestors, she is studying to be an accountant. She commutes by bus to Oaxaca and talks to her dad on her cell phone every weekend when he is away. Her big brother, Eduardo, stays home with the family while Vicente is gone and takes his place in the States when he returns. The family belongs to the Seventh-Day Adventist church, a fast-growing Protestant sect whose adherents are known in Mexico for their industry and upward mobility. They look out for Vicente when he's in the States, and the Catholics who predominate in Mexico let the Garcías worship in peace in the Adventists' new church back home.

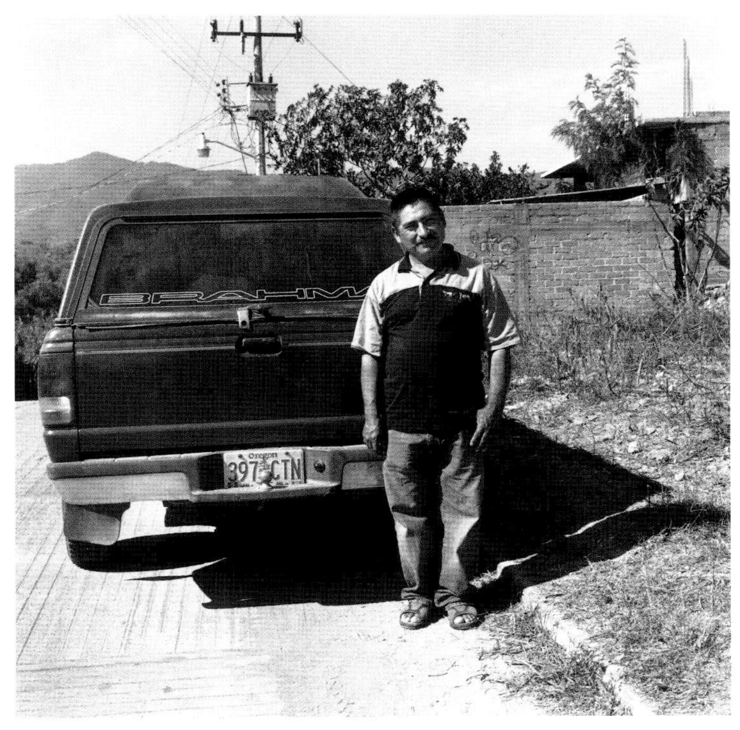

Vicente García. La Unión. 2006.

Life in Oaxaca as the Garcías are living it is progress in its most common form. The billions of dollars Mexicans send back to their families each year from the States is an extraordinary windfall that is being invested—out of reach of their meddlesome government—in as many ways as there are desires. The villagers today have more of almost everything—food, stoves, plumbing, cars—everything except the young men whose exodus has made the fulfillment of these desires possible. Accelerating changes, longer lives, absent men: such is the harvest of modernity in Oaxaca.

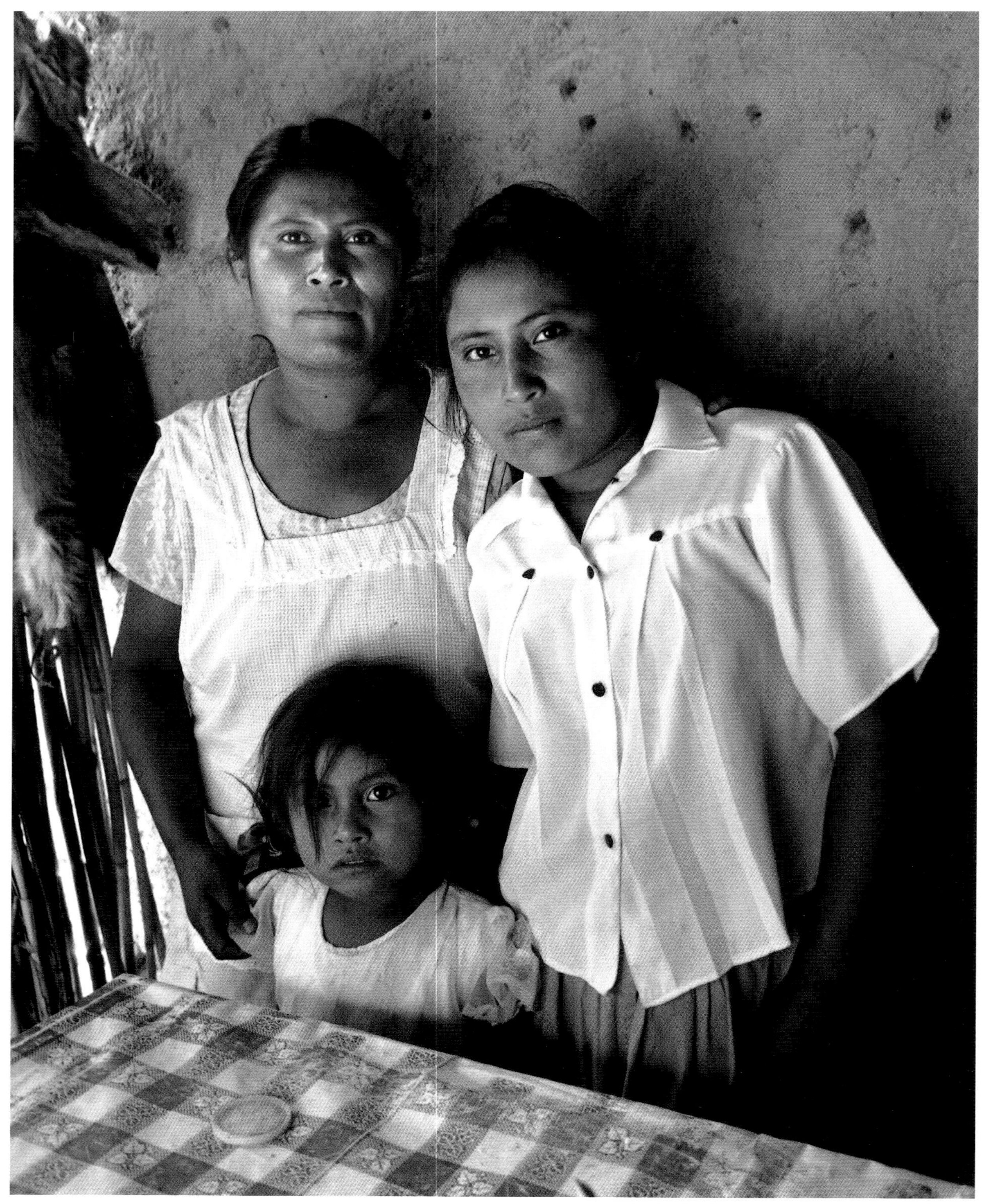

Vicente's wife, Soledad, with daughters Margarita (older) and Almadelia. La Unión, 1989.

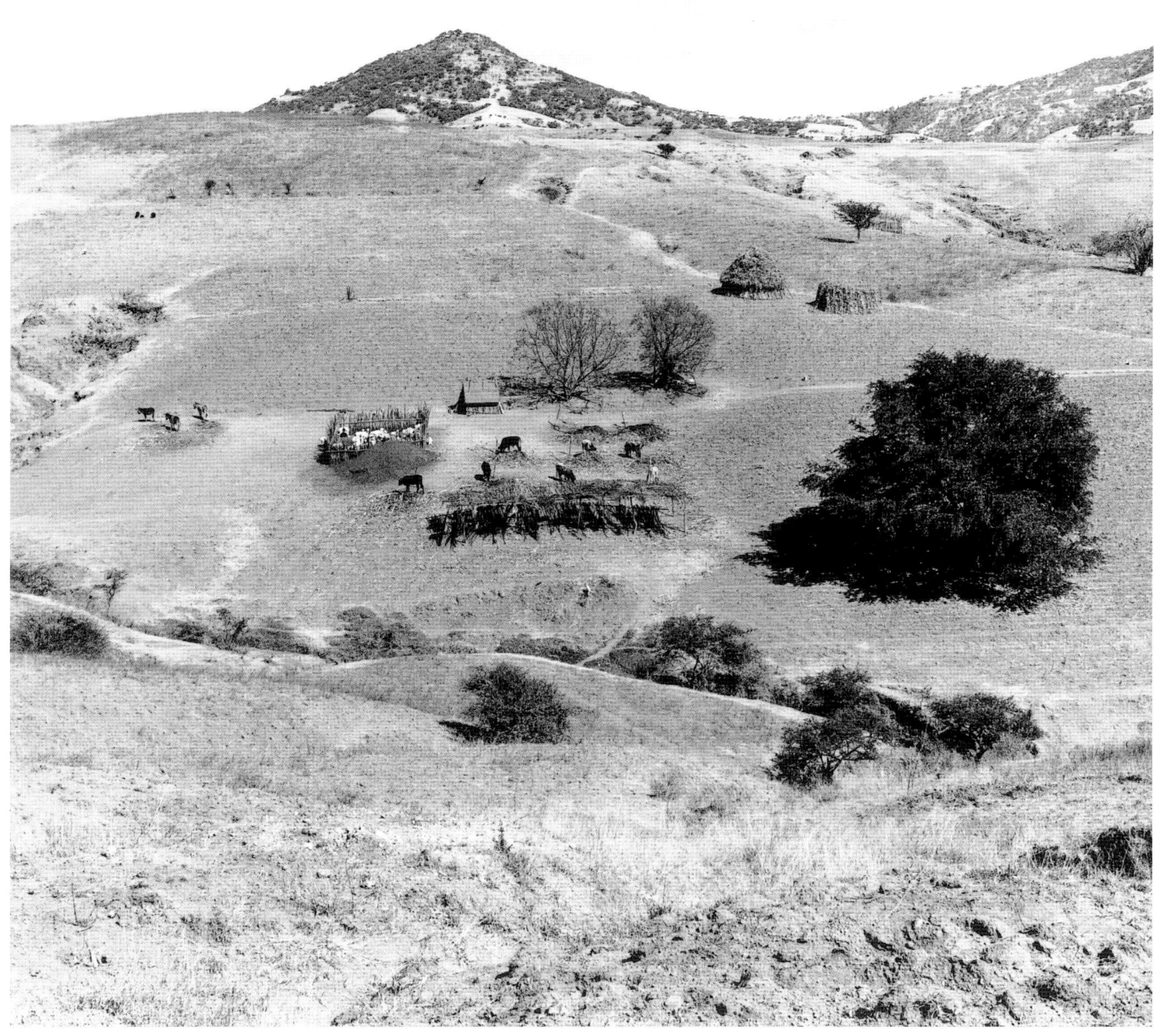

La Unión. 1989.

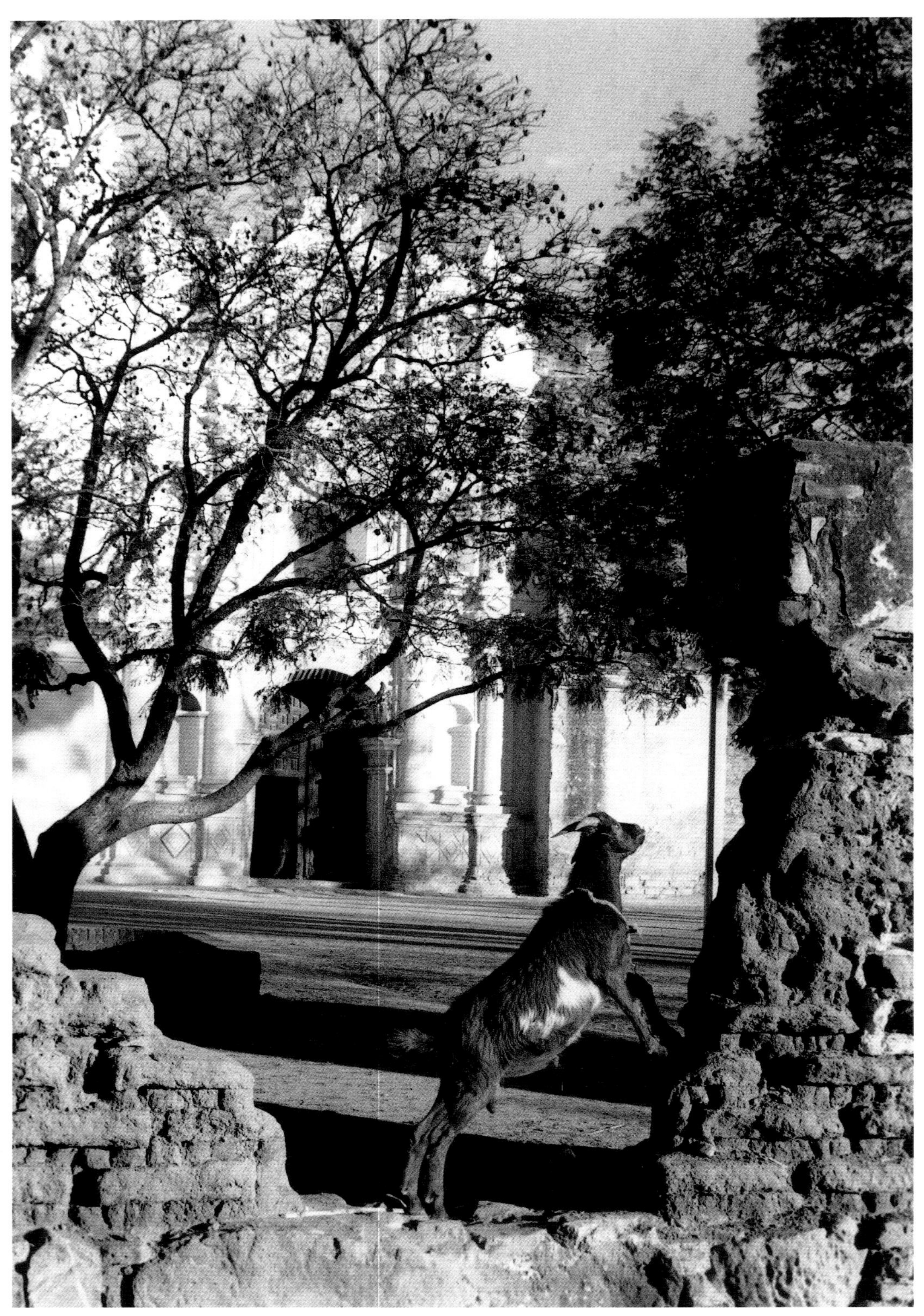

San Martín Tilcajete. 1989.

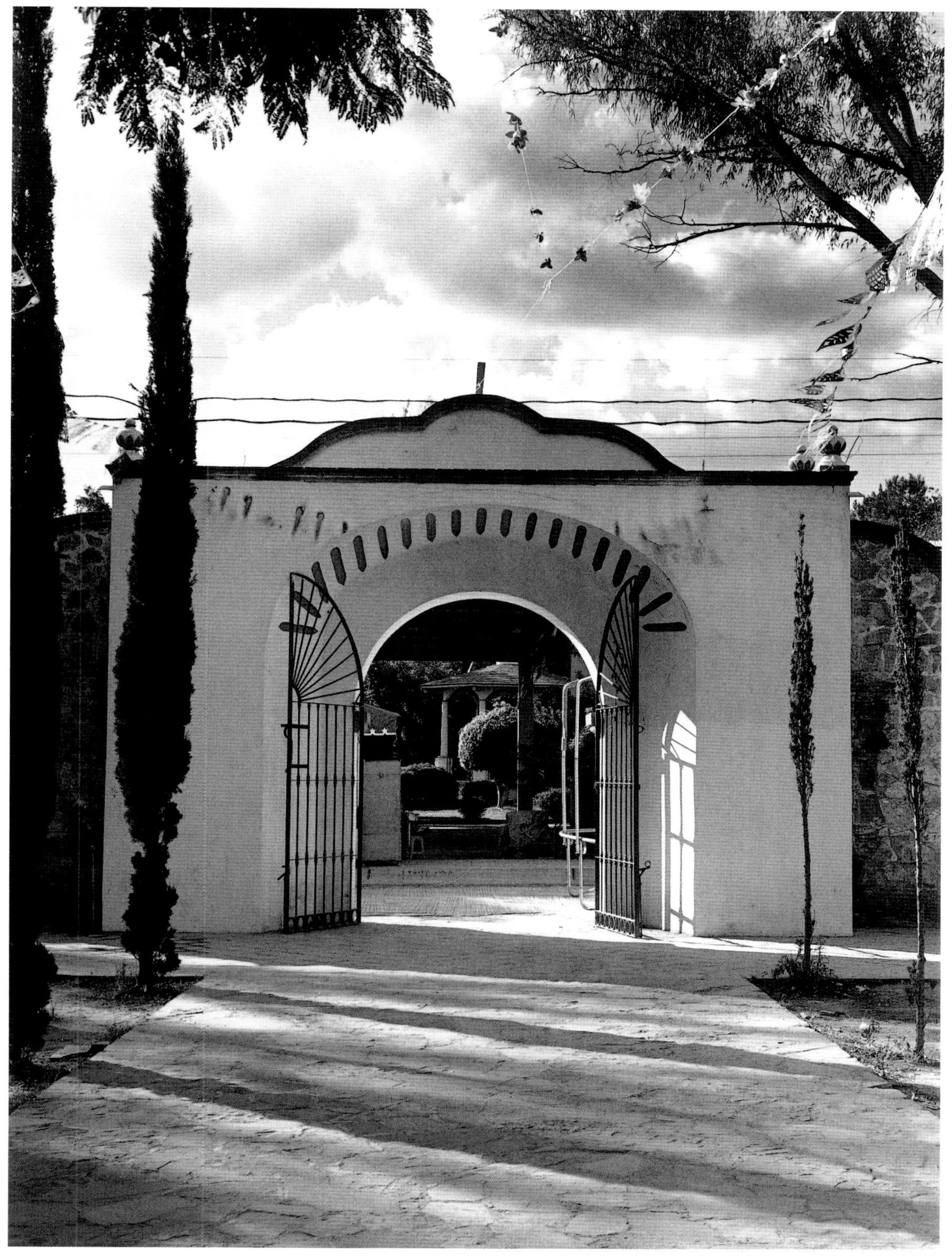

San Martín. 2004.

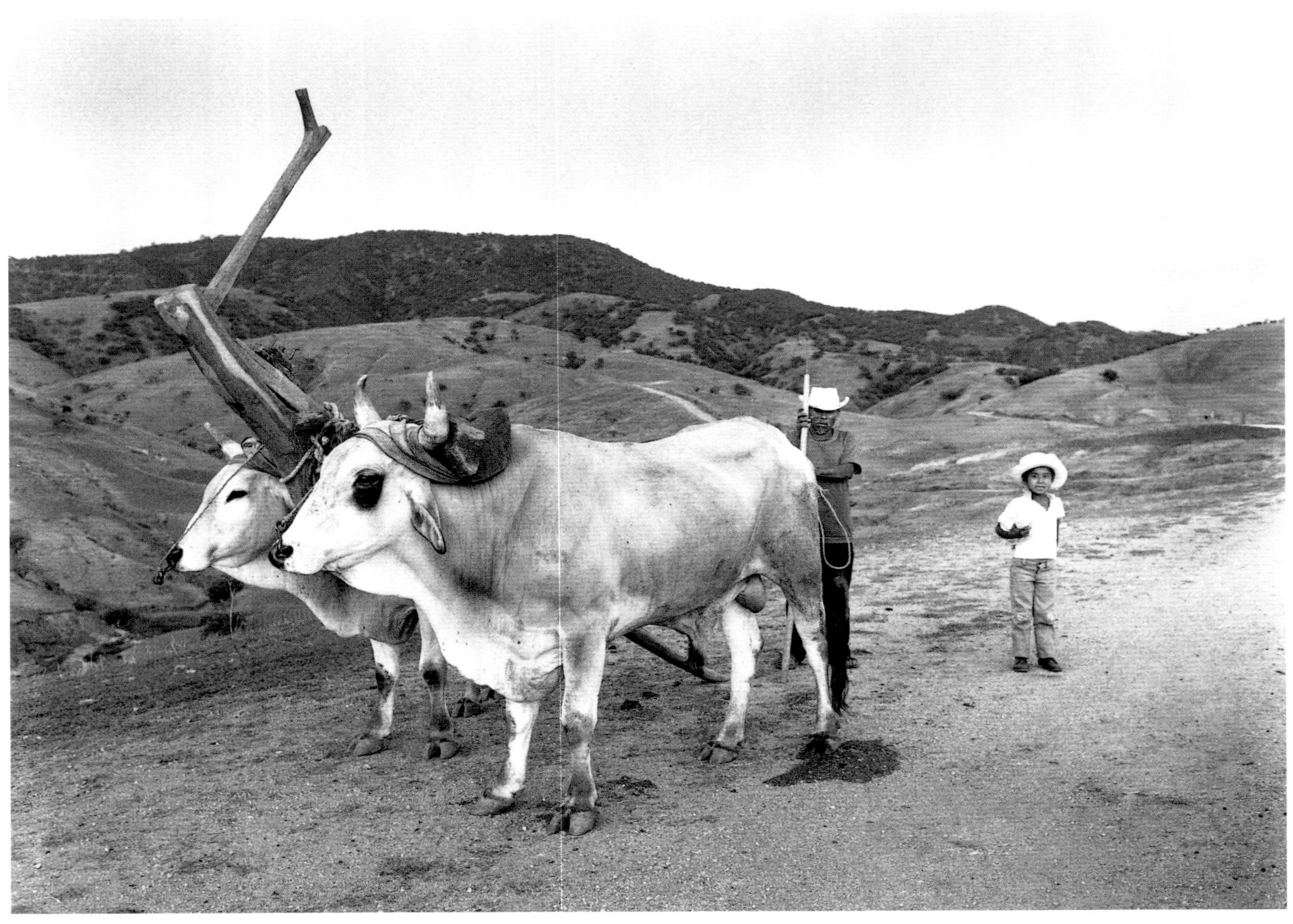

La Unión. 1989.

Farming

A FRESH HANDMADE TORTILLA hot off the fire is one of the great culinary pleasures of Oaxaca that seems destined to disappear, at least for a time, as the women who make them die off and their daughters are freed up to do other things. Oaxacans could spend the next few decades trying to figure out how to make the same delicious tortilla using a fraction of the manual labor they are now using—the hours plowing, planting, husking, grinding, and kneading on bended knee. Or, as seems more likely, they could stop farming and go into real estate instead.

Whether the Oaxaca valley becomes a farming center or a tourist-fed metropolis, its campesinos are fast disappearing into the mist of modern livelihoods. Less than half the people in San Martín and Arrazola now grow their own food—a sign of their growing prosperity. Most who still farm have replaced bulls and oxen with tractors, sold to them (along with diesel fuel) by the state at a steep discount. The more enterprising work their neighbors' land. After three years of cleaning college dorms and waiting on tables in California, Miguel Jiménez came home, bought a tractor with his savings, and, after a brief go at selling cowboy clothes in Oaxaca, became the biggest farmer in San Martín. He raises corn, beans, radishes, lettuce, and seasonal flowers on three hundred acres, few of them his. He also carves in his free time.

These baby steps beyond subsistence agriculture have been slowed by the lack of many basics that aspiring farmers in more affluent countries take for granted: adequate public infrastructure, access to credit and capital, a robust free market to buy and sell land, technical assistance from universities or the state. Oaxaca has none of these things. "You're on your own," Miguel says. Output per acre in the valley has increased, but the region still does not produce enough to feed its growing population, which every day takes up more land that can no longer be farmed. Food imports to the valley also are increasing—another sign not of the region's decline but of its growing wealth.

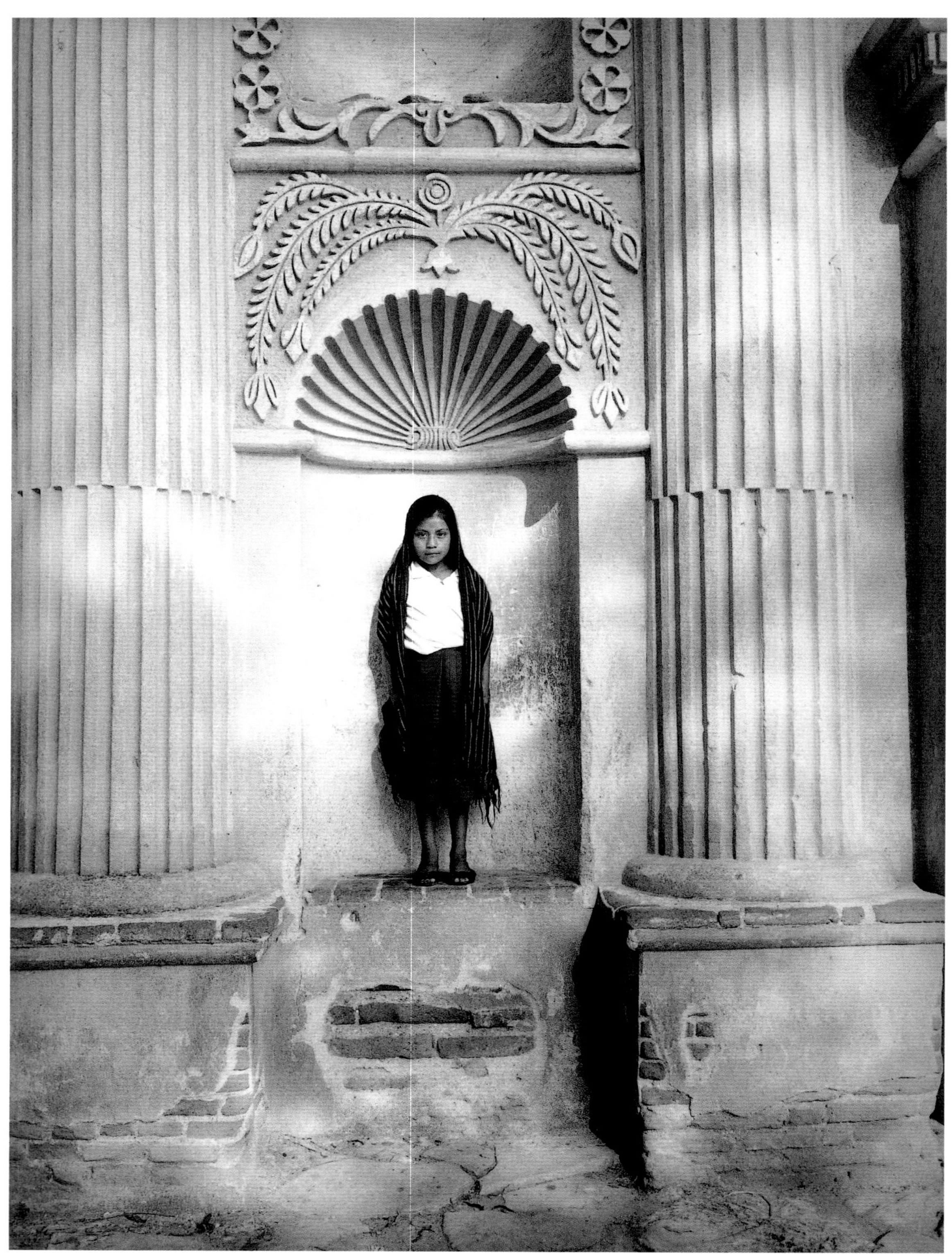

Santa Ana Zegache. 1990.

Women

THE GREATEST SOCIAL CHANGE IN OAXACA is that the girls no longer seem so different from American girls. More are staying in school, delaying marriage, and pursuing careers. They are more sociable and self-assured. (Teenage girls, daughters of the women who as girls themselves used to titter and hide from us, now snap cell-phone pictures of their girlfriends posing with our son—or they try to teach him how to dance.) Impoverished old Indians in handmade skirts can still be seen prostrate outside the market selling tortillas, but their granddaughters are more likely to be shop clerks in pants earning low but steady pay. Women have yet to achieve parity with men in education, wages, or participation in government and the workplace—indeed their progress may not have kept pace with that of women in other parts of the world—but the revolution in expectations is reason to hope that their gains will continue. Once painters of men's carvings, women now carve.

How this liberation will affect the region is not clear. So far, it has done little to lessen the state's interference in the economy, create new jobs, or reform the state's education system, one of the worst in the world. Nor has it reduced corruption in government or increased respect for the law. There is no reason to expect it would, but without progress in these areas, the benefits of greater freedom (except perhaps the freedom to leave the country as men do and work as *mojados* in the States) will likely be disappointing.

The Melchor daughters, Manuela and Nayeli, see the glass as half full. Both intend to get college degrees and have careers. Manuela is studying criminology and plans to go into police work—an occupation closed to women until recently. She wants to be a historian, but there are no good history departments in the state and the family can't afford to send her to study in Mexico City. Not to be denied, she found a part-time job summarizing historical documents at the municipal archives in Oaxaca. Nayeli, who plays soccer, wants to study foreign languages in college, or if that fails, medicine.

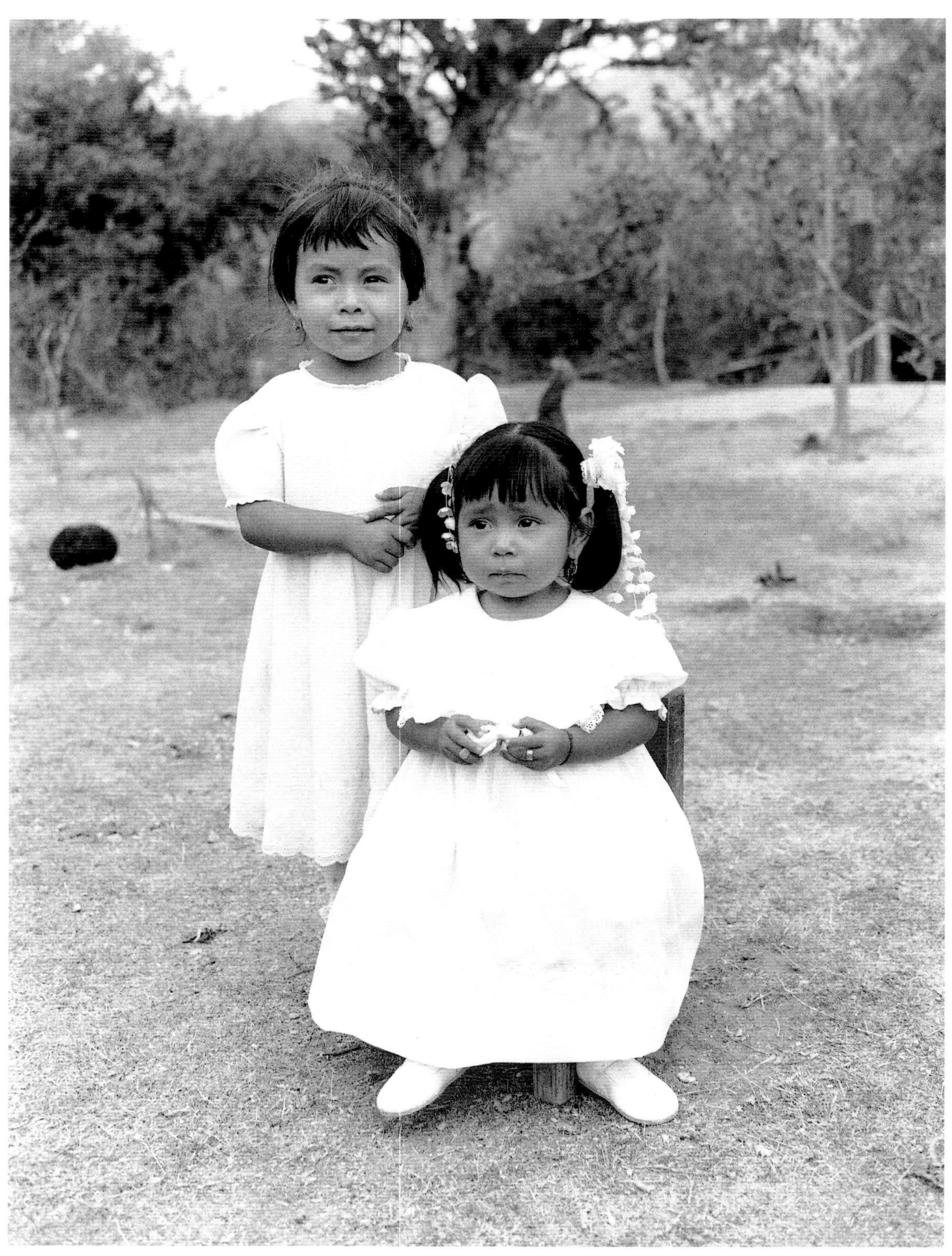

Manuela and Nayeli Melchor. San Martín. 1989.

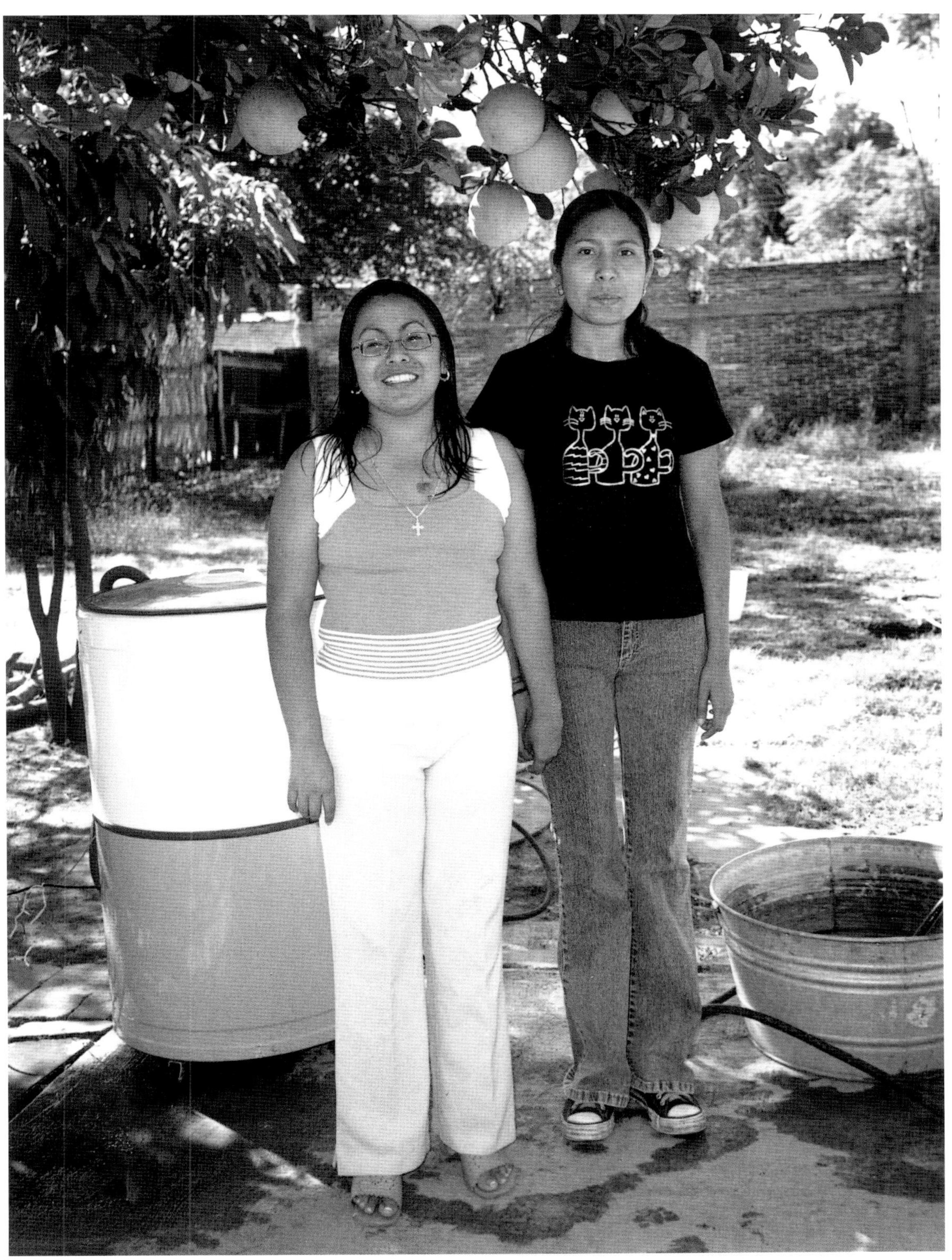

Manuela and Nayeli Melchor. San Martín. 2006.

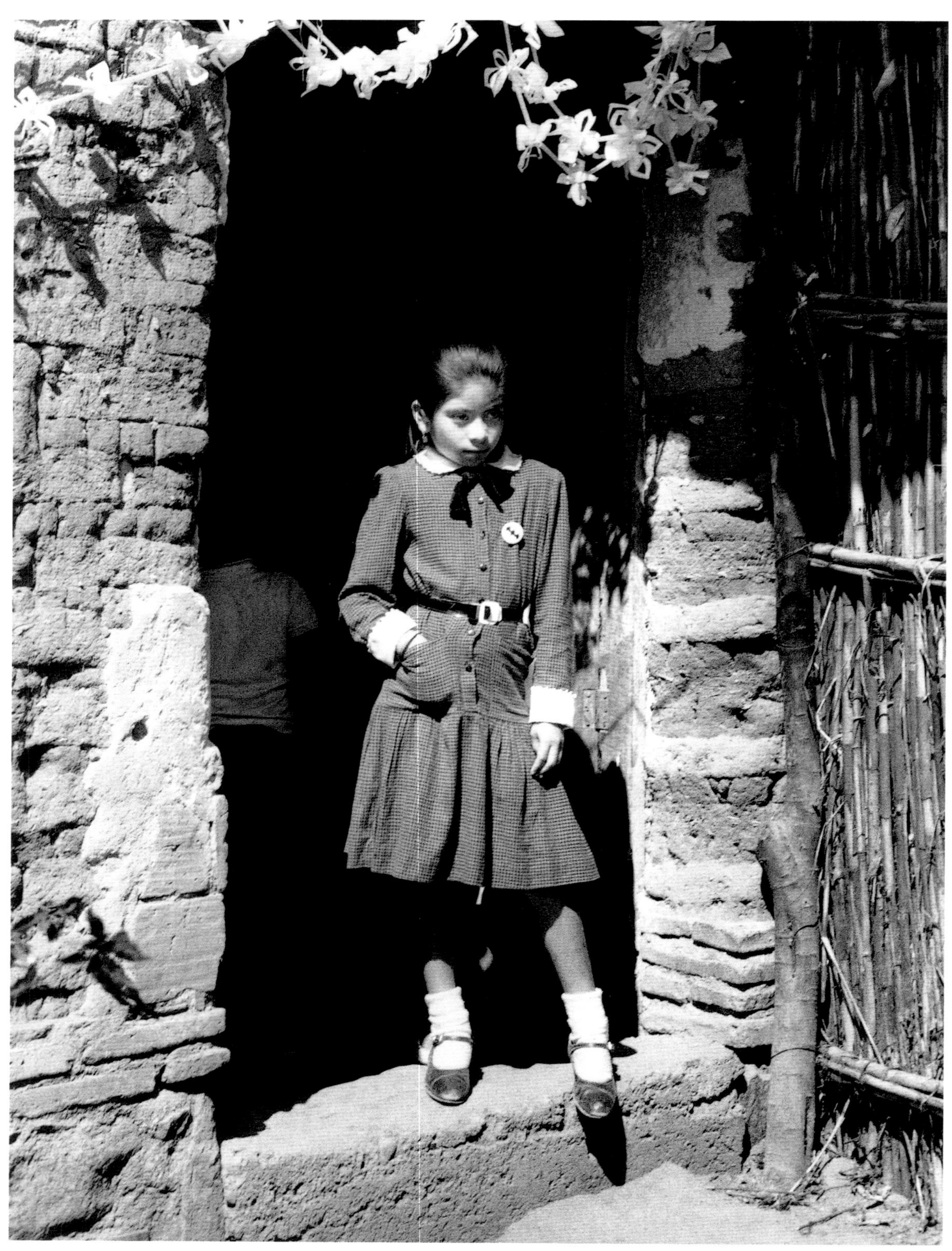

Nancy Martínez. San Martín. 1989.

Nancy Martínez

San Martín Tilcajete

BORN INTO A PEASANT FAMILY whose men worked as *mojados* in California, Nancy Martínez stayed home and became a lawyer. She works as a clerk in civil court for a judge whose calendar is taken up with complaints against deadbeats who won't repay their loans and fathers who won't pay their child support. Most of the judgments she writes up are not enforced or enforceable. Does she know what she is up against—what it will take to strengthen the rule of law in her country, how rare such a thing would be, how uncertain that it will happen in her lifetime?

Life in San Martín has little space for such concerns. Living at home amid her extended family and village traditions, Nancy does not agonize much about whether she is a cog in a vast, unyielding, malfunctioning machine. Her diploma is not her only prized possession. Her big brother, Leoncio, when he's not dry-cleaning uniforms as a *mojado* or crucifying wooden devils as a carver, teaches young children the famed Oaxacan *pluma* dance, a reenactment of the Spanish Conquest. Nancy helps him, doting on her nieces and nephews and joining in the communal fiestas where the dance is performed. She attends the late-night Mass honoring San Martín, the village's patron saint. Directly after Mass, joining in still another tradition she wraps herself in a heavy coat, fits a papier-mâché bull strung with fireworks over her head, lights the fuse, and dances through the crowd beneath a brilliant, deafening eruption of flames.

Nancy Martínez's law diploma. San Martín. 2004.

Gloria Inez Gómez

Arrazola

WHEN WE FIRST MET GLORIA INEZ GÓMEZ in 1989, her fifteen-day-old niece had just died and Gloria was waiting for everyone to get home from the hospital. The infant, whom her parents had just named Antonia the day before, was swept up a hillside in her hammock when a storm ripped the tin roof off the family's hut. Obeying a childhood instinct, Gloria had reassembled what remained of her toy tea set and was passing the time playing house.

When we last saw Gloria seventeen years later, she had just become the proprietor of Pooh's Presents and Novelties, a four-foot by eight-foot room made of recycled tin sheets and filled with fanny packs, toys, stuffed animals, and birthday cards. Known in the village as simply *La Gloria*, she was raising her three young children— their fathers had left them—and was living with her mother, who was helping support the family by selling tabloids in Puerto Escondido six hours away.

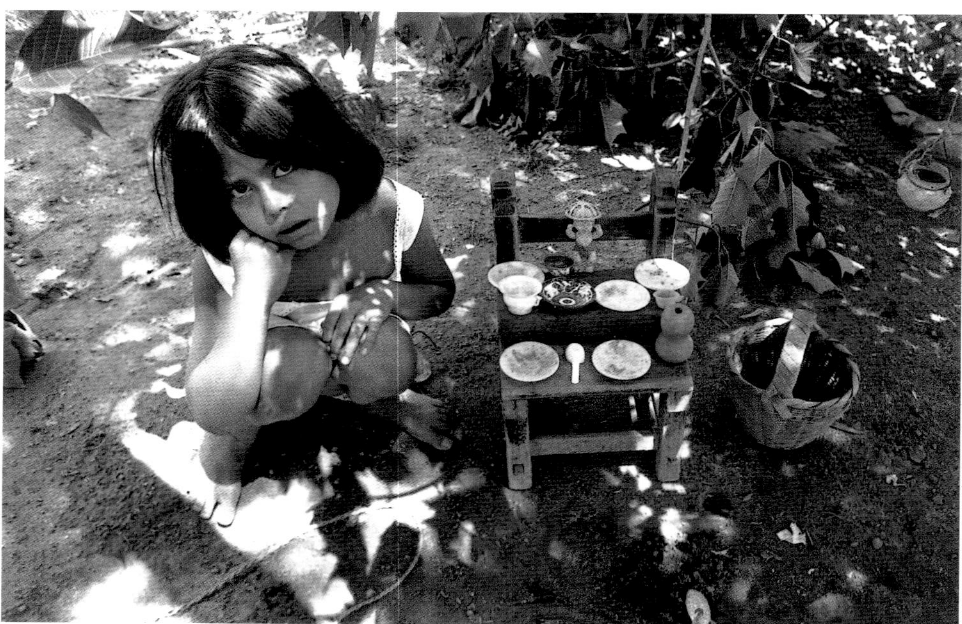

Gloria Inez Gómez. Arrazola. 1989.

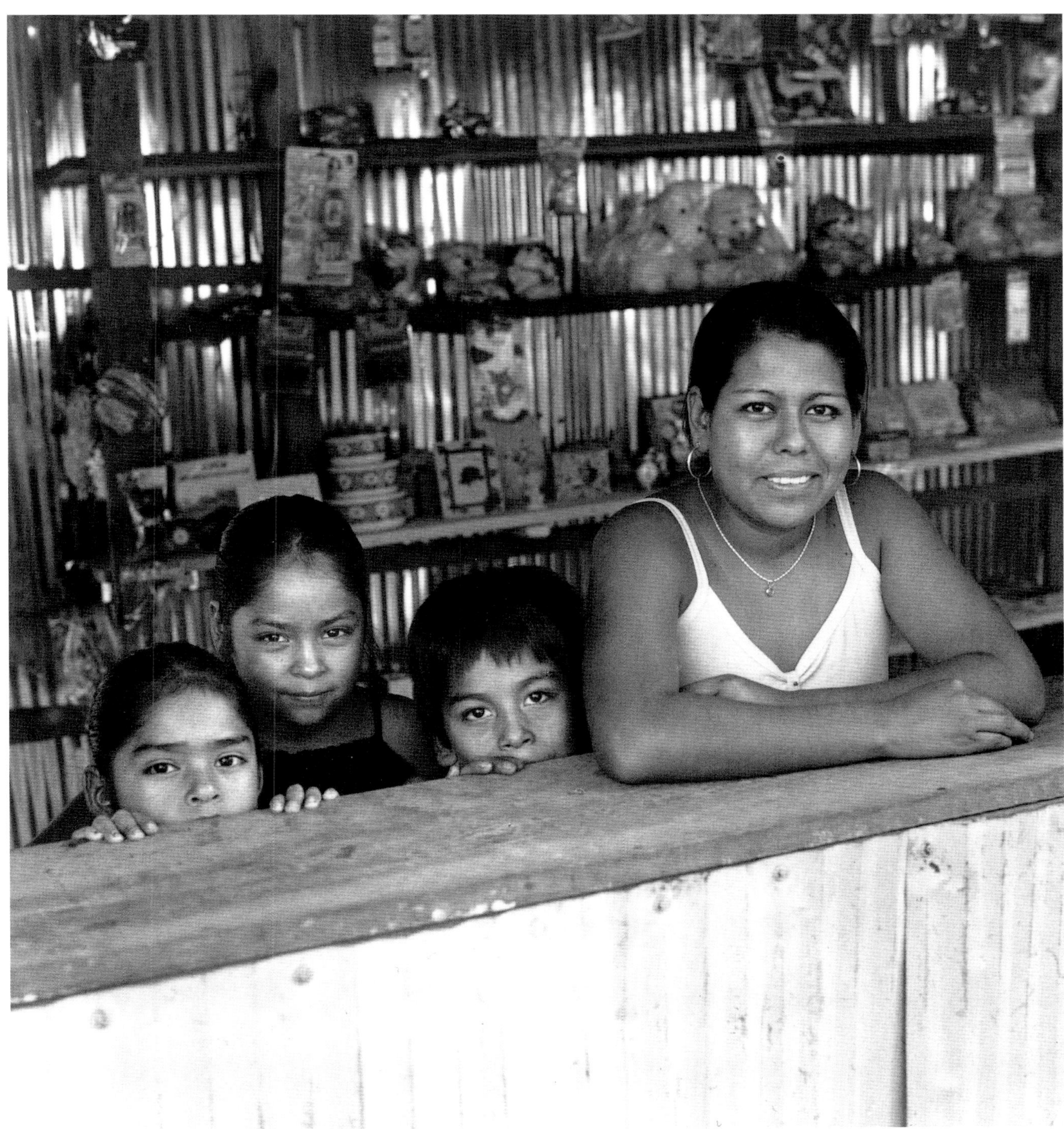

Gloria Inez Gómez. Arrazola. 2006.

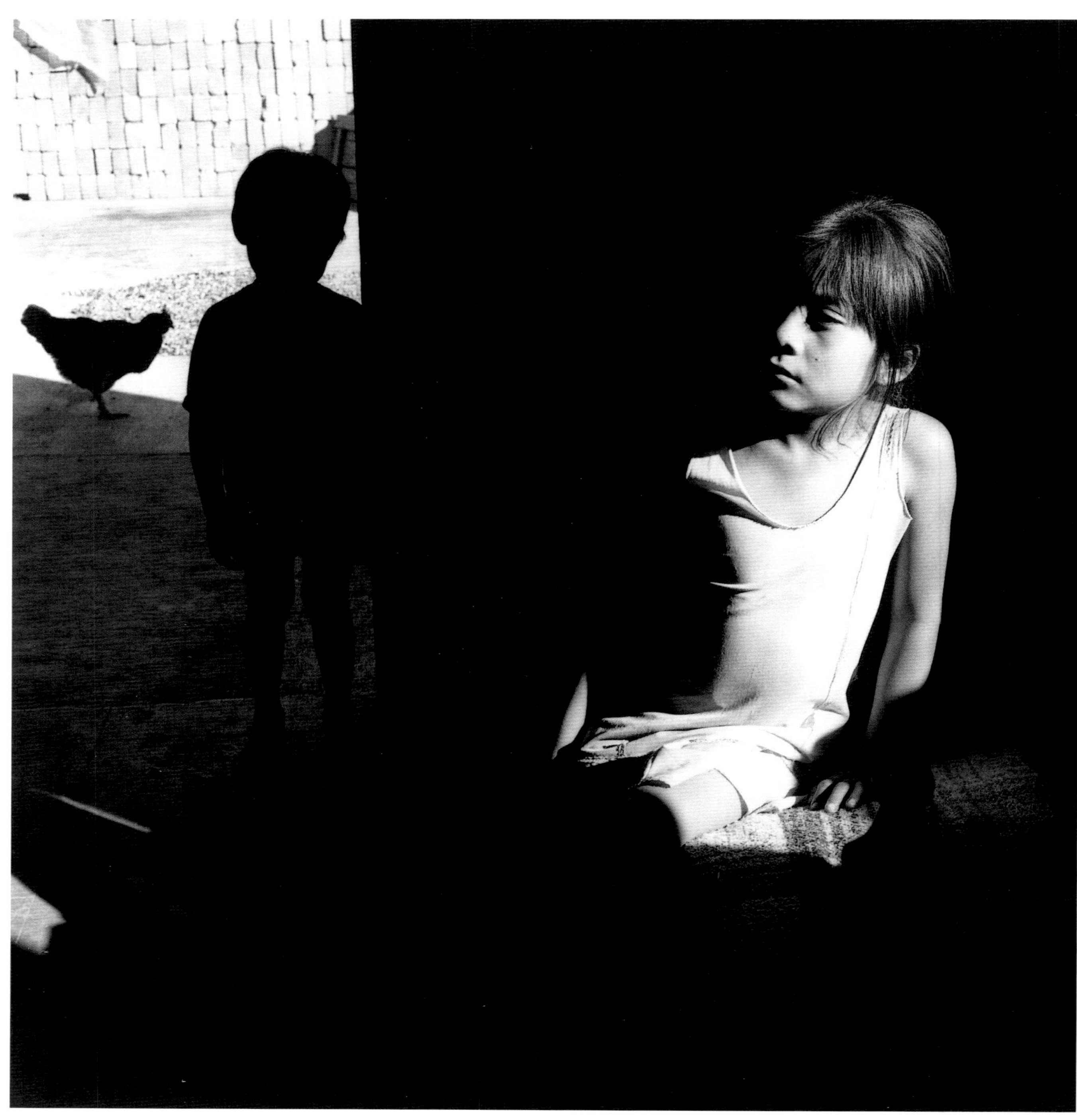

Juana Calvo. San Martín. 1989.

Juana Calvo
San Martín Tilcajete

THE DESIRE TO GO TO THE UNITED STATES is so strong, so prevalent, and so often gratified that, even for campesinos living a thousand miles away, the journey has become almost routine. Employment agencies come to Oaxaca offering round-trip transportation, three-month visas, housing, and guaranteed employment—all supposedly legal. At nineteen, Juana Calvo signed on with an outfit that took her to Tampa, Florida, where she was given a room with five other women and took a job mowing lawns for $7 an hour. She was one of six hundred women on the agency's sign-up list and waited two years for the opportunity. While waiting, she worked at a hardware store, saved her money, and bought a Carabela motorcycle. She watched with envy as her brother and brother-in-law left for New Jersey. When her turn finally came, her dad was perplexed that she would leave her job, family, and wheels to cut grass two thousand miles from home. Her grandmother, for whom motorcycles and trips to America were unthinkable as a child, approved of her going and understands why she hasn't come back.

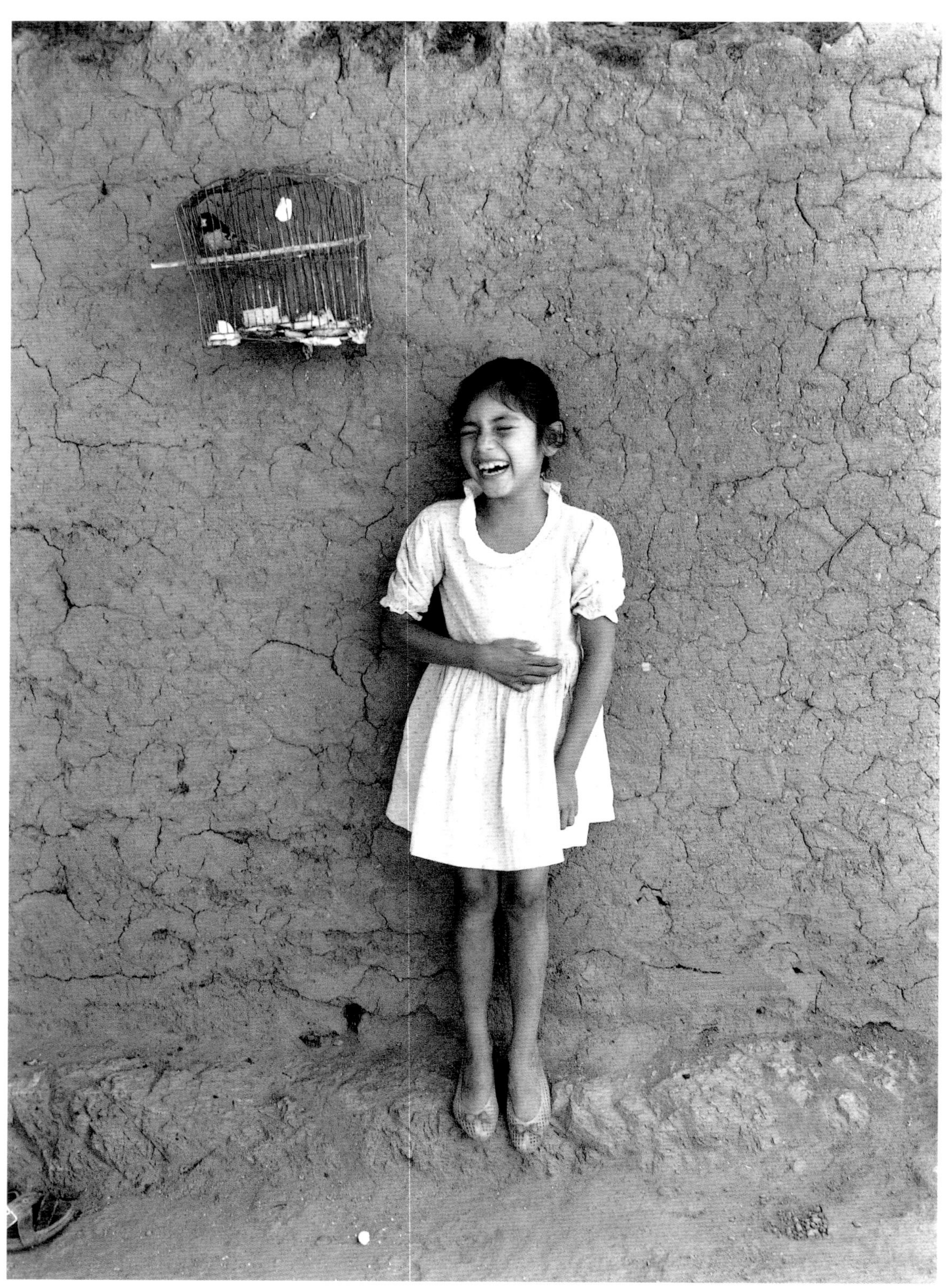

Edelmira Carreño. Arrazola. 1989.

Edelmira Carreño

Arrazola

THE GROWING FREEDOM OF WOMEN often expresses itself in a clear-eyed, wistful declaration of independence from the assumptions and solicitudes of men. "Better to dress saints than to undress drunks," goes the refrain, a mocking reference to the respective roles of spinsters who tend to the statues of the church and wives who minister to their husbands at home. More women are staying single, and more are becoming single mothers as well.

"He left us and I'm glad, I don't want him around," Edelmira Carreño says of her daughter's father, a young man from the city. Edie lives with her mother, helps out in her store, paints carvings to sell in the village square, and cares for the baby. She does not expect ever to be able to marry—tourism and prosperity haven't yet changed the sorts of things a man is willing to accept in a wife—but she does not yet use her liberty to rage against village mores. Indeed she is surprised to hear they are any different in the States.

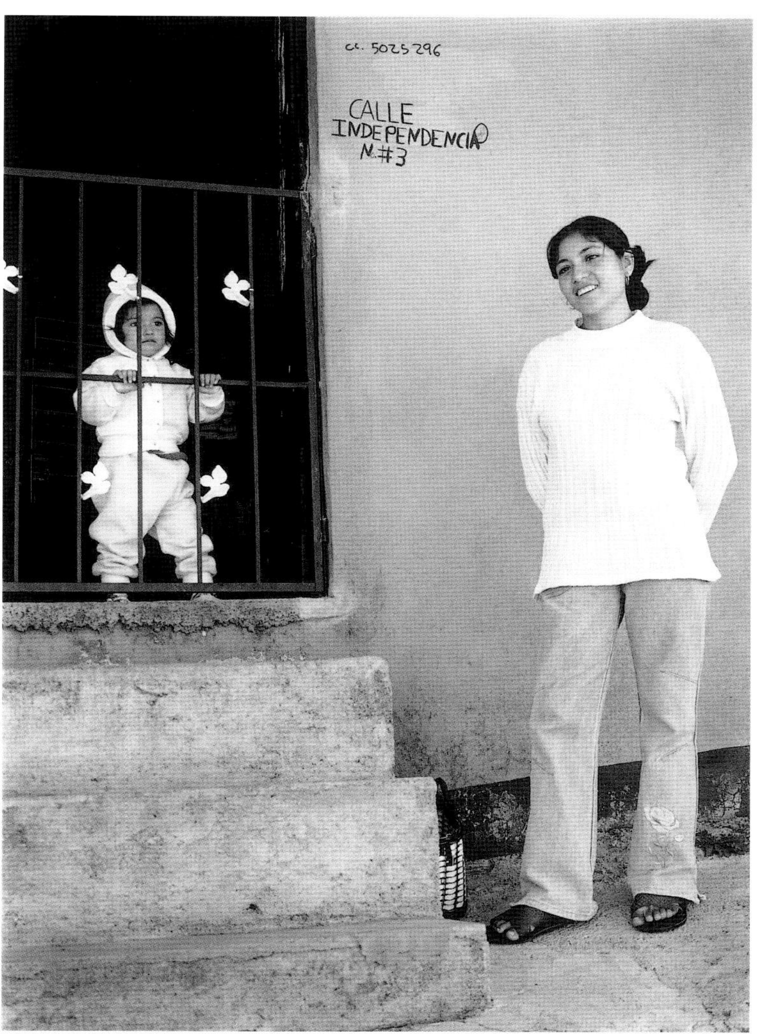

Edelmira Carreño. Arrazola. 2004.

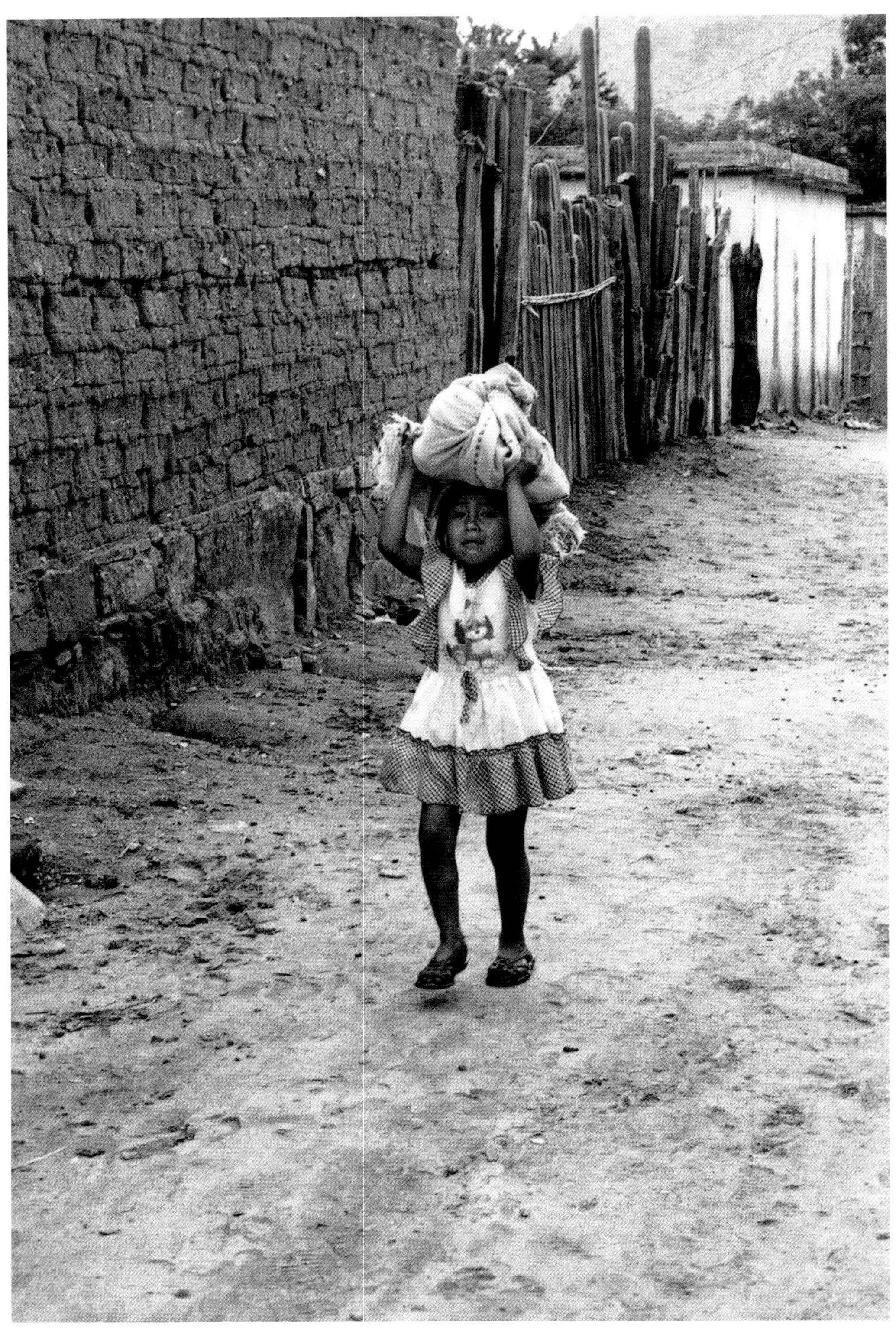

Catalina Julián. San Martín. 1989.

Catalina Julián

San Martín Tilcajete

From the time she could walk, Catalina Julián sought out responsibilities. As a small child she helped her grandparents bring in the crops. As a young adult, she studied to become an elementary-school teacher, then changed her mind and enrolled in a four-year program in tourist administration. She wants to be a hotel manager or open a travel agency. An optimist living in the poorest state of Mexico, she has no plans to sneak into the United States. If Mexico were somehow to become a nation of citizens like her, there would be no immigration problem: an industrious, forward-looking people would find good work close to home, and an honest, able government would stay out of their way or help them.

Catalina owns a Hewlett-Packard computer, paid for with money her dad earned working in California. She has traveled throughout Oaxaca and loves its fiestas, especially the rodeos. Few villagers have embraced modernity with more enthusiasm or less disdain for the past. Daughter of a bricklayer and the product of miserable schools, she has no trouble imagining herself as the manager of a five-star hotel. NAFTA seems made for her. "Everything is a question of strategy," she says. "You can't isolate yourself. Modernity arrives and replaces what you have. You have to adapt." She notes proudly that her sister is studying to become a nurse and that her dad has gone to the States three times to earn the money to put them both through school. U.S. dollars paying for Mexicans' education: thus may illegal immigration close the prosperity gap and erode its own future.

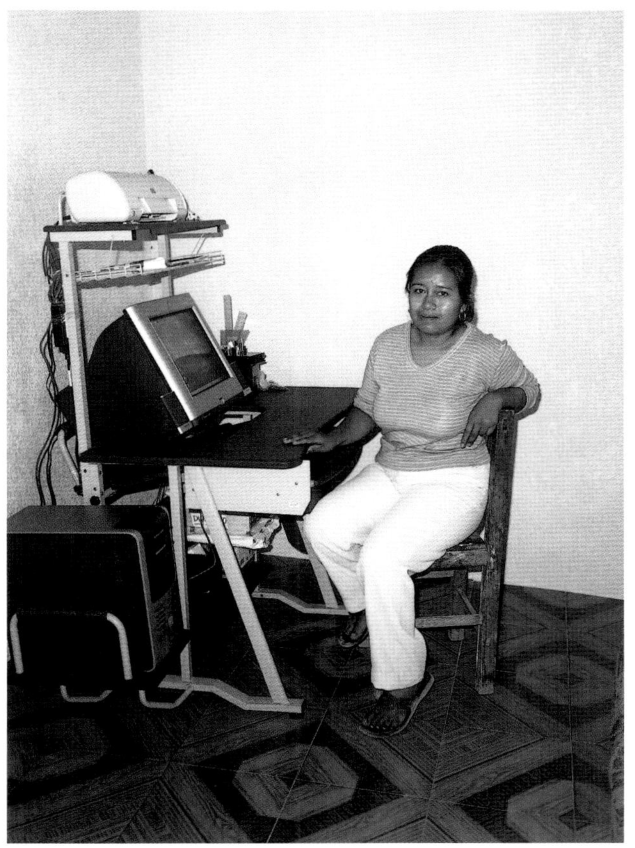

Catalina Julián. San Martín. 2004.

Juana Ortega and Maclovia Fuentes

San Martín Tilcajete

Campesino women work from dawn to dusk—planting crops by hand, tending smoky fires, scrubbing laundry, carrying water, de-graining corn, shoveling manure, sweeping, forever sweeping the dust and dirt of an unpaved life. Few teenage girls in the carving villages want or expect such a life—misshapen by bowlegs and stunted aspirations. But are their grandmothers really so miserable? They cook together at fiestas, gossip together at the mill, sit together at Mass, and live with family until the day they die.

Love and honor are nourished by freedom and prosperity, but they can be devoured by them as well, even as they grow in lives blessed with little of either. Eighty-five-year-old Maclovia Fuentes has few teeth remaining in her head, but that doesn't stop her from smiling broadly when she recalls her days as San Martín's premiere *pinolera*—the maker of the traditional *pinole* drink (a mixture of ground corn, cocoa, and cinnamon) served at weddings. Maclovia never got paid much for her work or traveled very far beyond her village, but she seems no less content than her nephew Jesús Sosa, an esteemed carver who has built his dream house for his family and has gone ten times to the States as a visiting artist. Jesús is the first to admit that his life is hectic and that neither wealth nor status has brought him much peace of mind. Indeed he doubts he will live as long as Maclovia. His wife, Juana, who paints his carvings but has yet to travel with him abroad, says his restlessness is congenital but that there does seem to be more of it in the village than when they were young.

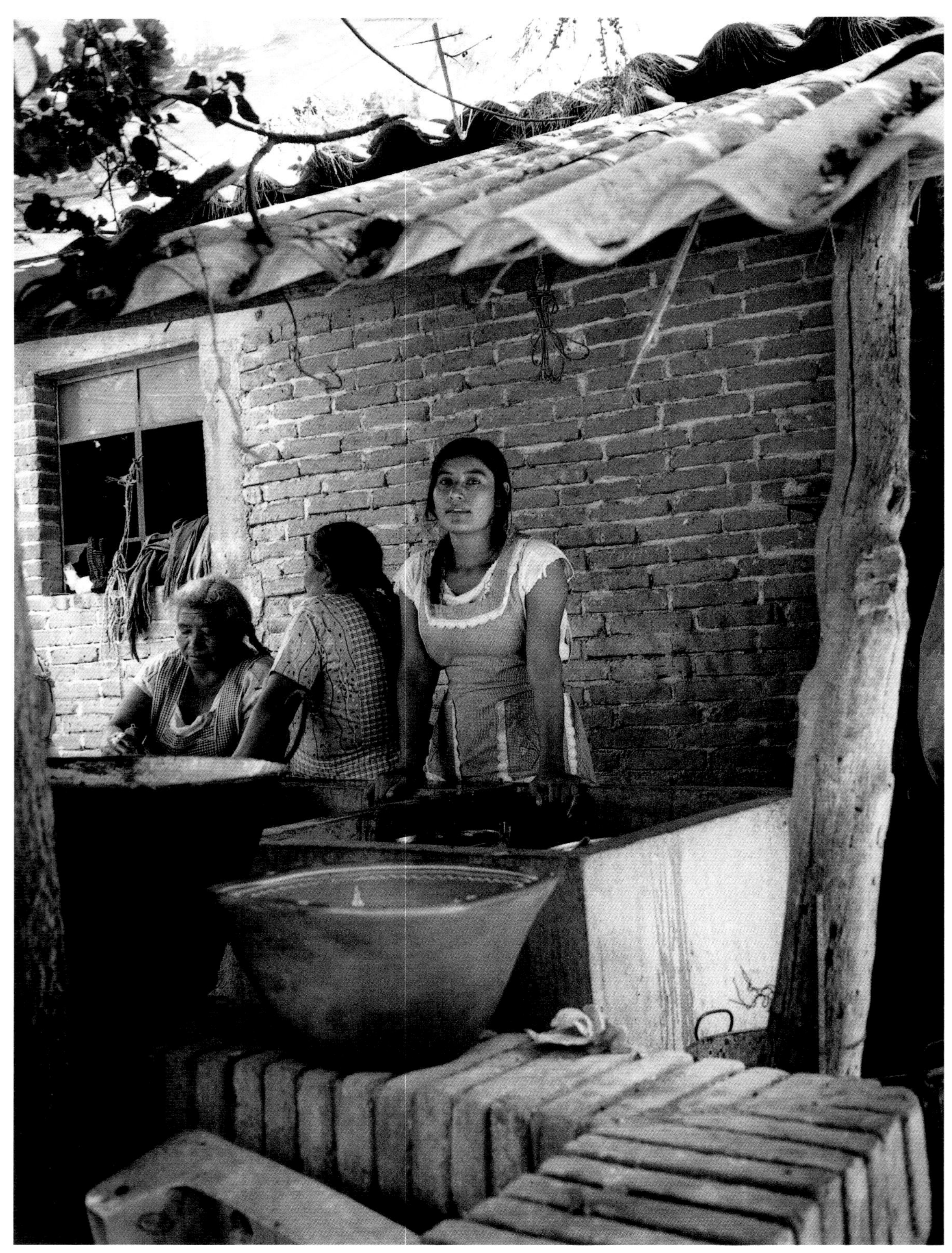

Juana Ortega. San Martín. 1989.

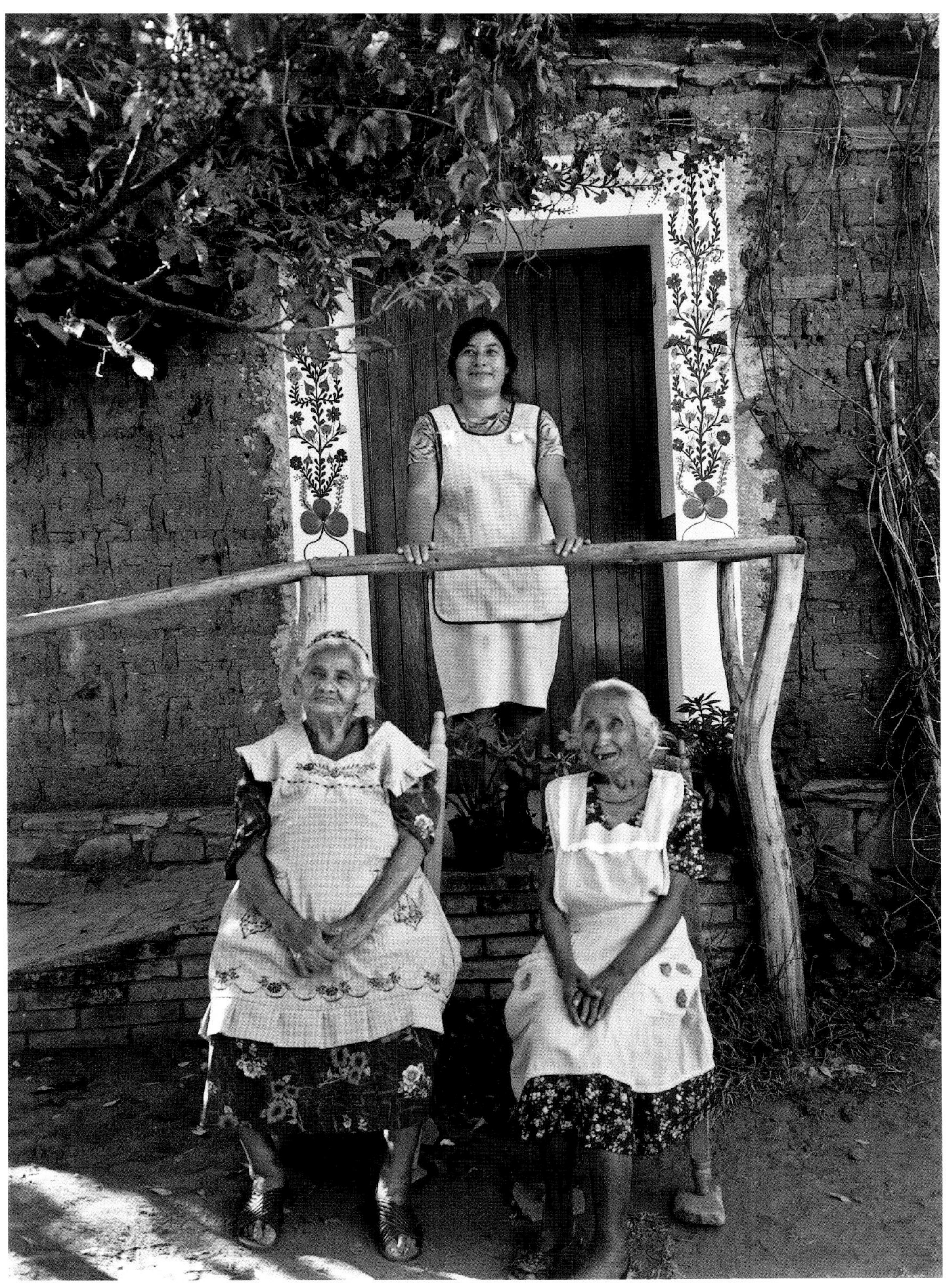

Juana Ortega with Maclovia Fuentes and Martína García. San Martín. 2004.

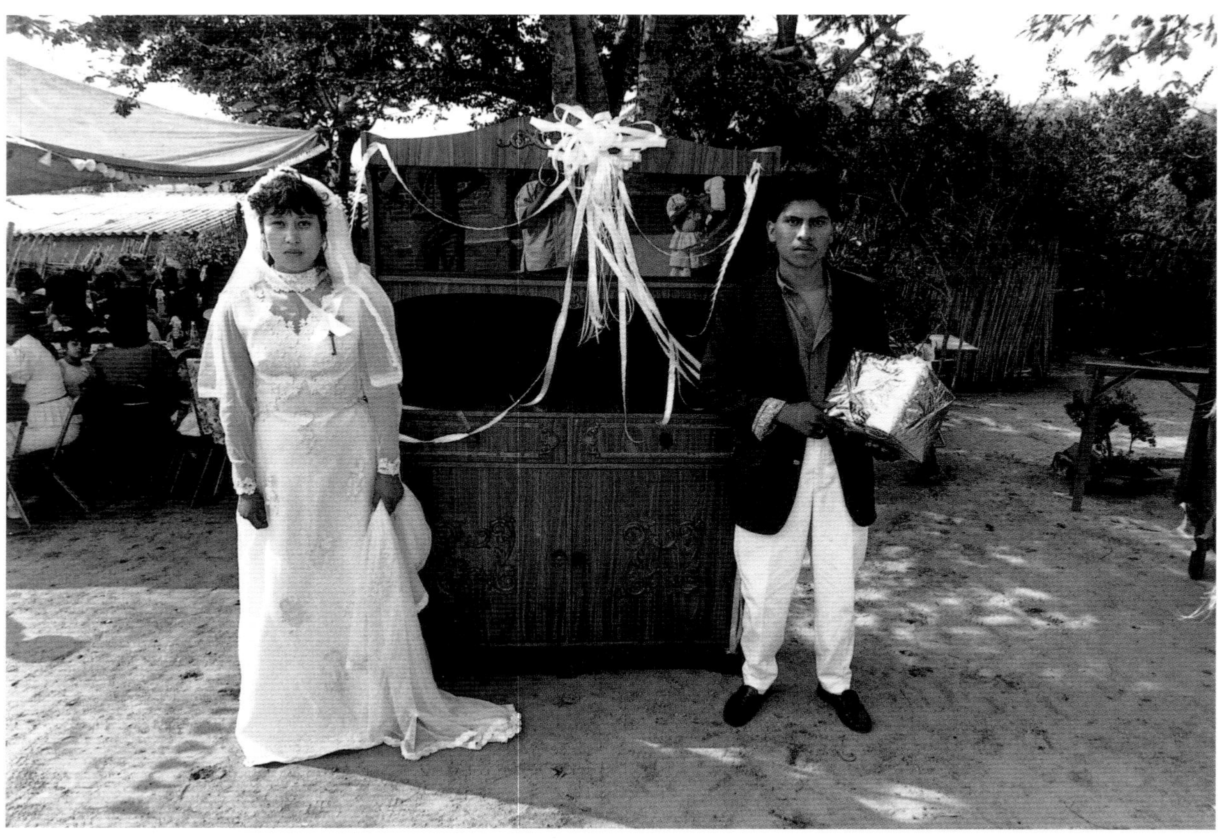

Leticia Aragón and Catarino
Carrillo. Arrazola. 1989.

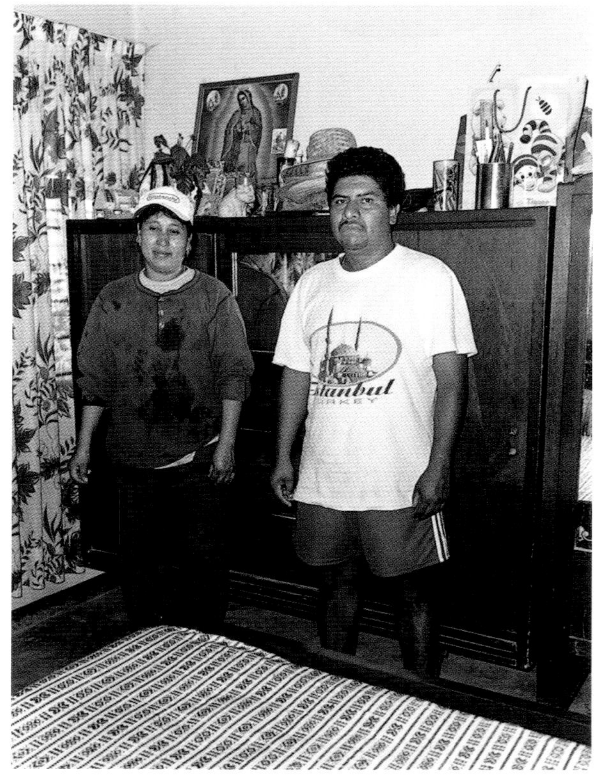

Leticia Aragón and Catarino Carrillo. Arrazola. 2004.

Leticia Aragón and Catarino Carrillo

THE WOOD WARDROBE IS a traditional village wedding gift, a symbol of a newlywed's independence and new home. Leticia Aragón and Catarino Carrillo have outlasted their first wardrobe.

Leticia says she was nervous on her wedding day. Catarino says he was not. The two met seven years earlier, when she was thirteen and he fifteen. They courted for a year (maneuvering around her six brothers), married after a two-year engagement, and began fighting immediately. "It took us four years to learn how to listen to each other," Catarino says.

Leticia thinks unhappy couples should try for "at least ten or twelve years" to make things right before separating. Whether or not such perseverance and forbearance are more common in peasant villages than elsewhere, the deeper mystery is what gives rise to these virtues *anywhere*. Catarino attributes his doggedness to his religious faith. But this doesn't answer the riddle so much as restate it: Whence comes this faith?

"I'm lucky to be alive," Catarino answers. On November 17, 2003, just before 1 AM, he set out by bicycle on a pilgrimage to the shrine of the Virgin of Juquila. Thirteen hours out, he fell on a steep downhill, tore up his cheek, and nearly ripped his ear off. Rather than turn back, he hitched a ride the rest of the way on the back of a truck and (after thanking the Virgin and soliciting her aid) came home two days later, faint with loss of blood. He needed forty stitches. Faith helped him heal, he says.

He and Leticia count their blessings. As artisans they earned enough money to build their own home before sales evaporated after 9/11. They have electricity, running water, a laptop with a printer, and e-mail, none of which they had growing up. They have two healthy sons—miraculously, Catarino says, because the first almost died of an infection at birth and the second almost went blind in one eye. They are respected in the village. (Catarino is president of the elementary school.) And they are still together.

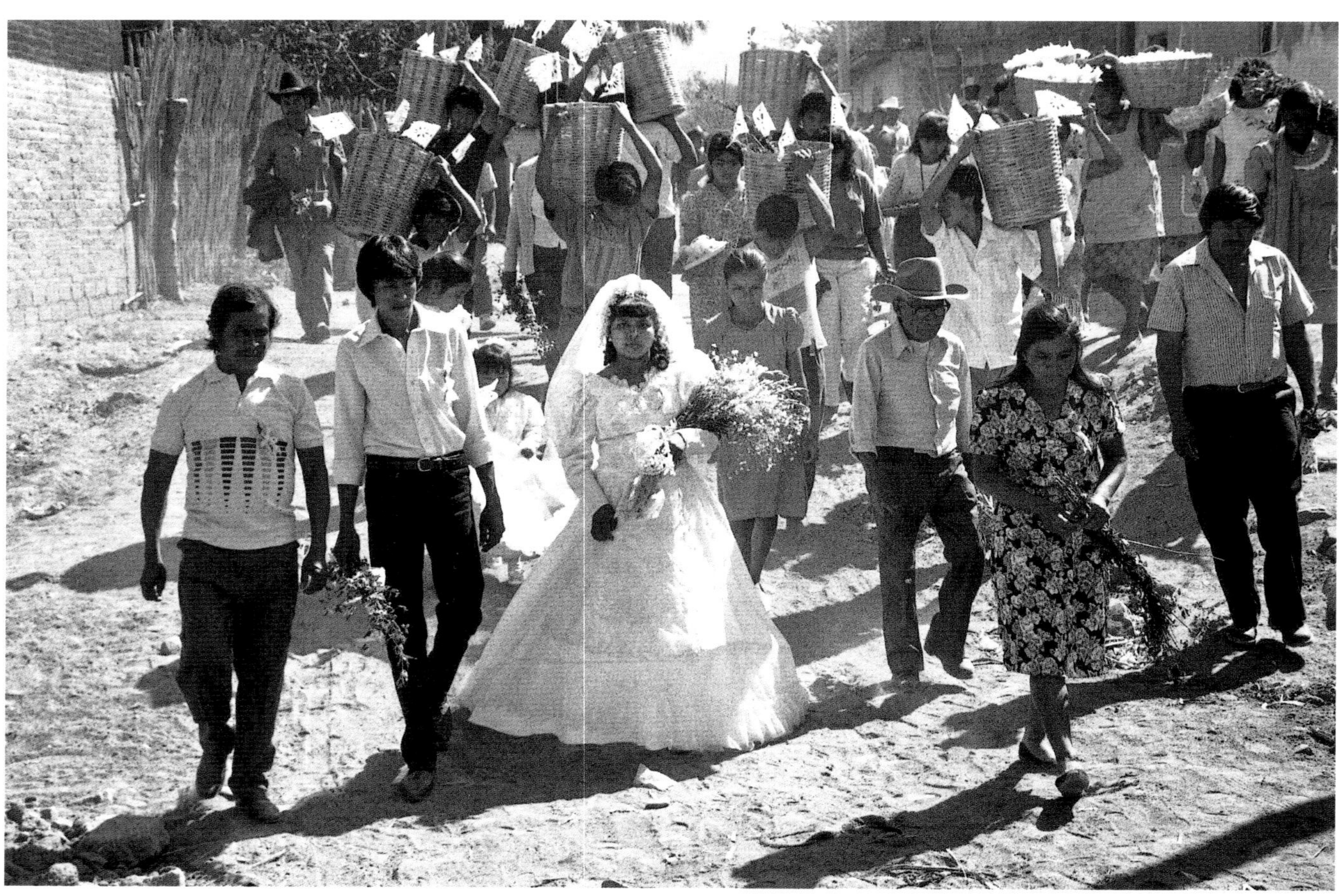

Teresa García. San Martín. 1990.

Teresa García
San Martín Tilcajete

Weddings in rural Mexico are an amalgam of Catholic and Indian traditions, reflecting Mexico's pre-Hispanic and colonial past. One surviving Indian custom is to shower wedding guests with candy and limes. These are carried to the groom's house in great baskets and tossed from the roof. The practice is said to reflect the belief that marriage, like life, is bittersweet.

Teresa García married Alberto Jiménez when she was eighteen and he was twenty. She was eight months pregnant at the wedding. The couple have three children. The love child, Maricela, now sixteen, is in high school. Her mom says she wants to be a biochemist. Marcos, fourteen, attends a school for the mentally handicapped. Alejandro is twelve. All three were born with heart problems. Alberto left for Santa Cruz early in the marriage to find work that would pay the medical bills. He was gone for five years, came back briefly, and has been gone for another two years. He lays tiles. Teresa says he plans to stay two more years. He sends money home for Maricela's expenses at school and to pay the doctors. When he's home, he admits he'd rather be back in California.

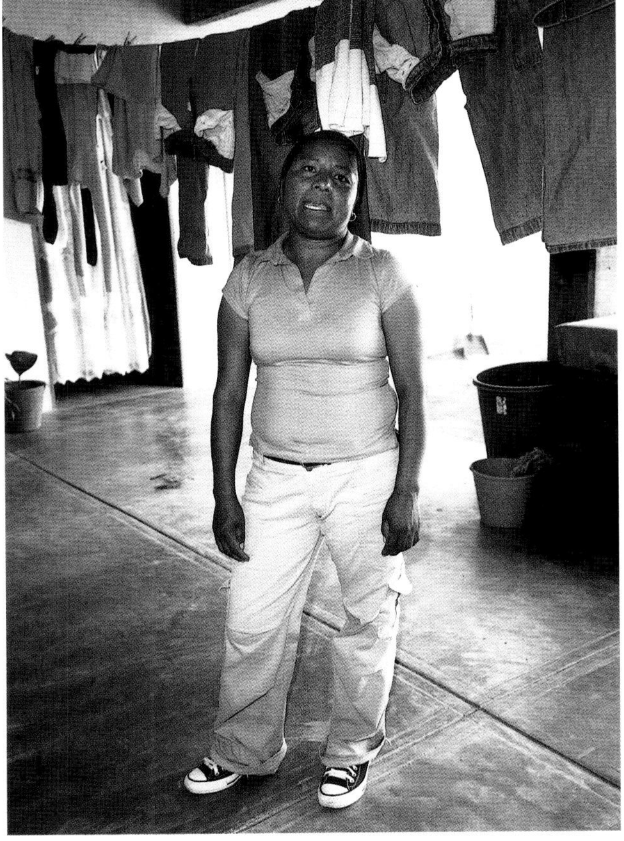

Teresa García. San Martín. 2006.

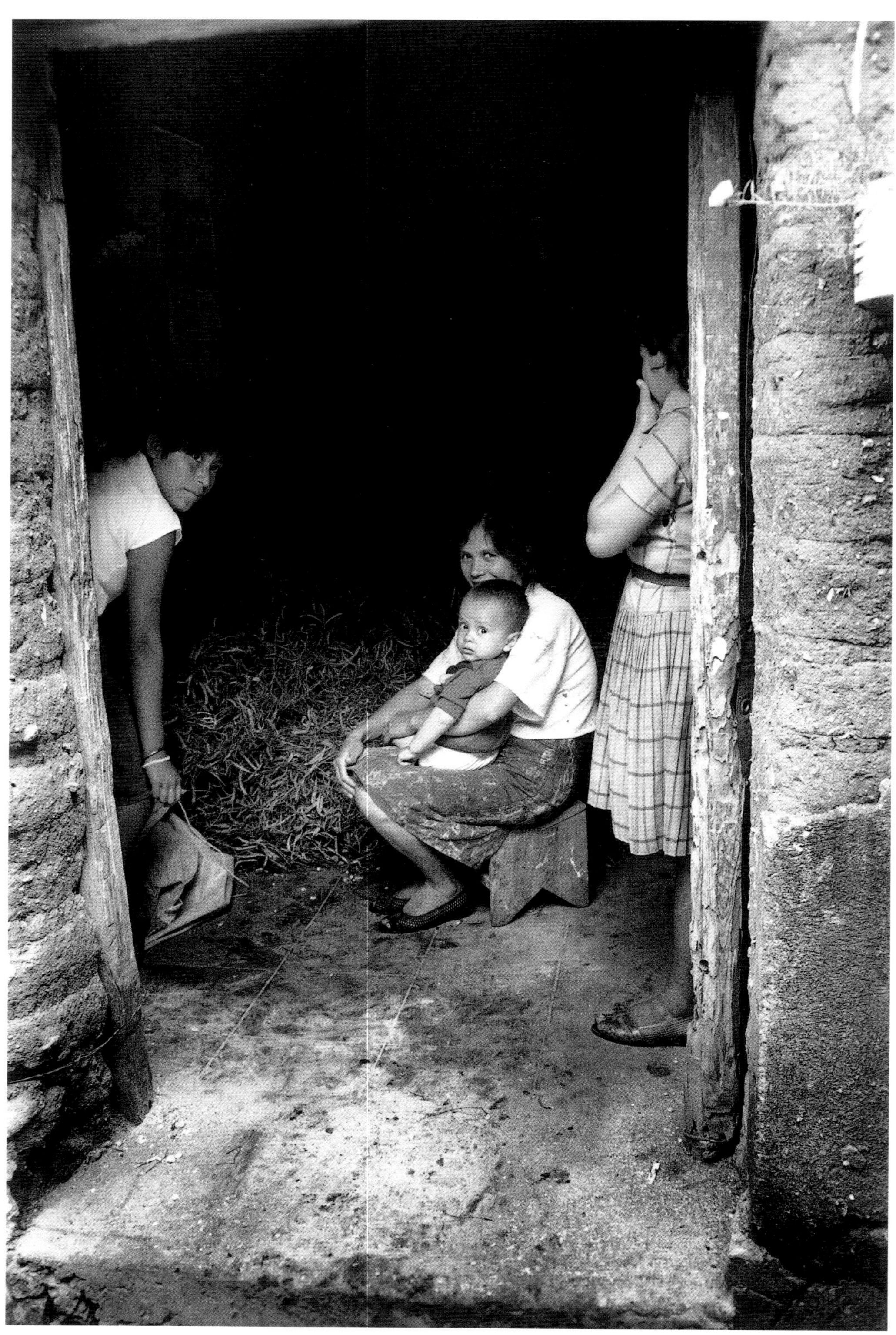

Maura Ramos holding her son Giovanni Melchor. San Martín. 1989.

Giovanni Melchor
San Martín Tilcajete

WHAT SHAPES A CHILD'S DESTINY? How much of it is beyond our understanding or control?

Giovanni Melchor is a few months older than our son, Eddie. The two were often together as babies when we lived in Oaxaca, and comparisons were affectionately made. Both boys were small for their age and strong willed, although Giovanni seemed active like his dad, Eddie attentive and skeptical like his mom. Both were prone to the respiratory ailments of childhood and the intestinal afflictions of Mexico. More alert than their peers—or so it seemed to us—both seemed likely to prosper.

And yet we secretly feared for Giovanni and felt sorry for him. Could he possibly thrive there in his pueblo, toddling through the filth of bulls and chickens outside his bedroom door? Would a loving family—the greatest ally of children everywhere—be enough to ward off the disasters and discouragements and bad doctors that are so much more common in Mexican village life than in ours?

Time makes fools of us all. Giovanni now towers over his family. He's even taller than Eddie. His parents, successful woodcarvers with a treasured U.S. visa, have left their adobe hovel and farm animals—their lives as campesinos—and built a two-story cement house closer to the highway. They have a bathroom with running water and a car. The numberless years of solitude are coming to an end. Giovanni's dad, Jesús, flies once a year to northern California to give wood-carving demonstrations and sell his work in computer-company lobbies and in schools. Leaving the family's cattle and goats to the care of his dad, Jesús talks of modernizing village politics. Giovanni plays the guitar and dreams of becoming a cartoonist, but Jesús thinks he could become a painter or an architect.

Meanwhile, my wife and I have moved the goalposts back. Clicking our tongues, we think to ourselves: What pipe dreams!

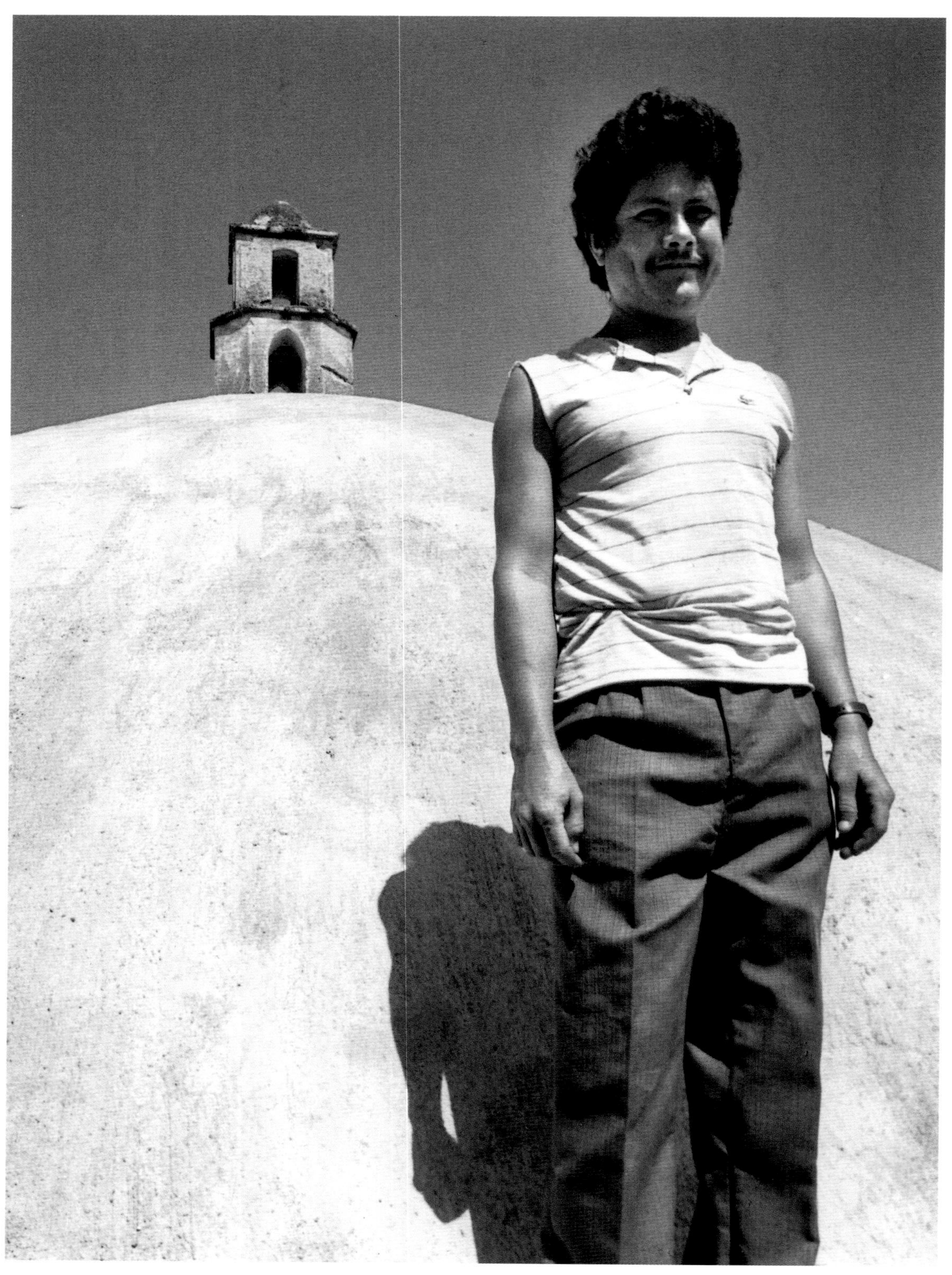

Jesús Melchor on church roof. San Martín. 1989.

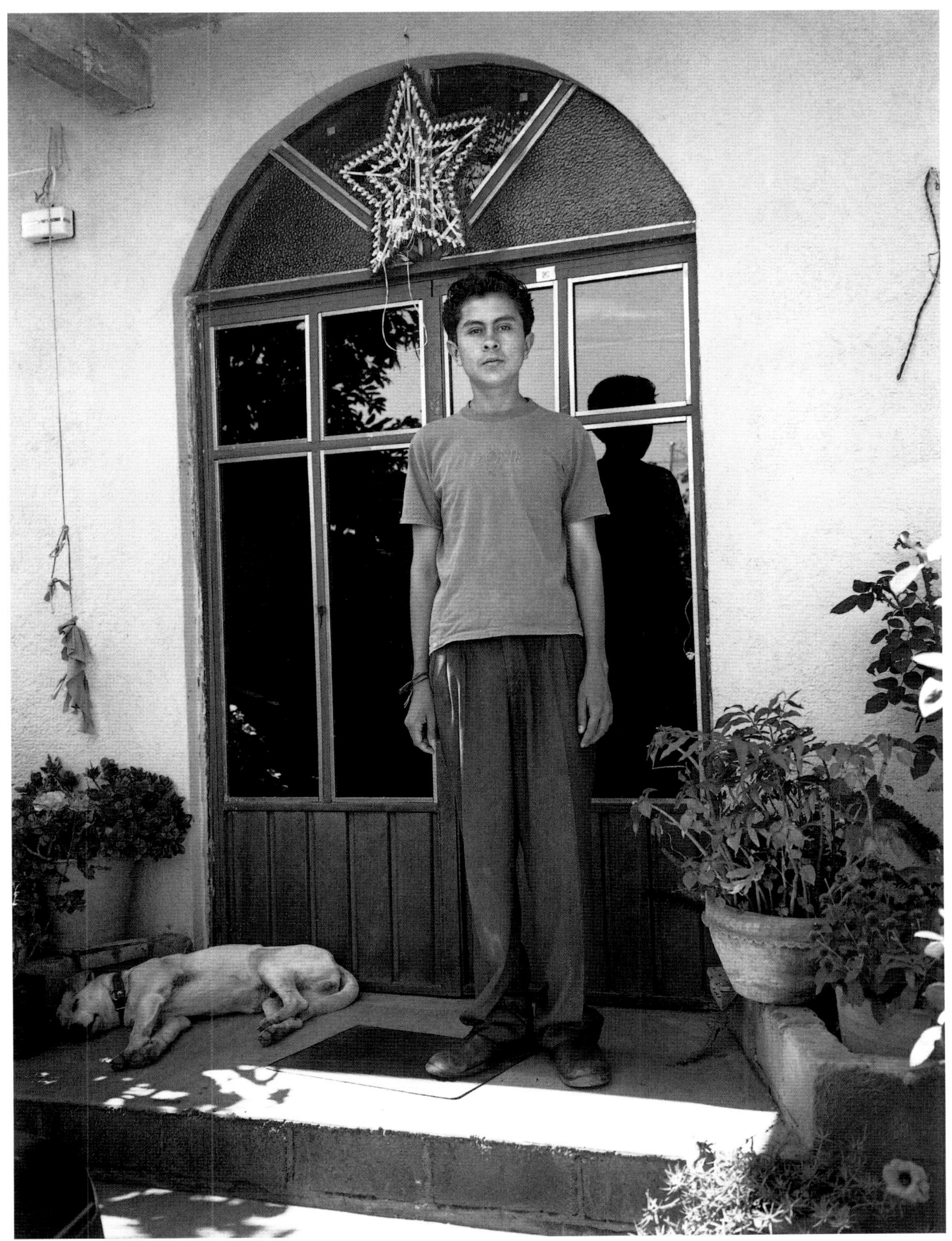

Giovanni Melchor. San Martín. 2004.

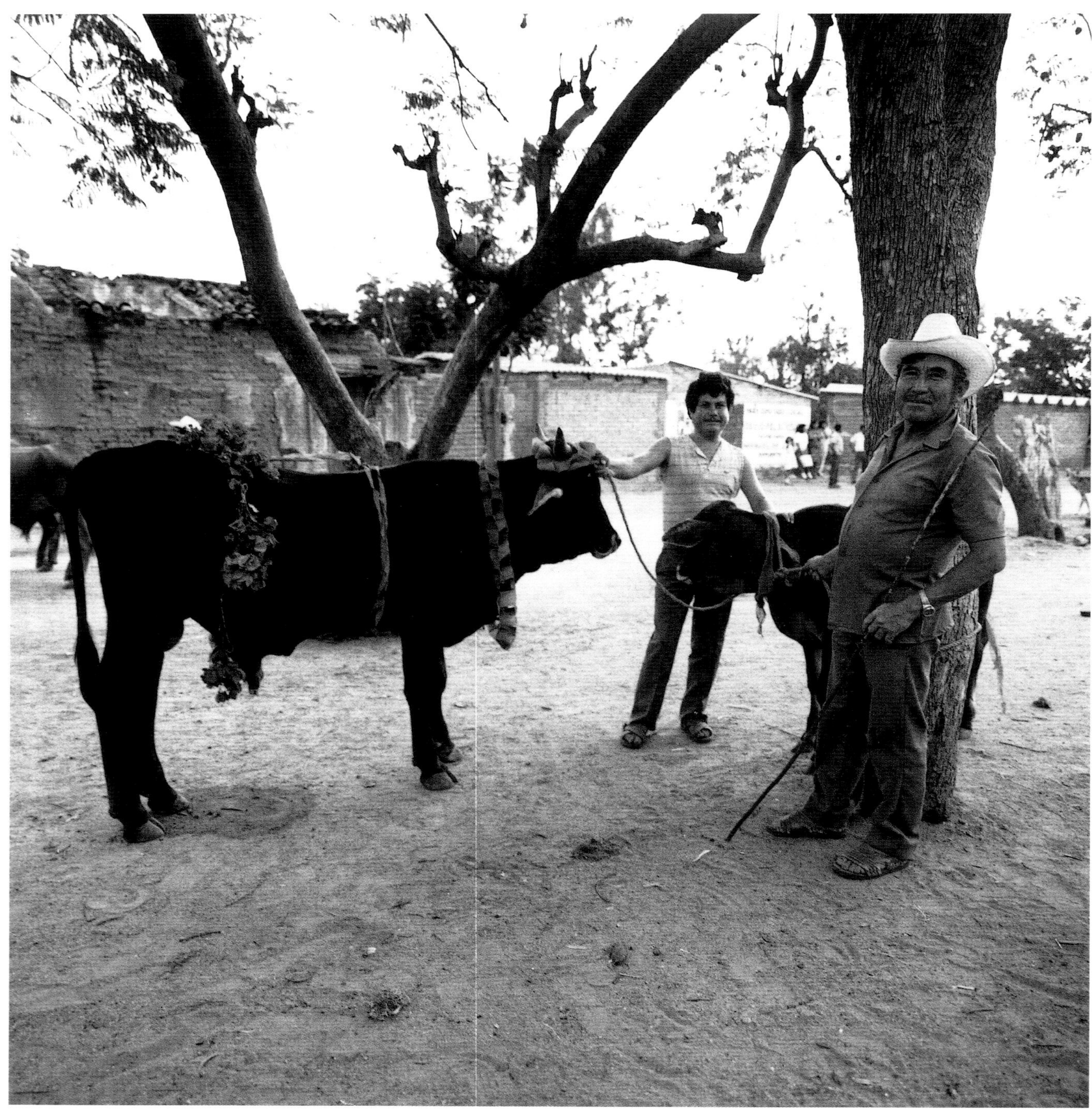

Jesús Melchor and his father, Coindo Melchor. San Martín. 1990.

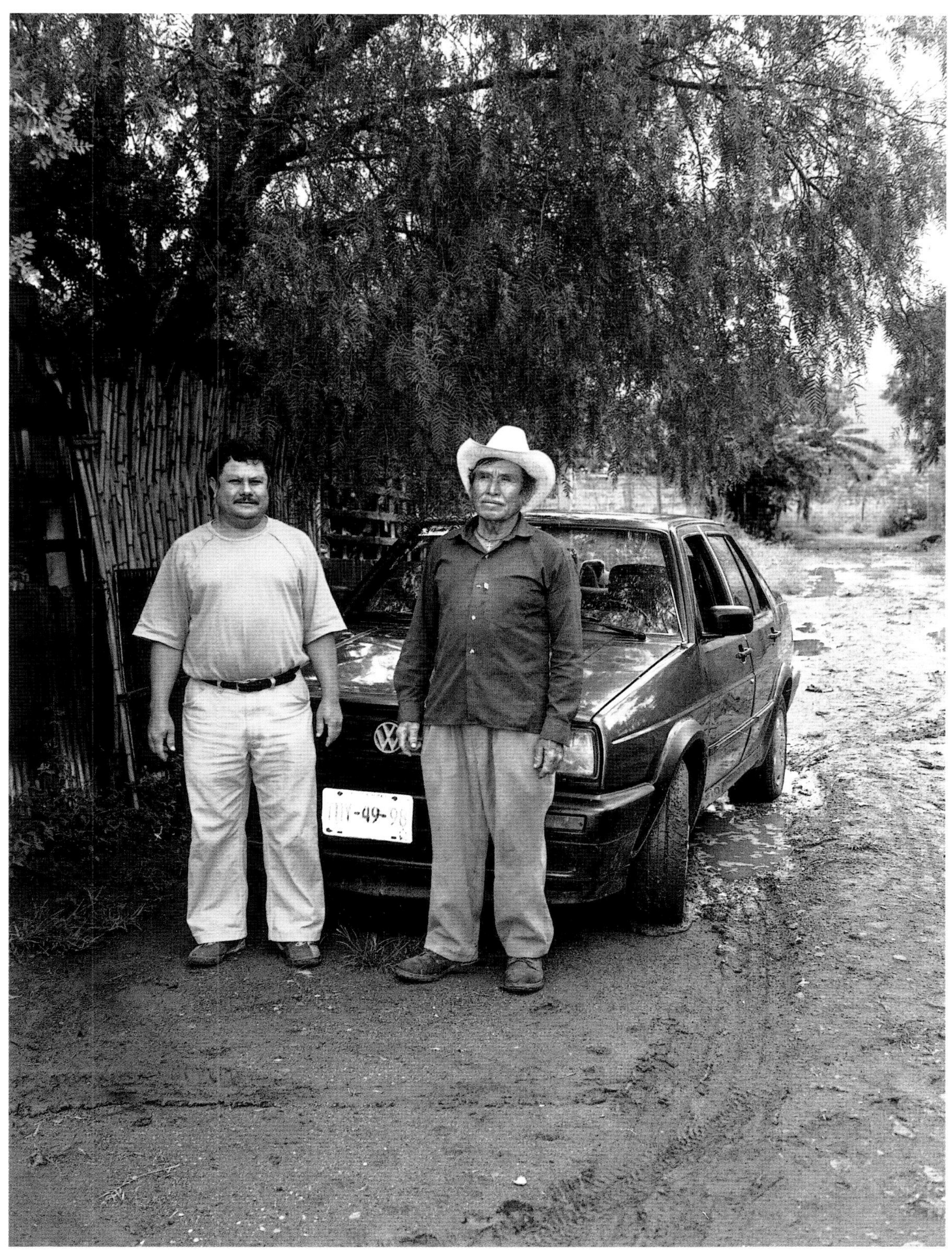

Jesús Melchor and Coindo Melchor. San Martín. 2004.

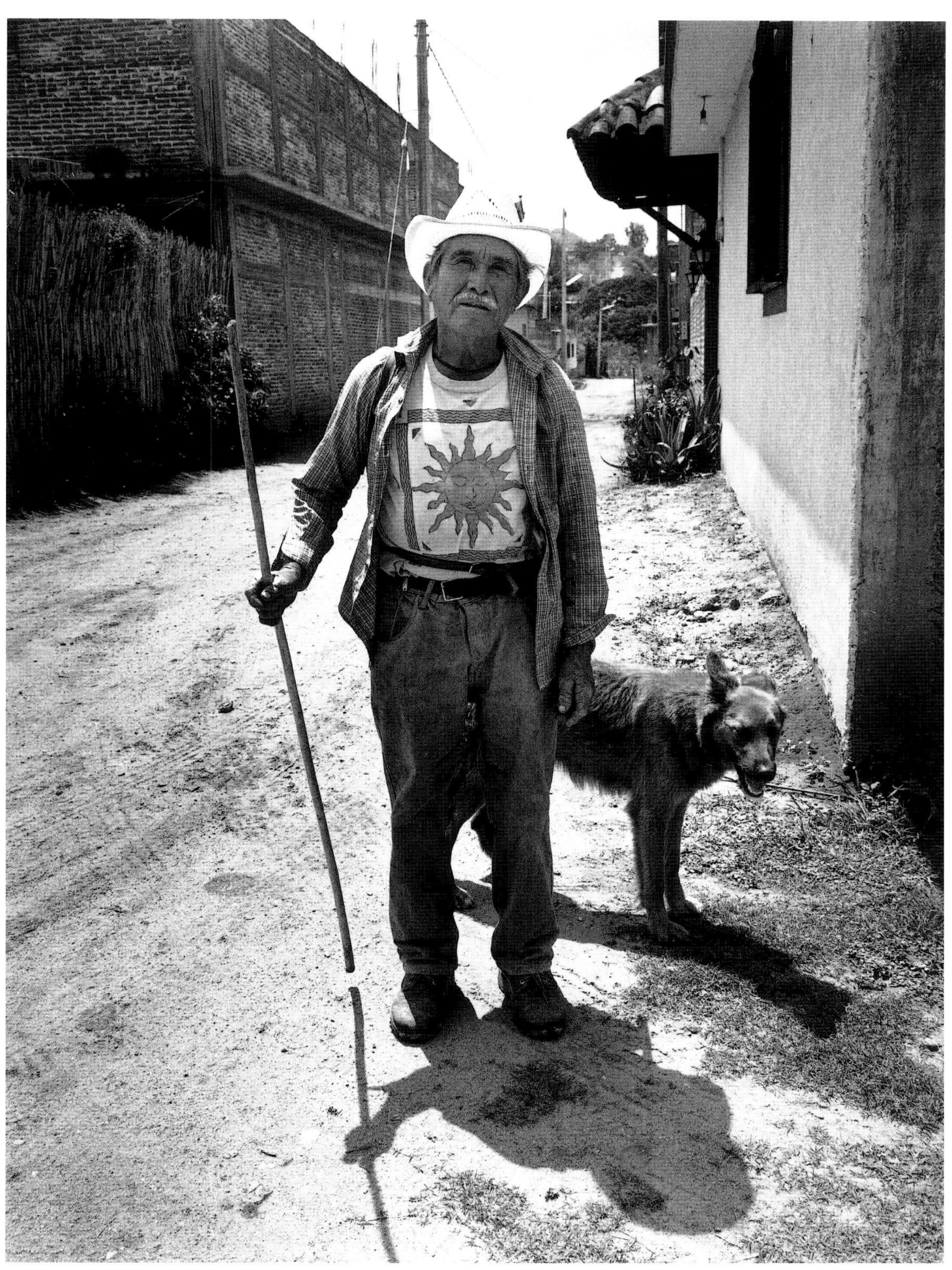

Coindo Melchor. San Martín. 2004.

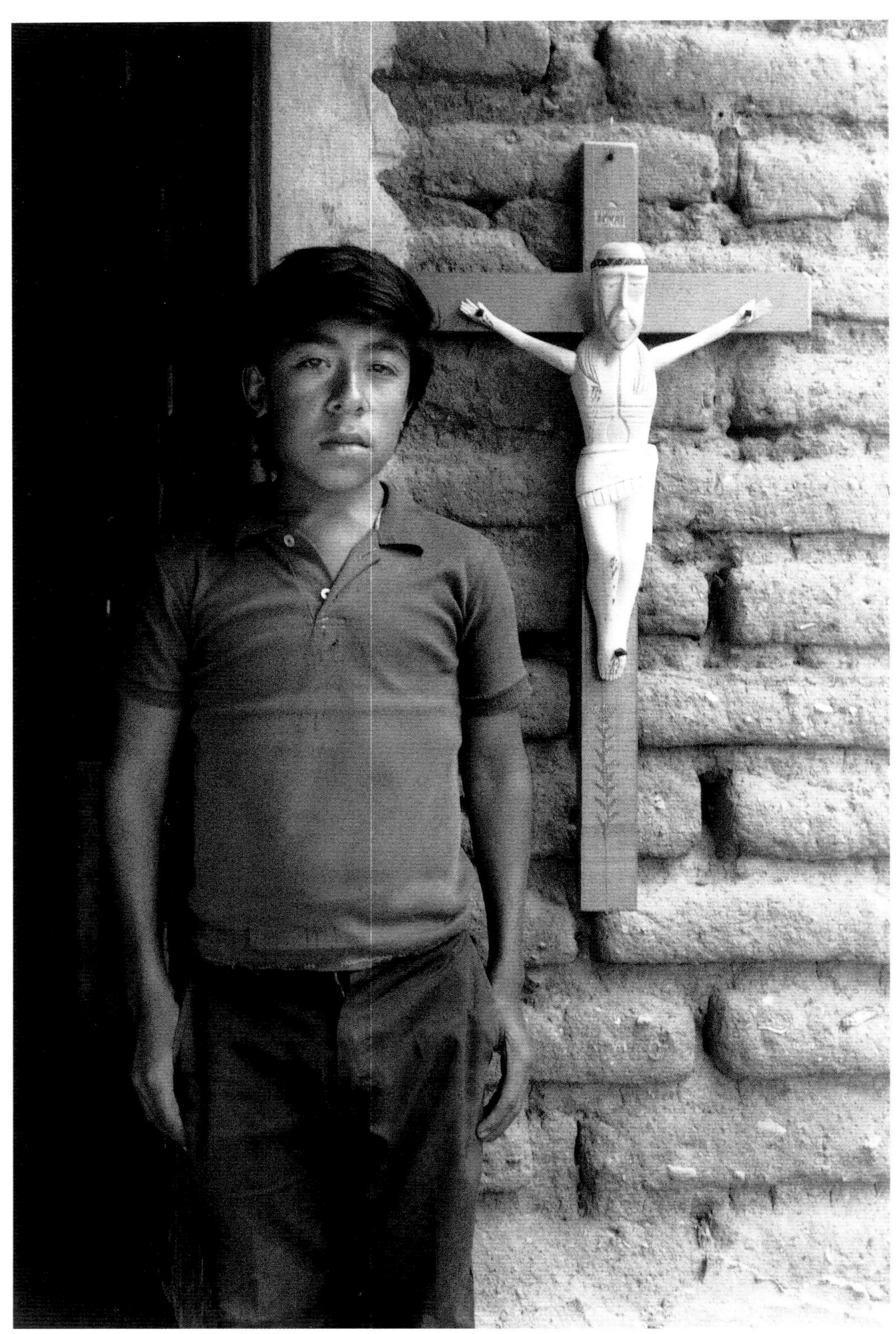

Gilberto Aquino. San Martín. 1989.

Gilberto Aquino

San Martín Tilcajete

IN THE MOST DYNAMIC PLACES and tumultuous times, there will always be those who opt for solitude. Gilberto Aquino lives a quiet life alone with his parents. He has never had much contact with foreigners. During the height of the carving boom, in the early 1990s, he moved to the outskirts of town to get away from the tourist traffic everyone else was so avidly seeking. Gilberto now carves figures for sale, but he is too shy to offer them to strangers. He leaves them unpainted and sells them to his neighbors, who paint, sign, and resell them as their own at triple the price. He is one of a dwindling number of his generation who supports himself by farming. He rarely goes to Oaxaca, rarely receives visitors, and rarely misses a Mass. He has six dogs and prefers them to the company of outsiders. San Martín was once filled with people like him.

Police and Protests

STRENGTHENING THE RULE OF LAW in Mexico is the work of generations. Occasionally the effort breaks down and the nation's most debilitating weaknesses are alarmingly exposed, disturbing the complacency of visitors and would-be foreign partners and sapping the will of even the most capable members of society. Such periods typically end not with steps to better safeguard individual liberties, improve the operation of government, identify wrongdoing, or bring wrongdoers (in or out of government) to account, but with the state using its oil money to placate or put down the contending parties. In such periods, the tenuousness of the people's acceptance of the state's legitimacy is revealed by a surge of violent lawlessness that is fomented (and promptly disowned) by forces that remain in shadows. In such times, the carvers count their relative solitude as a blessing. Their buyers may be gone but their villages are at peace.

In May of 2006, the Oaxaca teachers union, the most powerful force in the state, went on strike over wages and took over the city's zócalo—something they have done every year for three decades. In most years, the occupation lasts no more than a week before the federal government steps in and satisfies most of the teachers' demands. But 2006 was a presidential election year and the first year that the party controlling the presidency, the National Action Party (PAN), was not the same as the party in control of Oaxaca, the Institutional Revolutionary Party (PRI), whose long national reign the PAN had ended six years earlier. Perhaps hoping to weaken the PRI on the eve of the elections, perhaps wanting to confront an infamously corrupt and unproductive union, the feds this time refused to bail out the state. When the governor ill-advisedly tried to evict the teachers by force, elements of the union, in concert with the left-wing Revolutionary Democratic Party and a local newspaper, orchestrated a massive statewide protest aimed at forcing him from office. Six months of mayhem ensued, during which at least nine people (some say more) were killed, including an American photographer; government buildings, banks, hotels, and other businesses were taken over, damaged, looted, and/or destroyed by fire; traffic to, from, and within the city was shut down by protest barricades, causing food shortages in poorer neighborhoods; street crime soared as local police, poorly trained and badly outnumbered, abandoned their duties; thousands of buildings were defaced with graffiti; dozens of city buses were seized and burned; schools remained closed, the despised governor remained in office, and the state remained ungovernable.

By the time federal police were belatedly sent to restore order in November, hundreds of businesses in the city had closed and another wave of *mojados*-to-be had left the carving villages for the States. The teachers, whose students fair worse on tests than students in any other state in Mexico, got their pay raise. Very few tourists came for the holidays, which passed without incident.

The total cost to settle the strike, end the uprising, and repair the damages to the city was estimated at forty-six billion pesos—four hundred times more than what the union had asked for back in May. As of May 2007, no one had been formally charged with the killings, the number of which remains in dispute.

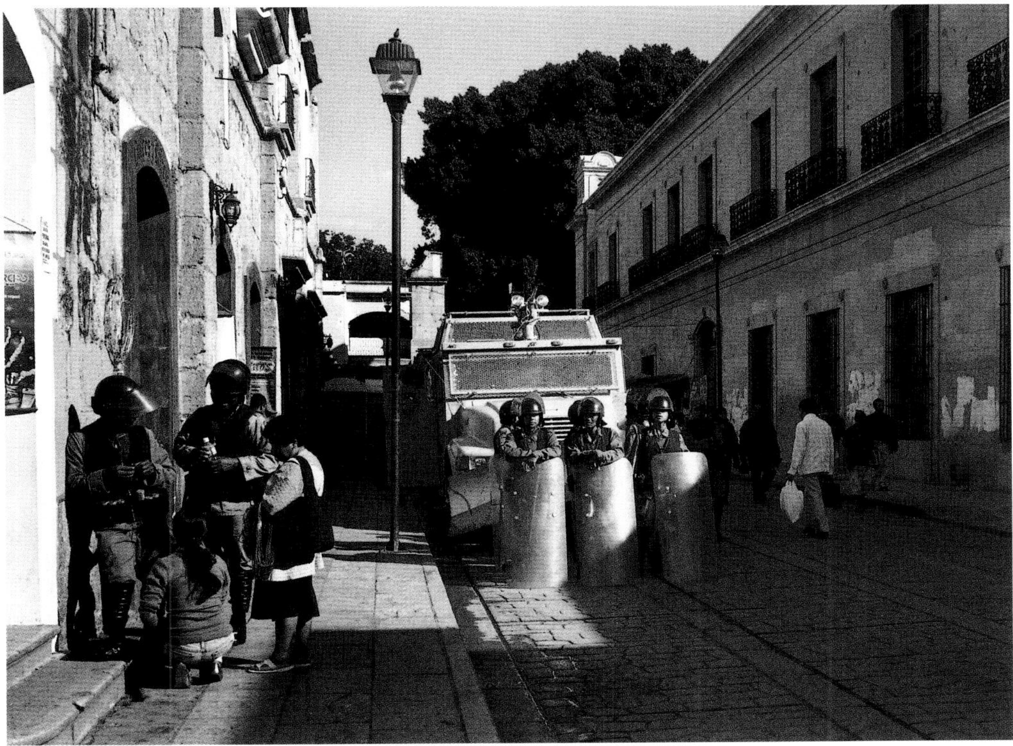

Federal police guarding zócalo. Oaxaca. 2006.

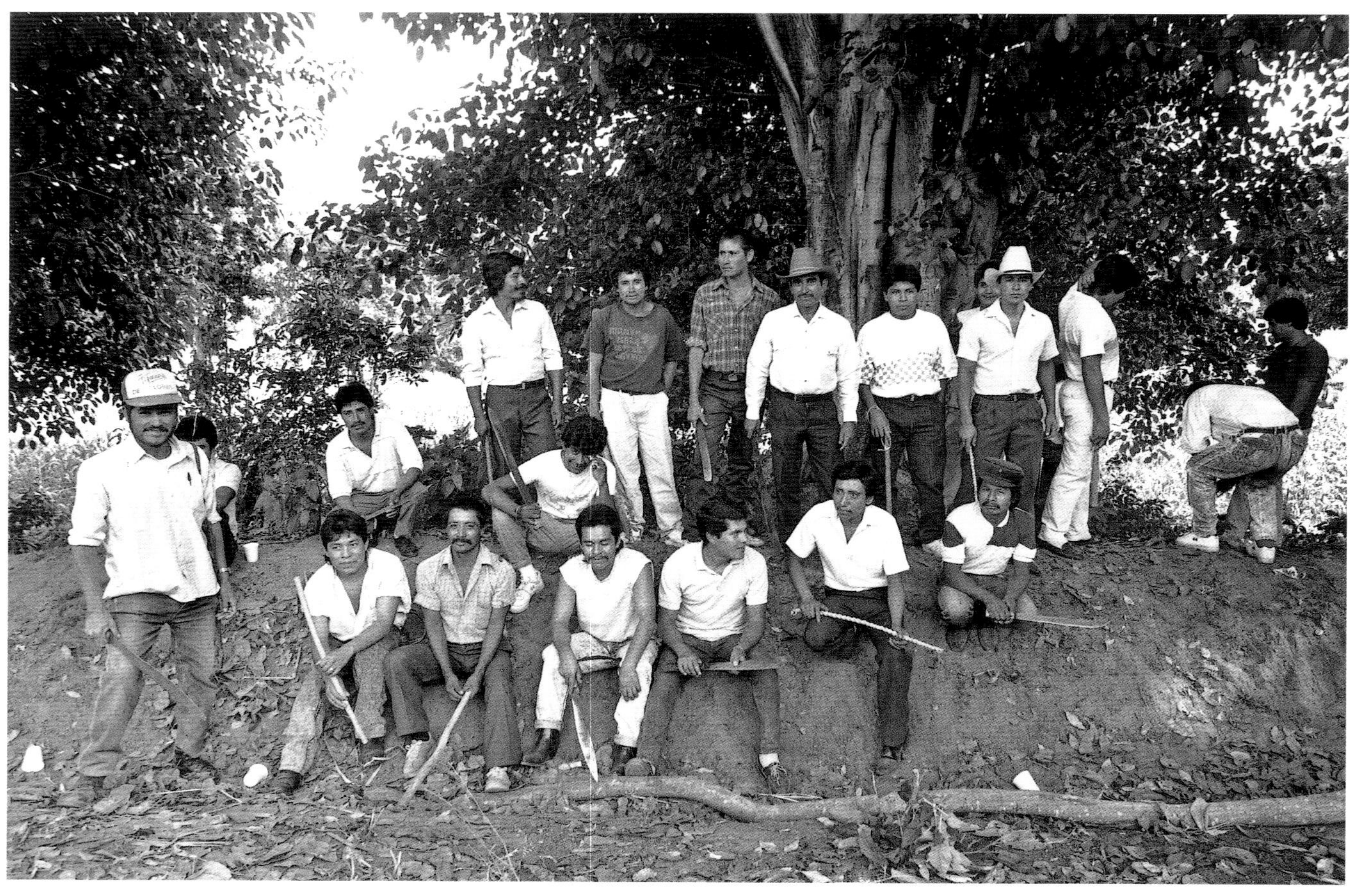

Volunteer police force. Arrazola. 1990.

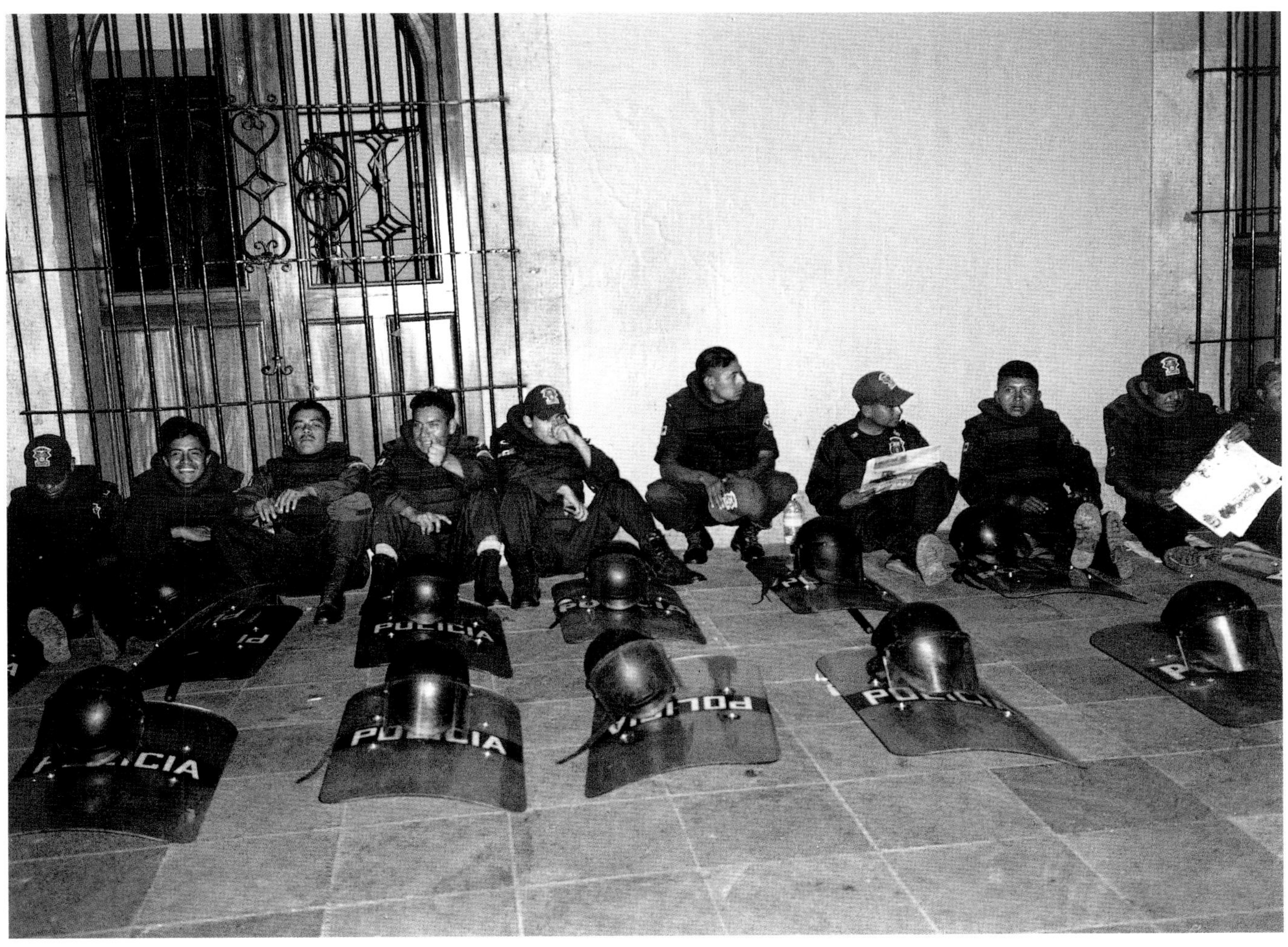

State police in zócalo. Oaxaca. 2006.

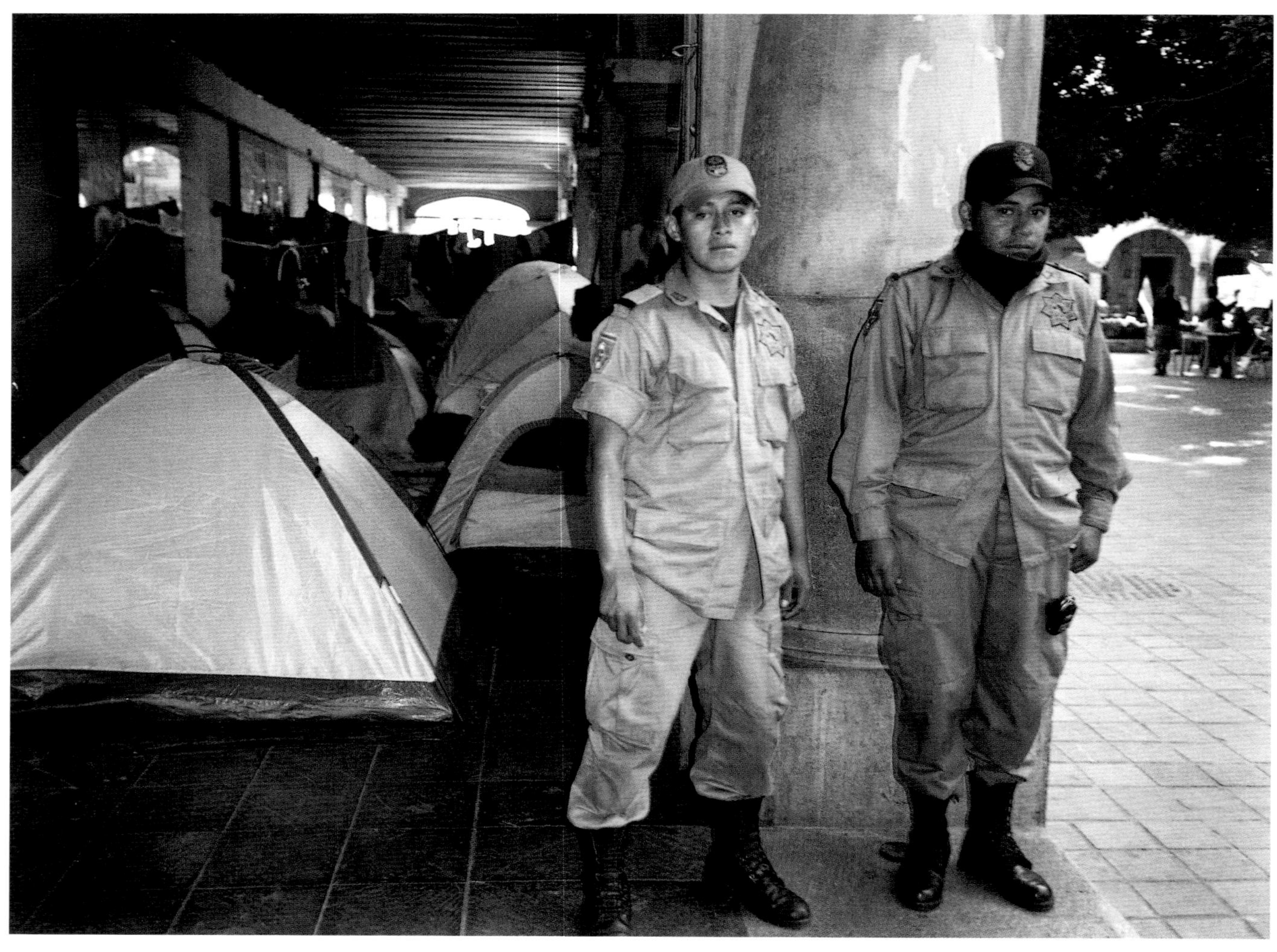

Camped out in zócalo. Oaxaca. 2006.

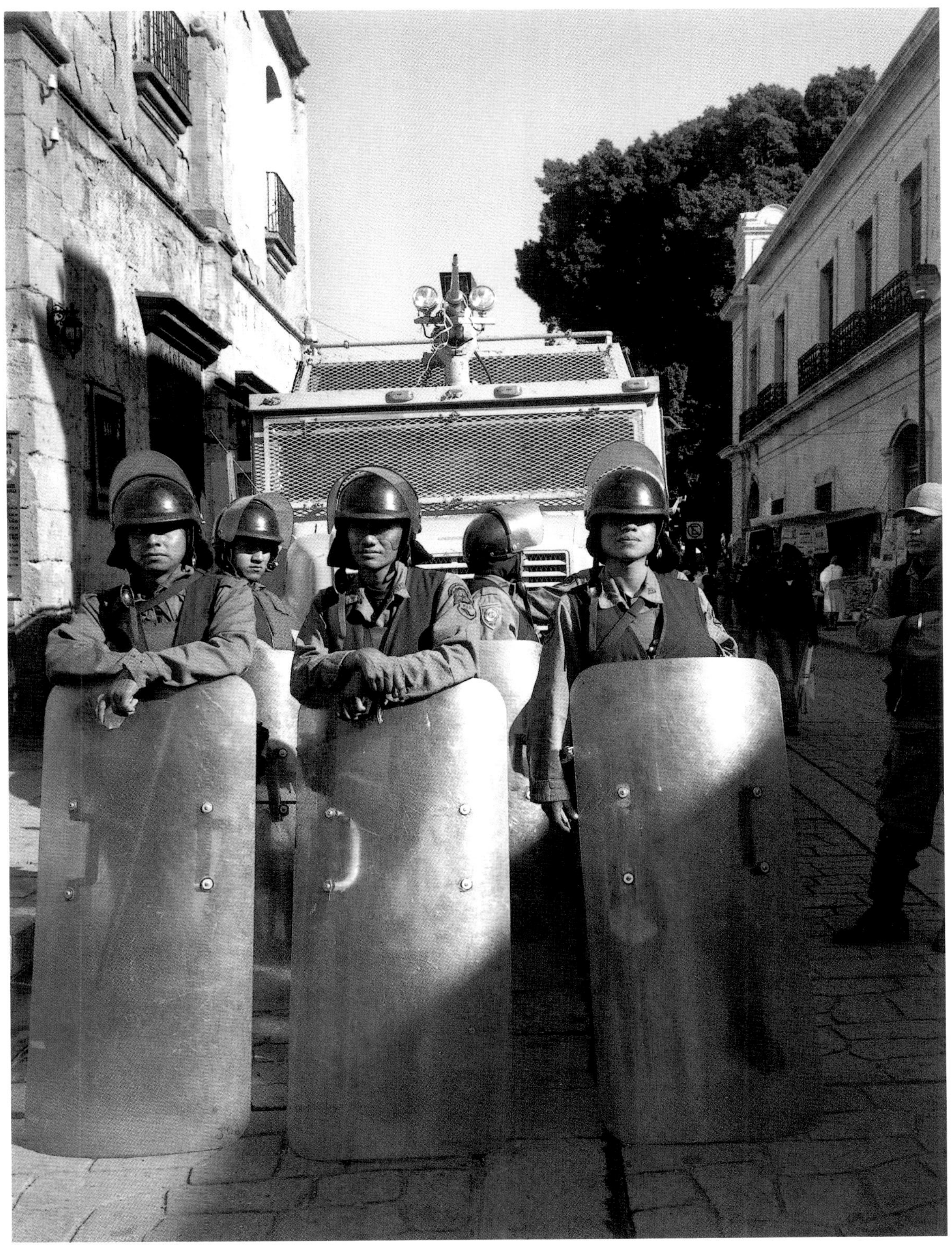

Federal police outside zócalo. Oaxaca. 2006.

Ismael Carrillo

Arrazola

ISMAEL CARRILLO WAS A POLICEMAN in the municipal force of Xoxocotlán, the district seat between Arrazola and Oaxaca. He worked three twenty-four-hour shifts a week and earned about $1.20 per hour. The income, though small, was steadier than what he was making as a carver, and he liked the work better. He wanted to be a role model for his sons and "fight juvenile delinquency," he said. He got the job through a friend.

Notwithstanding his employment in a profession that is often accused of abetting more than combating the country's lawlessness, Ismael was proud to be a cop. He talked at length about the physical training (calisthenics and a ten-kilometer run three times a week), the mental training (a high-school diploma plus a three-month course in police work), the discipline, the honor, and above all, the bravery it took to do his job well. Xoxo's force (fifty men divided into two teams) carries no firearms and must impose its will on drunks, abusive spouses, vagrants, and the like armed only with clubs, tear gas, handcuffs, and persuasion. Serious crimes are turned over to the state. With fewer responsibilities, lower pay, and less weaponry than big-city and state police, the force has fewer opportunities and incentives for the sort of corruption and abuse that have been unchanging features of Mexico's law enforcement apparatus for decades and that flourish even now under the country's new multiparty democracy. As with the volunteer police that patrol Ismael's village and others like it throughout the country (teams of young men armed with sticks and pressed into service by their elders), the Xoxo police seem, if not quite professional, then at least well intentioned and, in a land where disputes are unending, conciliatory. At worst they are harmless beneficiaries of the country's welfare state, staying close to home to support their families, resisting the lure of higher wages and lawless adventure in the States.

"Little by little, we are earning people's respect," Ismael said in 2004. Two years later, with protests against the governor sweeping the state, police everywhere in retreat, and federal forces preparing to intervene, he gave up his job and took off for California.

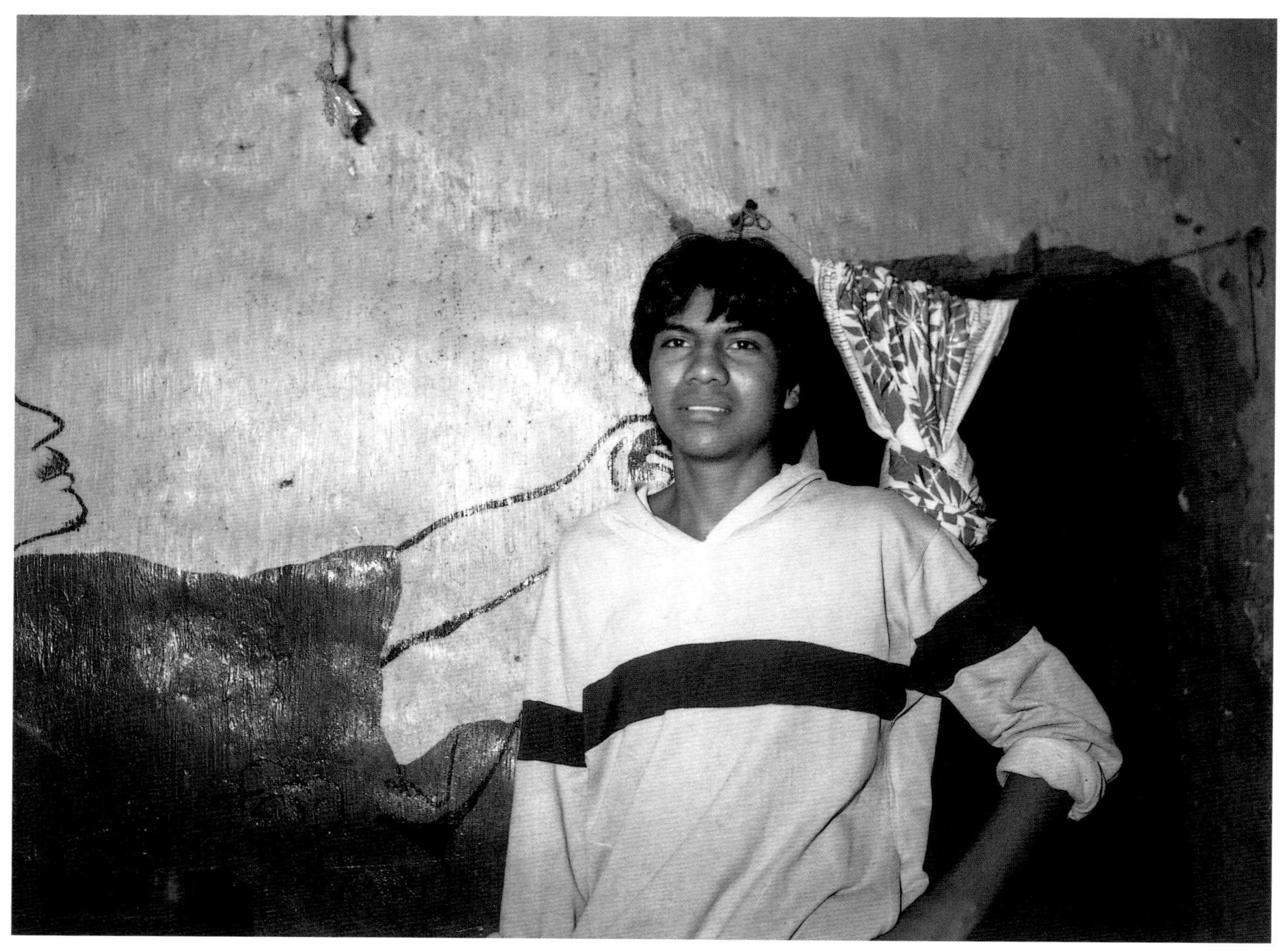

Ismael Carrillo. Arrazola. 1989.

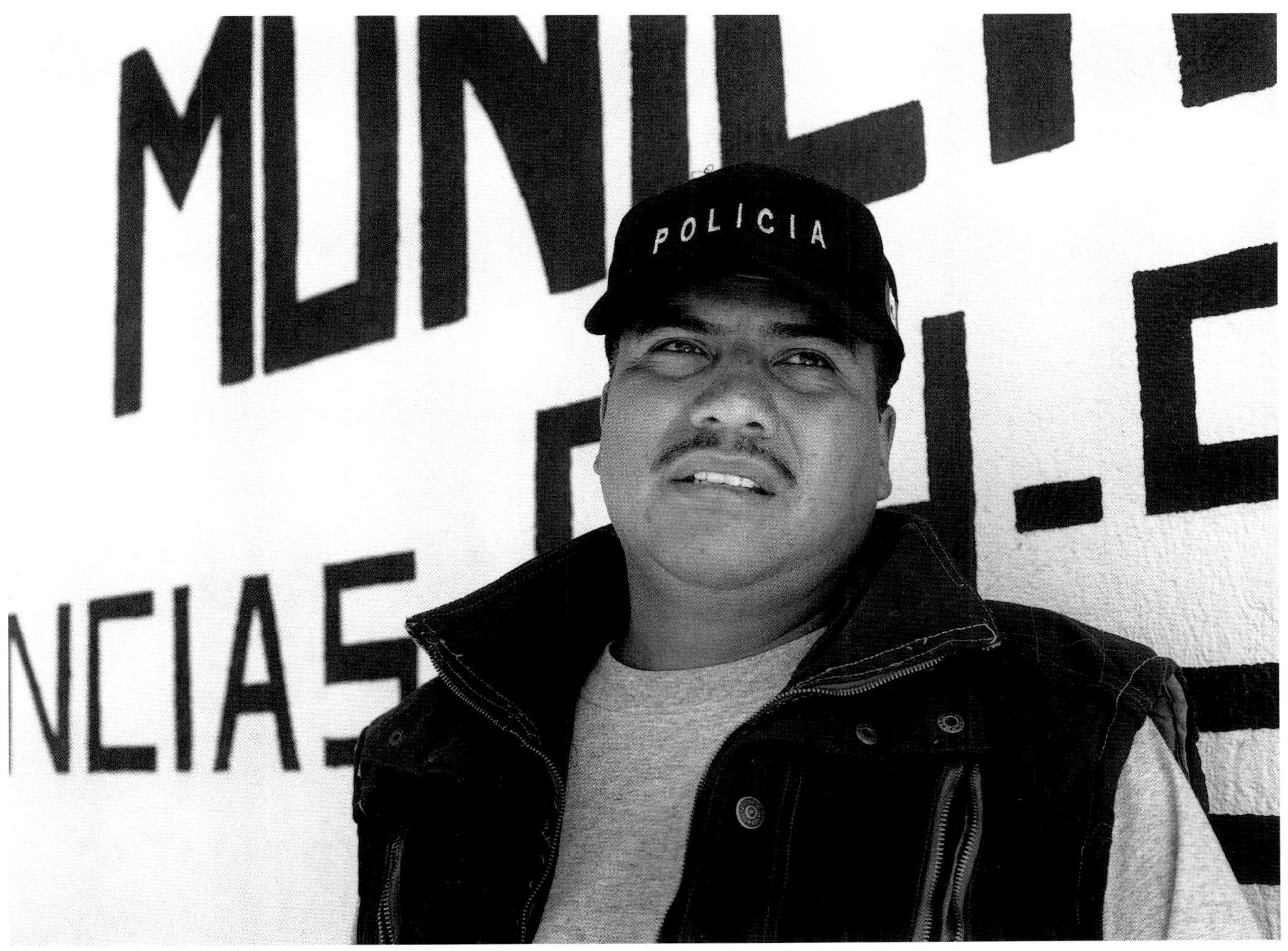

Ismael Carrillo. Xoxocotlán. 2004.

The Fuentes Family

San Martín Tilcajete

Carver Alejandrino Fuentes proposed to his wife, Elizabeth, when he was twenty-five and she was fourteen. They were married a year later. The priest, concerned that the bride was too young, joined them reluctantly and with admonishment. The idea of a college graduate wooing a girl not yet out of junior high school seemed to us at the time like just another example of the backwardness of the "developing world" and a measure of our distance from it.

Today Alejandrino and Elizabeth live a sophisticated bilateral existence. The couple divide their time between San Martín, where they sell sundries and wood carvings out of their house, and Santa Fe, New Mexico, where they are employed by a folkart store to sell carvings and give demonstrations. If neighbors like young Catalina Julián are Mexico's hope for the future, the Fuentes are that hope fully realized: a prosperous, hardworking family, sensible, self-reliant, at home in the world and content with each other. San Martín's youth, nowadays wise enough (most of them) to wait a little longer before marrying, would do well to marry as wisely.

Alejandrino, who studied engineering but found that wood carving paid better, says his goal in life was never just to build a nice house, although he has done that, but to be able to pay for his children's education and help them chase dreams bigger than his own. This sounds familiar. Born into a music-loving family of no great talent, our son wants to be a jazz musician. Born into a village society of no great means, Fuentes's daughter Emmy wants to become a pop singer. I scour the land for the best teachers and cheer Eddie along, but I fret about whether he will achieve his goals. Alejandrino, who met his wife when he was a singer in her uncle's band, doesn't mind paying for Emmy's music lessons but admits he'd rather she also study something else.

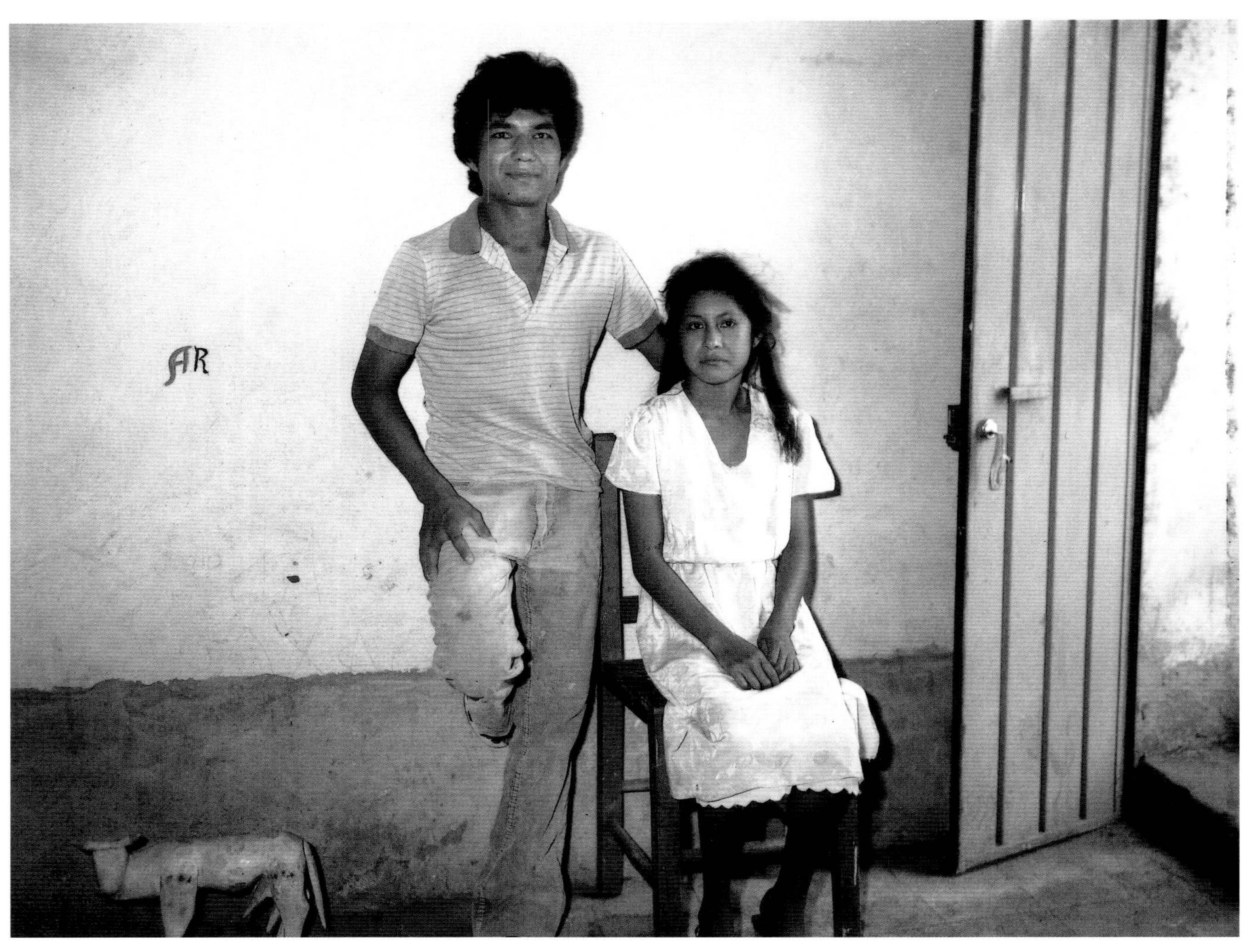

Alejandrino Fuentes, Elizabeth Díaz. San Martín. 1989.

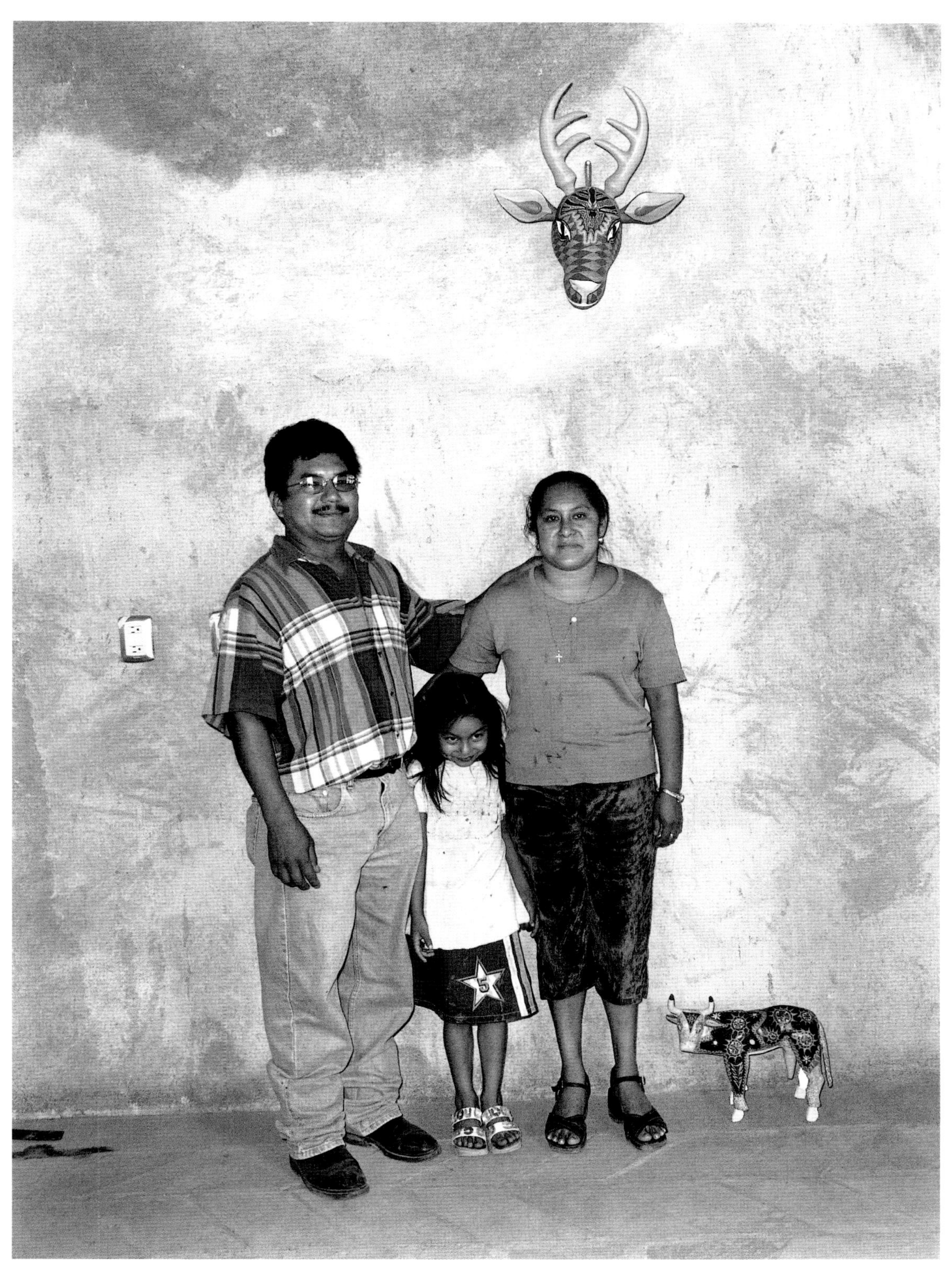

Alejandrino Fuentes, Elizabeth Díaz, and daughter Ivón. Ocotlán de Morelos. 2004.

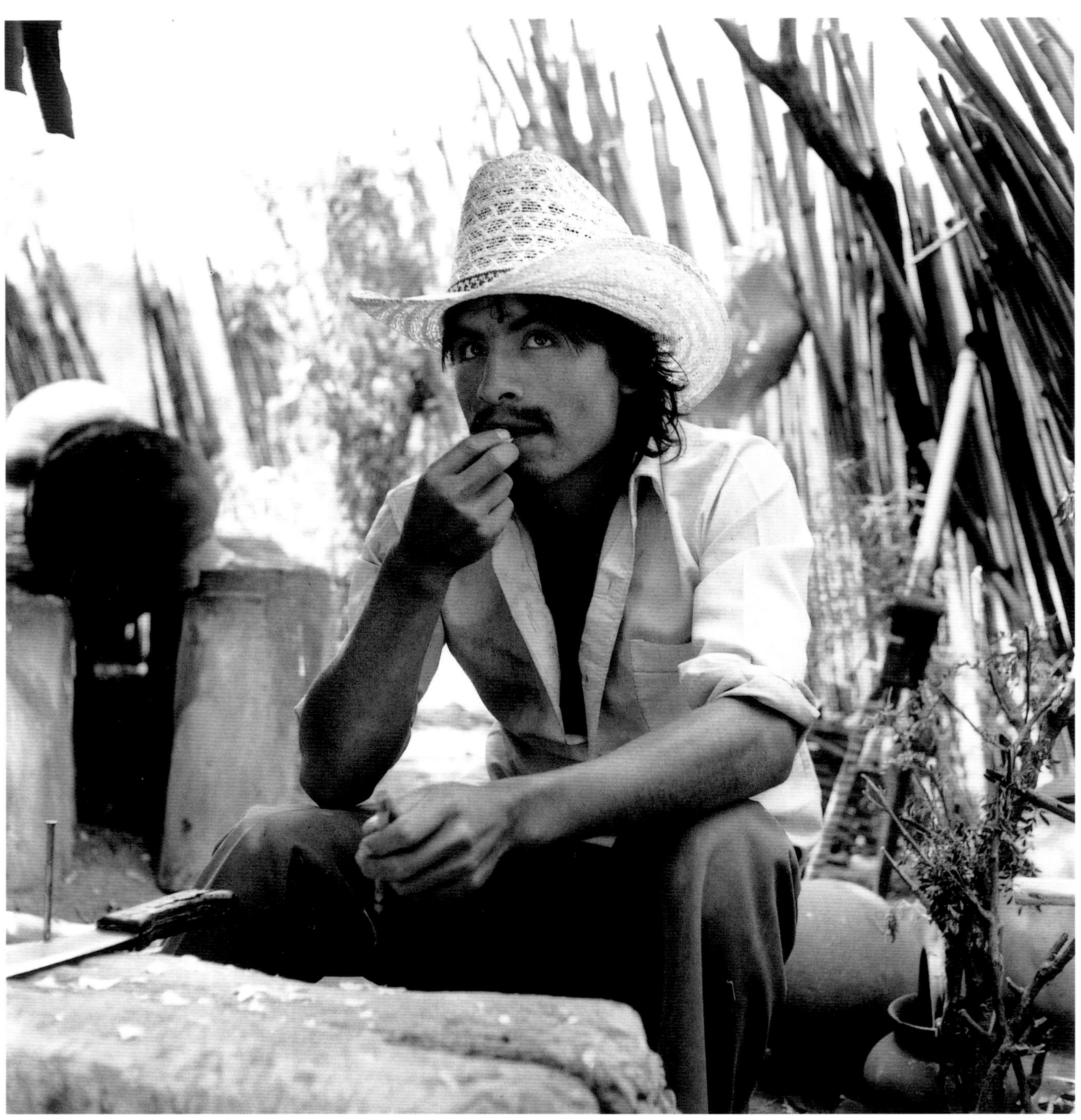

Gabino Reyes. La Unión. 1987.

Gabino Reyes

La Unión Tejalapan

A WOODCARVER who considers himself talented pointed to a *tunillo* cactus in our bathroom and said, "If I had to choose one carving I wish I had made myself, it would be this."

Carvers can be harsh critics, but the carvings of Gabino Reyes provoke nothing but admiration. The cactus (which has a tiny bird's nest) is typical of his oeuvre: wondrously detailed and lifelike. Most carvers worry about being copied and undersold. Gabino, blessed with more talent than vanity and more sense than ambition, knows he cannot be copied.

Reyes's pieces are hard to come by. He works slowly and refuses to leave his fields to carve full-time. Folk-art dealers futilely press

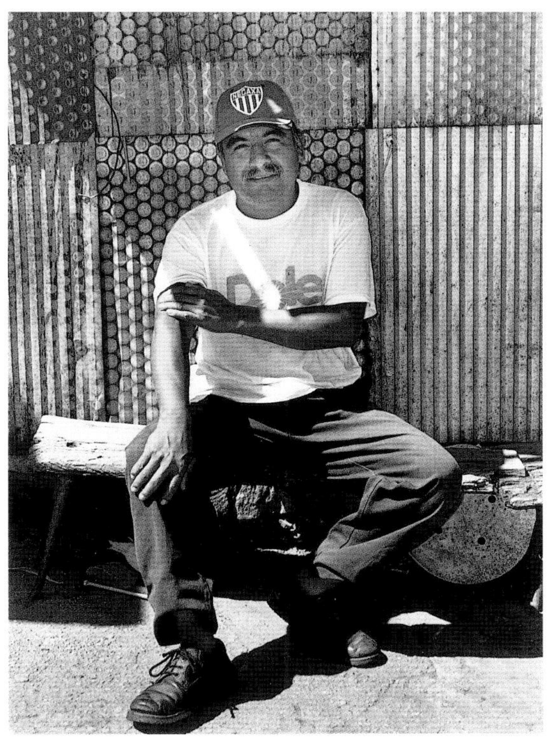

Gabino Reyes. La Unión. 2004.

him to produce more. "They want you to have a motor in your hands," he says. As it is, he is going blind from farming in the sun's glare and from carving and painting his tiny details. His meager output, phlegmatic temperament, and continued attachment to the land explain why he has not yet made it to the States as a guest of some museum or gallery. Watching him work would be dull, and there would be little to buy to reward one's patience.

Fortune scatters her gifts at random. Gabino was born and raised in a village so poor and with so few prospects that most of its young men have left to find work elsewhere. He started carving in the late 1980s at the encouragement of an American. He knows he could earn far more, and save his eyesight, if he joined his friends in the States, but he does not want to be separated from his aging mother—a high-spirited octogenarian—or from his wife and two teenage sons. "Families fall apart when the husband leaves home," he says. He is proud that his boys are studying algebra and computers in school, and though he can't help them with their homework in either subject, he likes being around to make sure they do it.

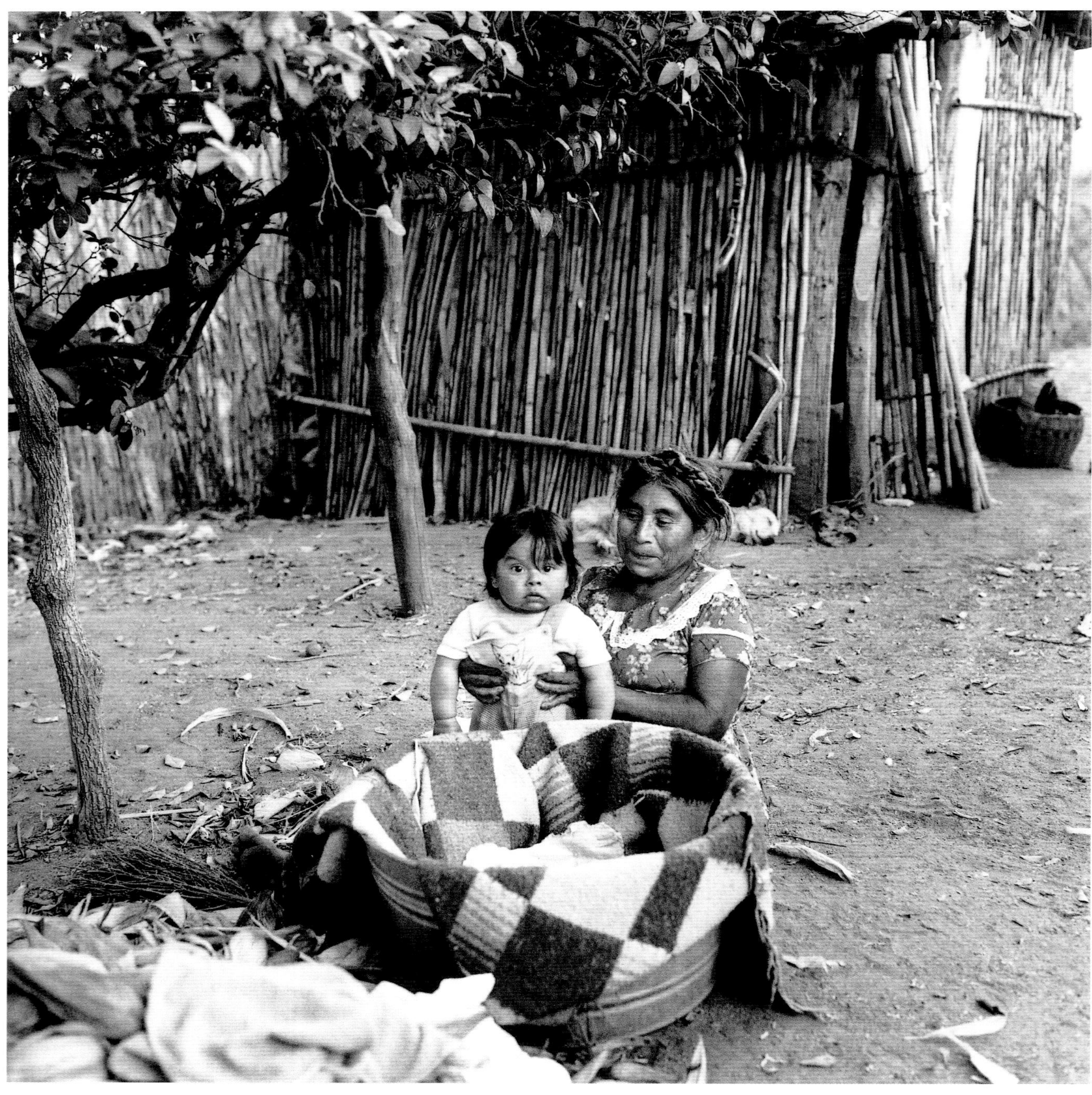

Gabino's mother, Ricarda López, with his son Giovanni. La Unión. 1988.

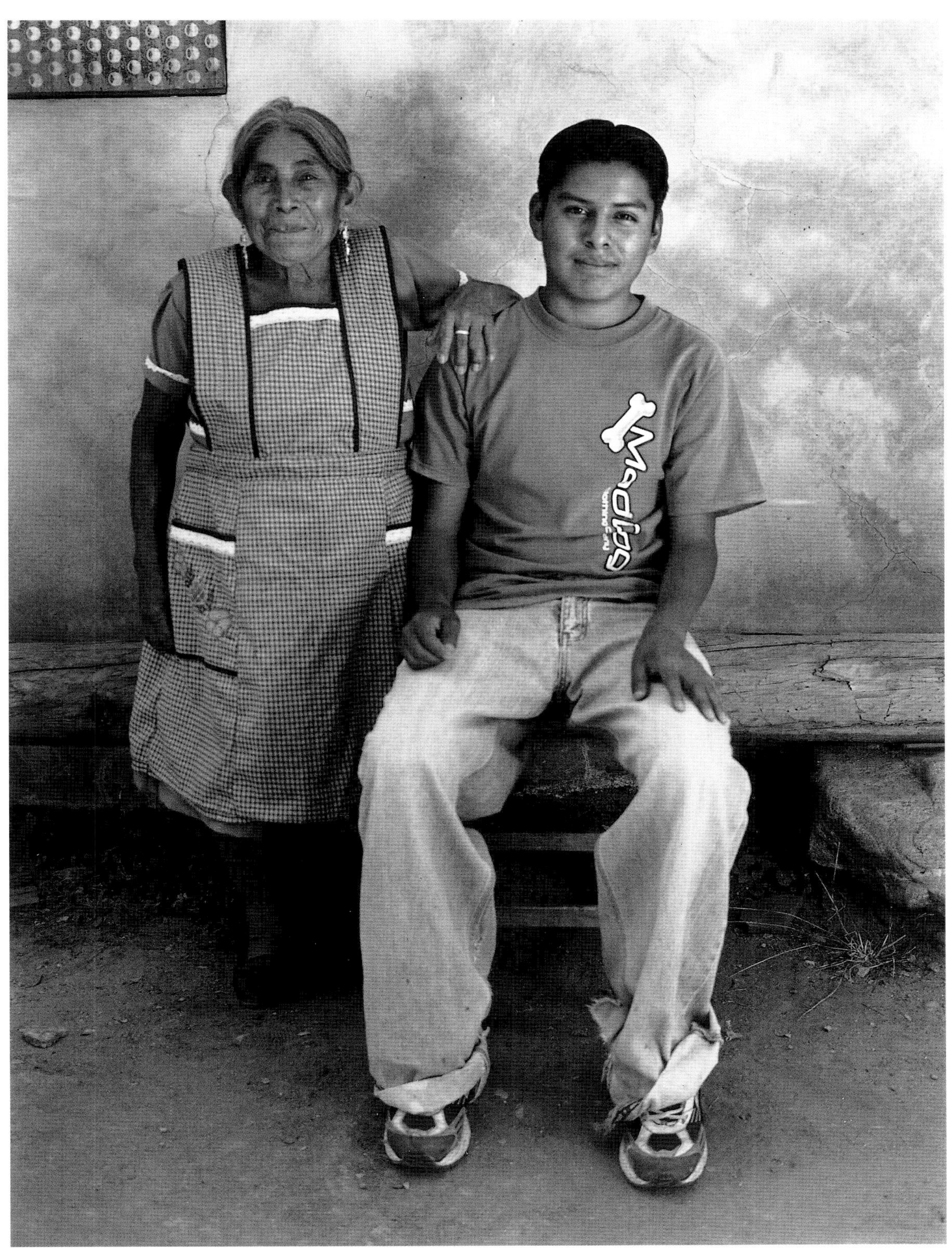

Ricarda López and her grandson Giovanni. La Unión. 2004.

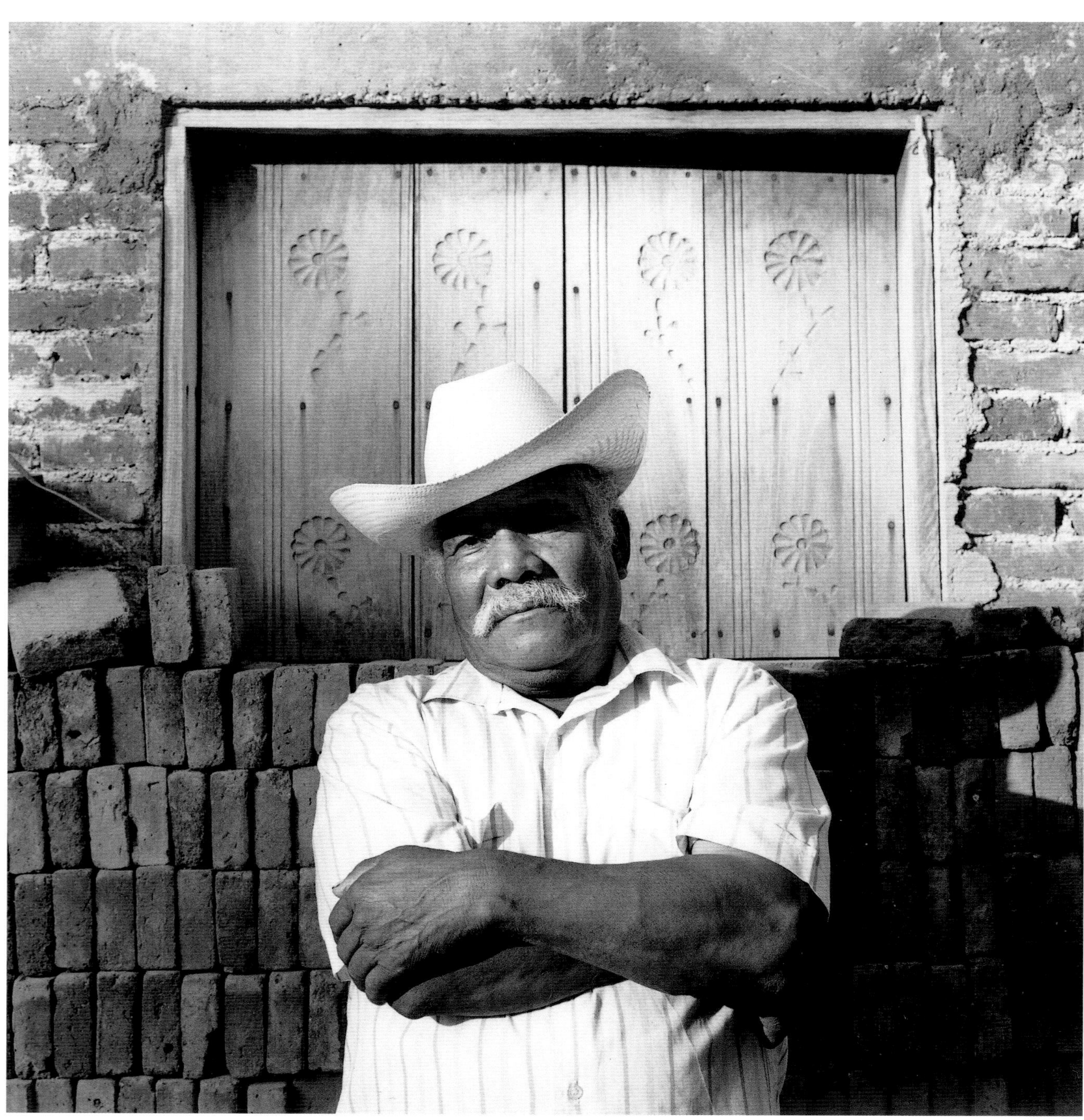

Zenén Fuentes. San Martín. 1989.

Zenén Fuentes

San Martín Tilcajete

ZENÉN FUENTES ADMITS he is more comfortable with the laws of nature, which never change, than with the laws of men, which are always in dispute. Village president for a year and campesino for life, he knows both worlds well. Over the years he has grown corn, beans, and garbanzos and raised goats, burros, and cattle. Now in his eighties, he sells milk to his neighbors and carvings to tourists.

"The time for peasants is past," he told us fifteen years ago. "It's not a good business. We do it out of habit." Five of his children are schoolteachers. Two others, Epifanio and Alejandrino, are successful carvers. None are campesinos.

Habits of governance are changing, but here, too, Zenén resists. Like most villages, San Martín manages its politics through "uses and customs"—a system of conventions whereby leaders are selected and policies set through loosely run elections at assemblies. The government comprises mostly volunteers who are cajoled into assuming their duties. Presidents are selected more than elected and are considered unqualified unless they have ascended a ladder of different posts. Detractors call the system "*abuses* and customs," but Zenén fears the alternatives, which he sees as opening up the village to the corrupt factionalism of political parties and accepting a new set of laws on how villages are to be run that neither citizen nor state would likely apply with justice. "I was a good president without those things," he says.

But reform seems inevitable. The post of president in San Martín now receives a small salary. Some of the younger, more educated villagers are pushing to open up the nominating system by eliminating the "ladder of service," which they see as poor preparation for a job that has changed. Zenén was president in 1980, when there were no budgets or salaries to disburse, most people were campesinos, and one party ruled the country. But today Mexico is a competitive democracy, and lawyers, doctors, teachers, and accountants now live in San Martín. Noting that their present incumbent didn't finish junior high and can barely read, some of them are ready for a change.

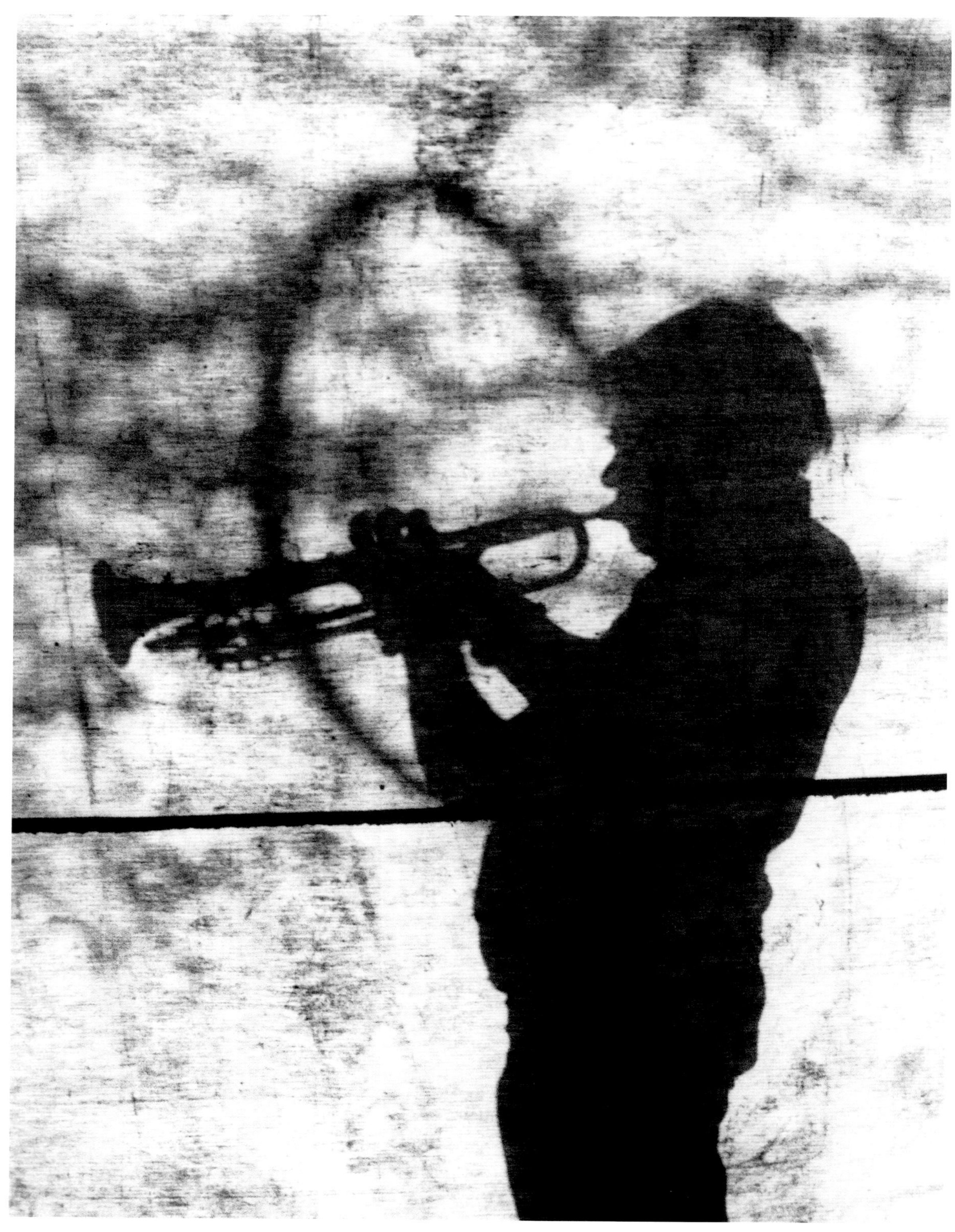
Epifanio Fuentes. San Martín. 1989.

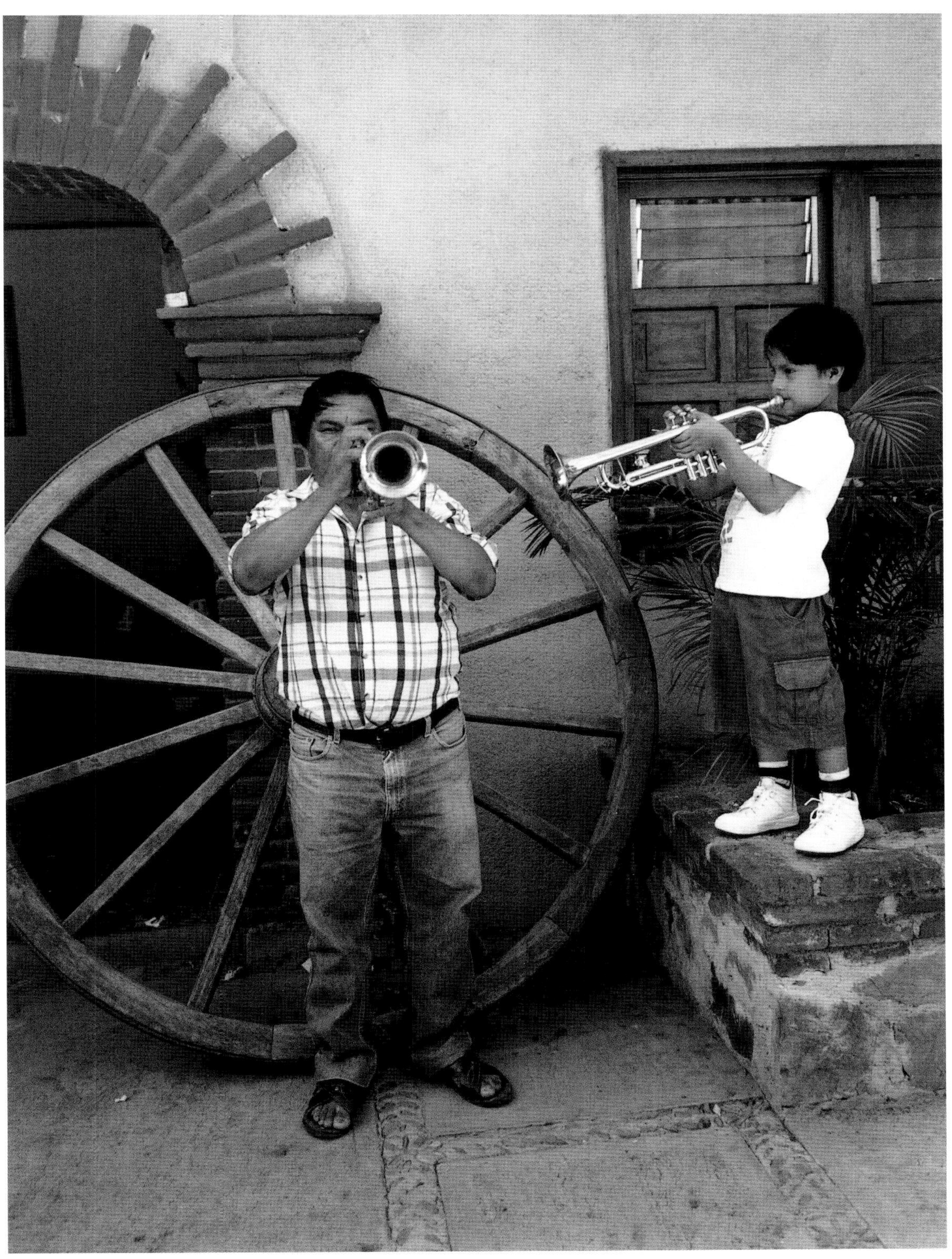

Epifanio Fuentes and his son, José Alberto. San Martín. 2004.

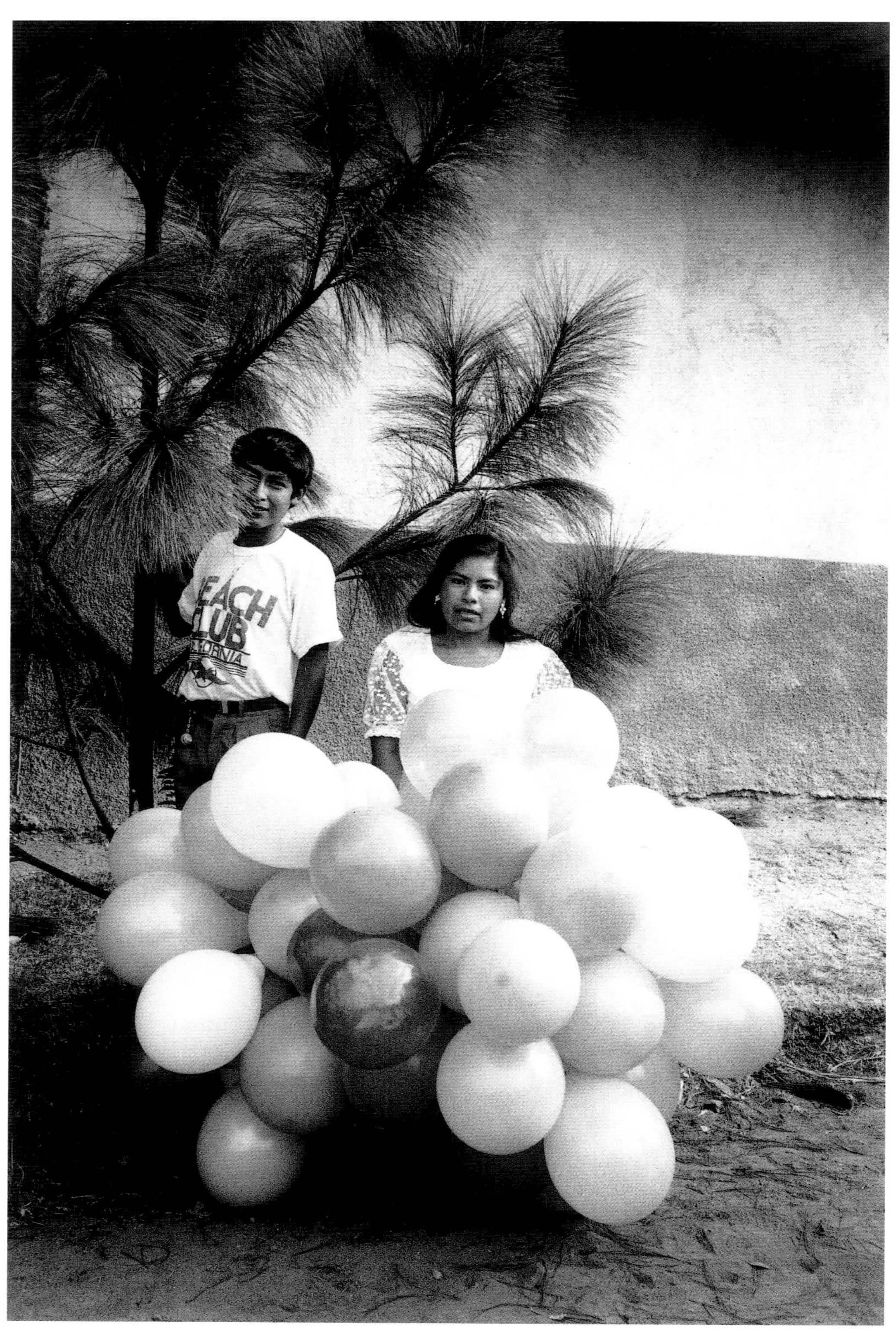

Alberto Melchor and María Jiménez. San Martín. 1989.

María Jiménez
San Martín Tilcajete

Sweet-tempered María Jiménez is determined to remain single, even as her village opens up to the world and her fortunes grow. Four brothers, a vigilant father, and the innumerable influences of village life have no doubt fed her resolve. But her own talents and thoughtful reserve have marked her for solitude as well, contenting her to live out her life as the beloved aunt of her brothers' children.

In the last fifteen years, María has established herself as a successful artisan. In an art form where men get most of the credit, she has earned renown as the indefatigable ornamentalist who paints her brothers' carvings. She has been to Virginia as a visiting artist and has been featured in books. Rising onto the narrow radar screen of Oaxaca's political elite, in 2004 she was invited by the state to contribute an angel to its new Popular Art Museum, at whose inauguration she and her brothers were honored guests.

María lives with her sisters and parents. Her brothers live next door, on lots given to them by their father, a successful mason. The family is upstanding and enterprising. One brother, Miguel, is a prospering farmer, another is San Martín's police chief. Their dad has been village president, a post he served with distinction.

"Work, health, and family are the three most important things to me," María says. Why marry? A man from the village would only want her to keep house and would interfere with her work. A more liberal-minded suitor from beyond San Martín is unlikely to appear, and in any case would be dismissed as a stranger whom she could never get to know well enough to trust with her affections.

"You only really know someone when you've grown up with him and seen him with his family," María says. She also understands that the carvers' lives, while transparent to one another, are inscrutable to everyone else. She is sensitive to her foreign patrons and patient with their naive demands—demands that, unlike those of the boy next door, she gets paid to meet and graciously endures as the price of her independence.

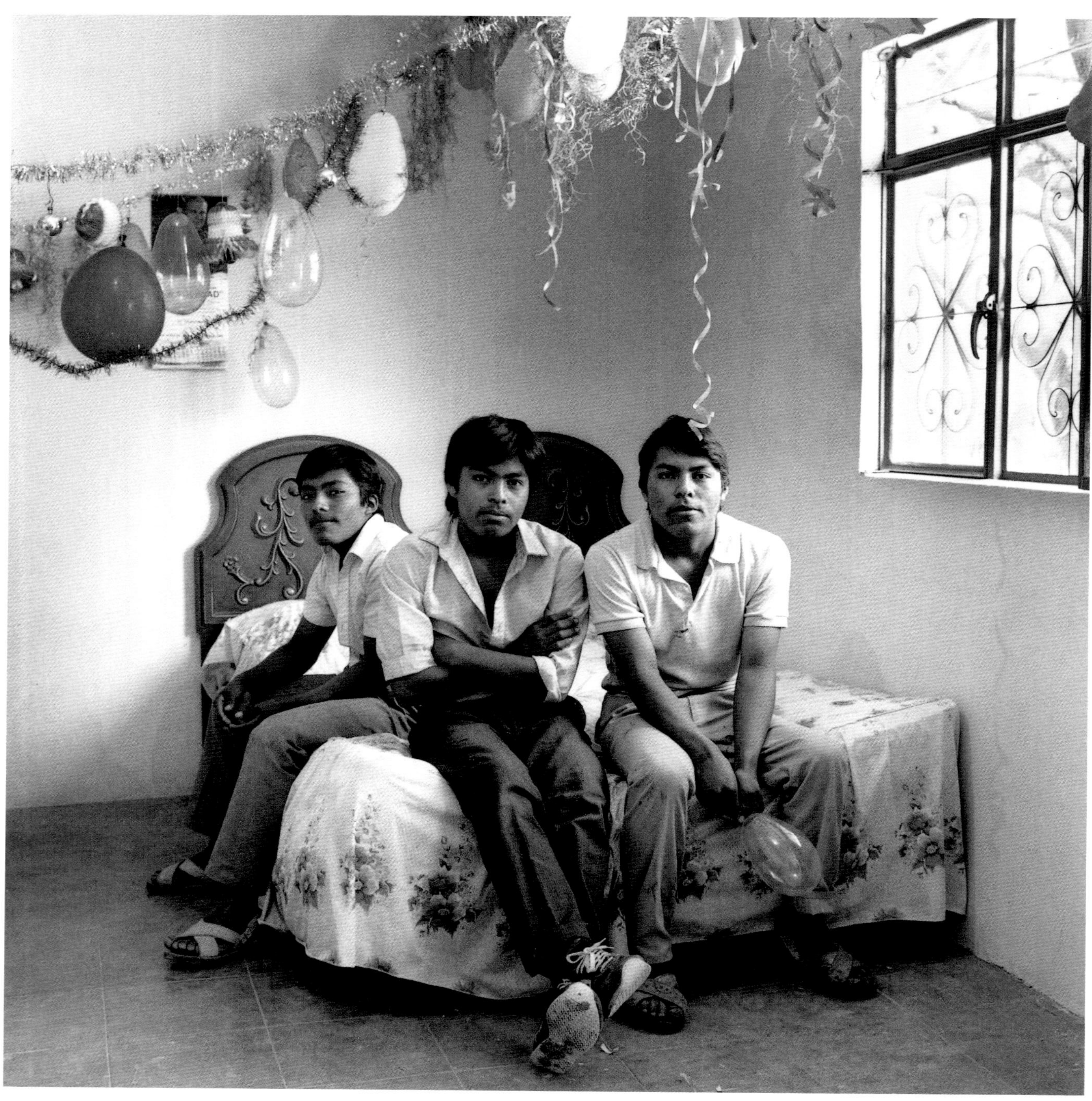

Miguel, Cándido, and Alberto Jiménez. San Martín. 1989.

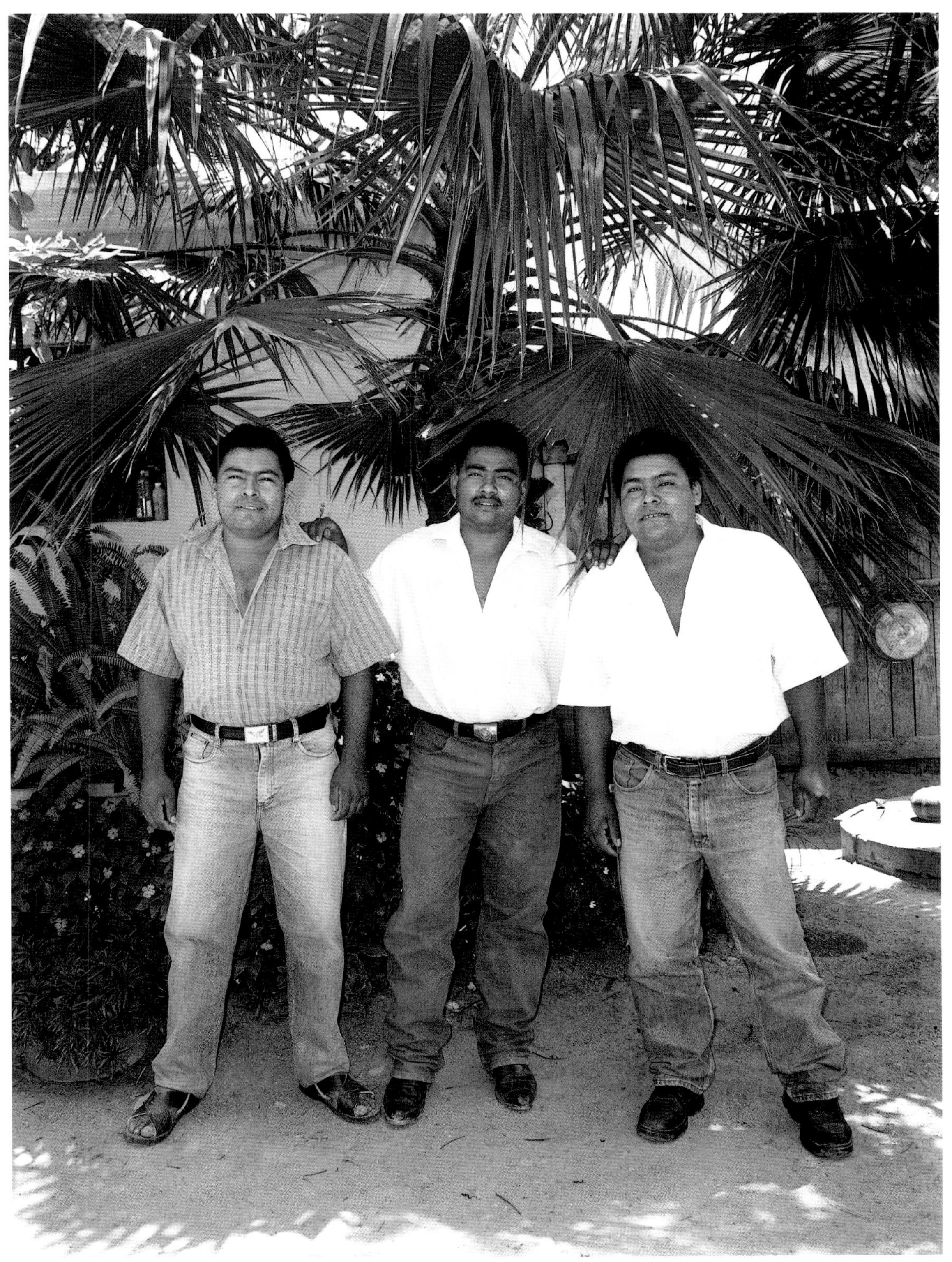

Cándido, Arón, and Alberto Jiménez. San Martín. 2004.

María Teresa Santiago
San Martín Tilcajete

THE DEATH OF MARÍA TERESA SANTIAGO came not long after the death of her youngest son, Arturo, whose own death at age fourteen followed the death of her oldest son, Alberto, a few years earlier. Both boys died of juvenile nephritis, an inherited kidney disease passed down to them by their mother. Arturo died at home, lying face down, surrounded by candles and a crowd of praying villagers. Following village tradition, the boys were buried dressed as angels.

María Teresa had a high, lyrical voice, which fluttered like a calling bird when she got excited, which was often. She was an adoring mother but gripped by superstitions, which competed with the arduous regime of medicines and diet prescribed by the doctors for her sons. From her we learned that eating an avocado when angry causes hysteria and that a woman who wants to conceive should truss up her womb with a tourniquet. She worried about people casting spells on her and her children. Her demise remains a topic of mystery in San Martín. Some say she died of a broken heart. Others suspect foul play. Still others insist that supernatural agents ought not be ruled out. Indeed her fears outlived her.

María Teresa was married to Margarito Melchor, one of the most talented woodcarvers in Oaxaca. She painted his figures with bright, florid patterns, fastidiously executed. The couple was renowned for their cats, one of which was chosen for the cover of our first book, *Oaxacan Wood Carving*, which described them:

> Murderous tigers and playful kittens, lions devouring sheep and house cats batting balls, smiling jaguars drowsing in the sun . . . [painted] in riots of color—polka-dot reds inside oblong yellows against solid cobalt blues . . . true-to-life, fantastic, and mysterious.

Margarito and Teresa were a great team. They went to Palo Alto—Oaxaca's sister city—as visiting artists. And yet somehow their notoriety didn't seem to help with the things that mattered most. They never saved enough money to pay for their sons' medical care—inferior in Oaxaca though it was—and they never benefited much from advice. Even the most well-meaning clients—who came bearing Nikes, paint-brushes, and medical referrals from New Mexico—found their world of curses and demons impenetrable, just as our world of Darwin and dialysis remained alien to them. Some walls are too high even for love and kindness to scale.

Margarito, now a grandfather, has remarried and started a second family. He still carves and his new wife paints, but things aren't the same and sales have declined. His three surviving children from Teresa are grown and married to spouses from San Martín. The oldest, Margarito Jr., lives with his dad and carves; the youngest, Isaura, lives illegally in Santa Cruz with her husband, who works in construction; the middle child, Maricela, married the son of a successful carver. Though none is likely to wind up on the cover of a book, the life prospects for all three seem brighter than they were for the generation before them. They have more education than their parents, neither of whom finished junior high school. Medical care in the Oaxaca valley has improved and access to care has increased, as has the villagers' willingness to use it. Best of all, neither Margarito Jr.'s two children nor Maricela's two children have juvenile nephritis—confirming once again the adage that it is better to be lucky than good. It is an adage María Teresa might have understood.

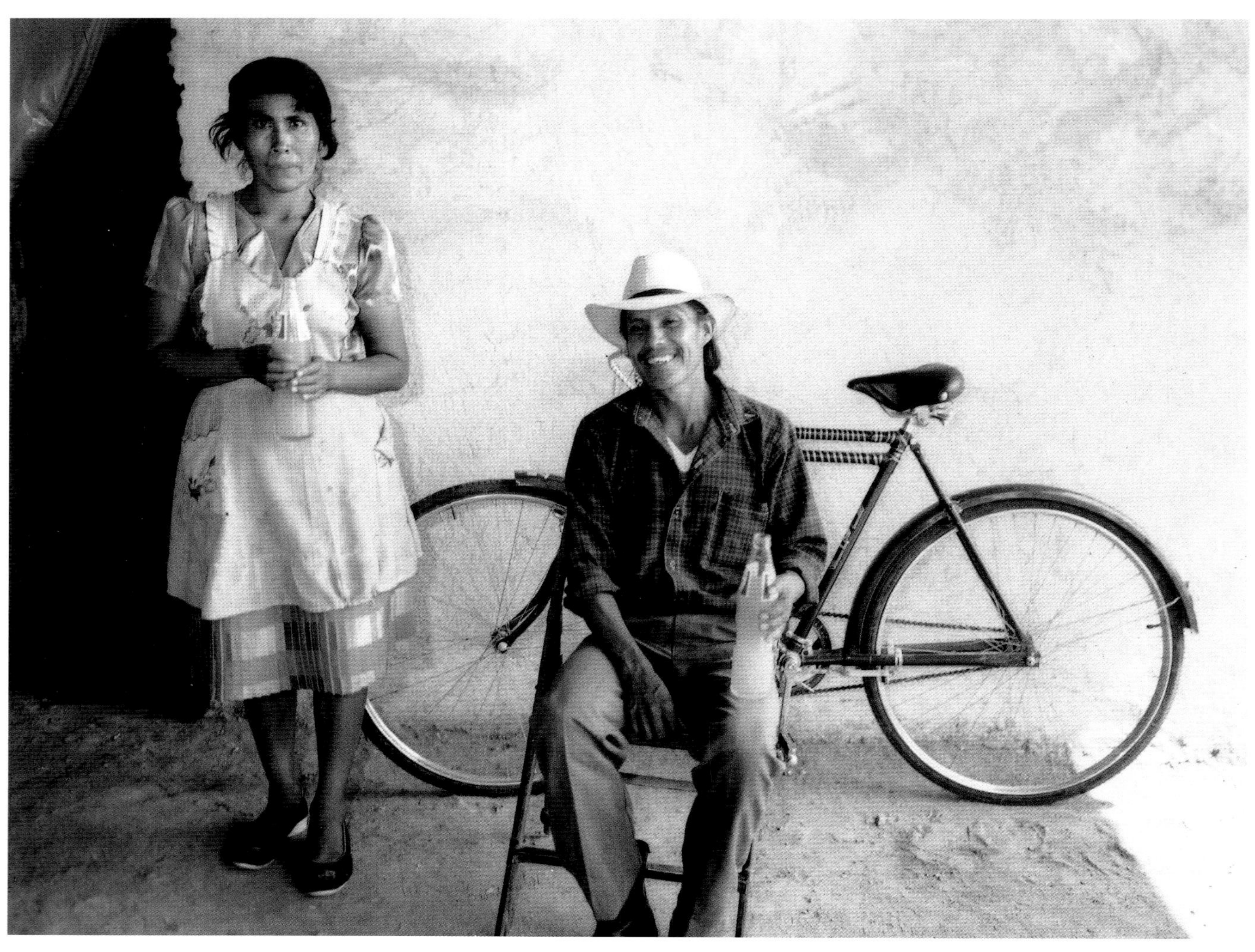

María Teresa Santiago and Margarito Melchor. San Martín. 1987.

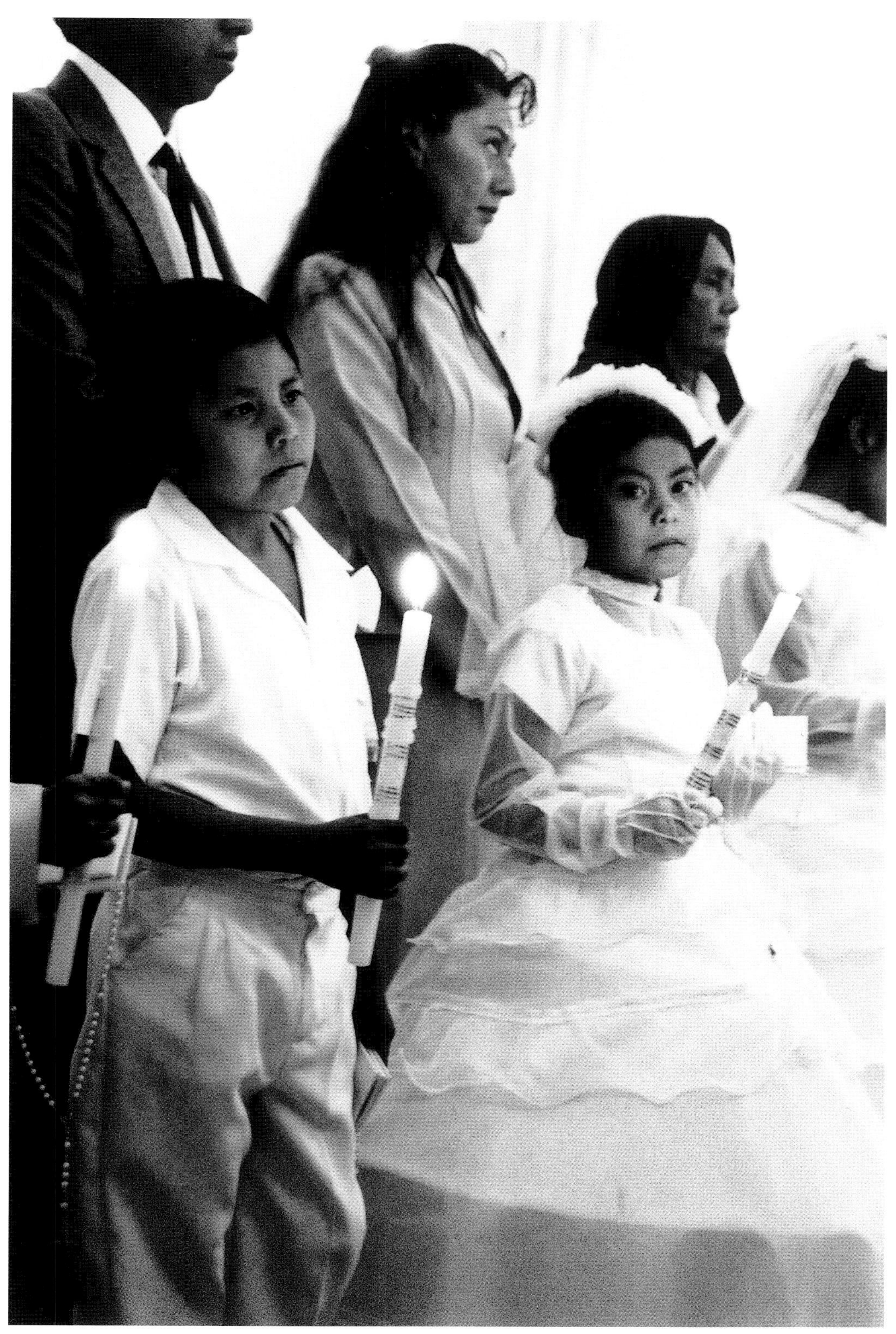

Arturo and Isaura Melchor. First Communion. San Martín. 1990.

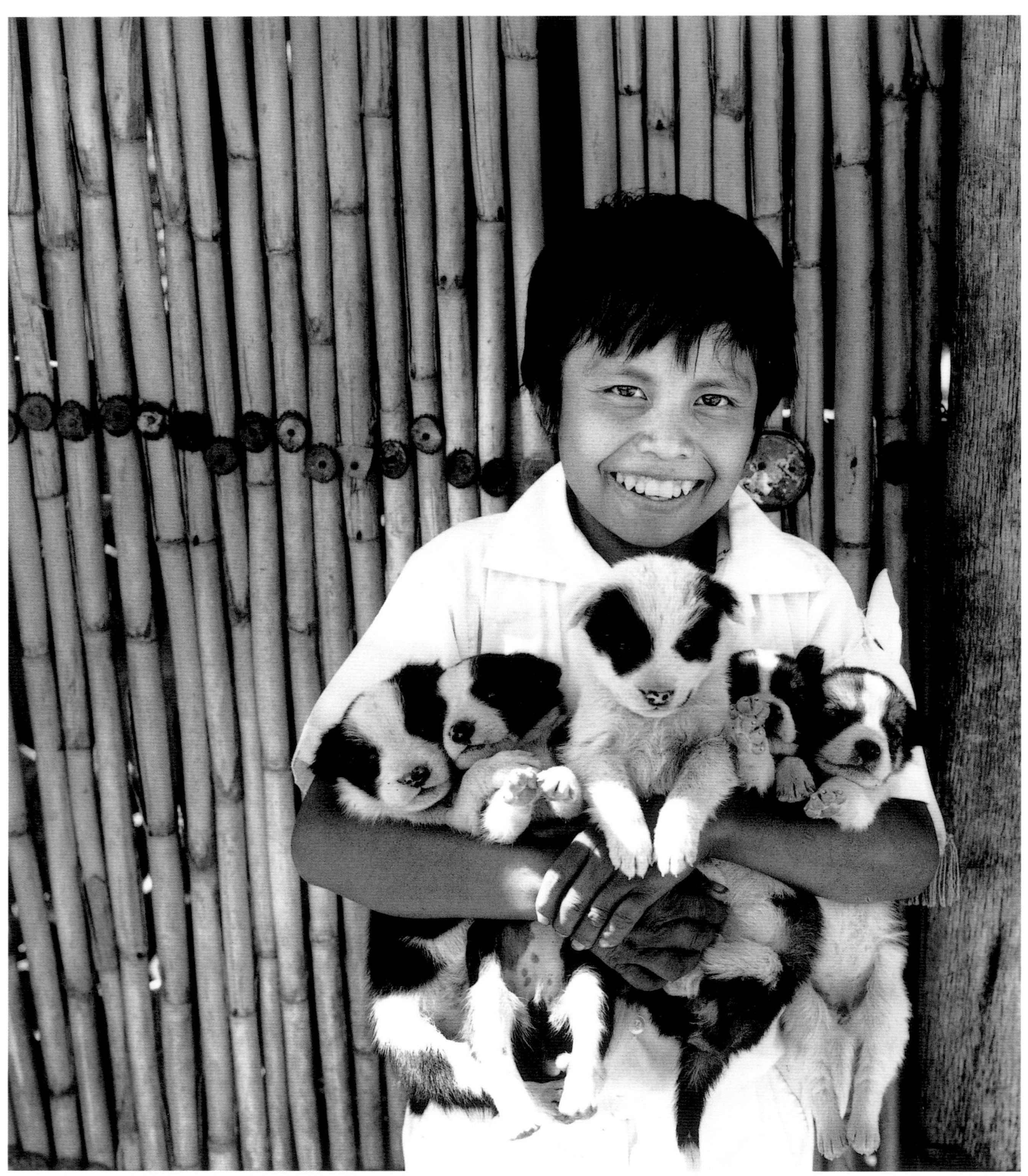

Arturo Melchor. San Martín. 1989.

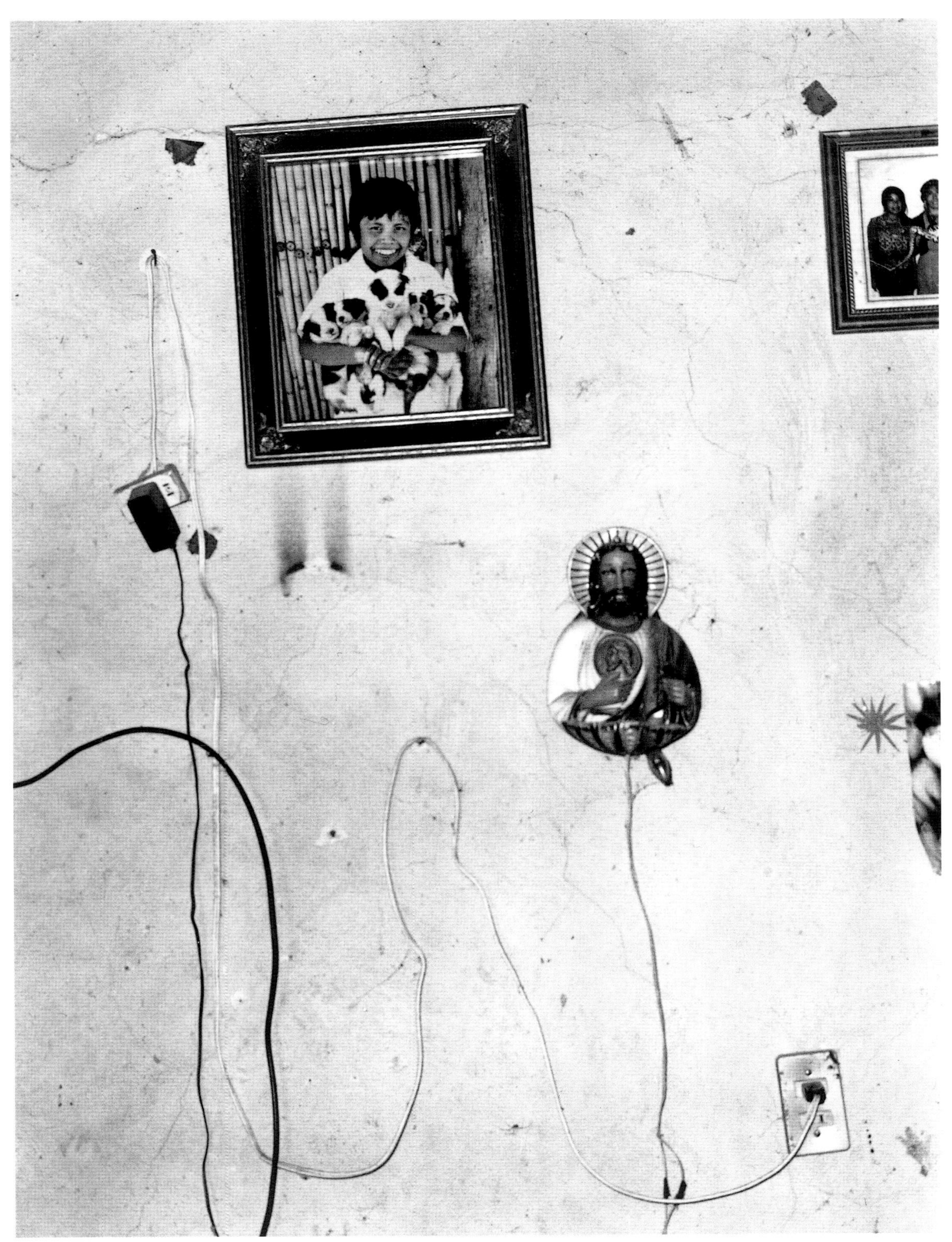

Wall in house of Margarito Melchor. San Martín. 2004.

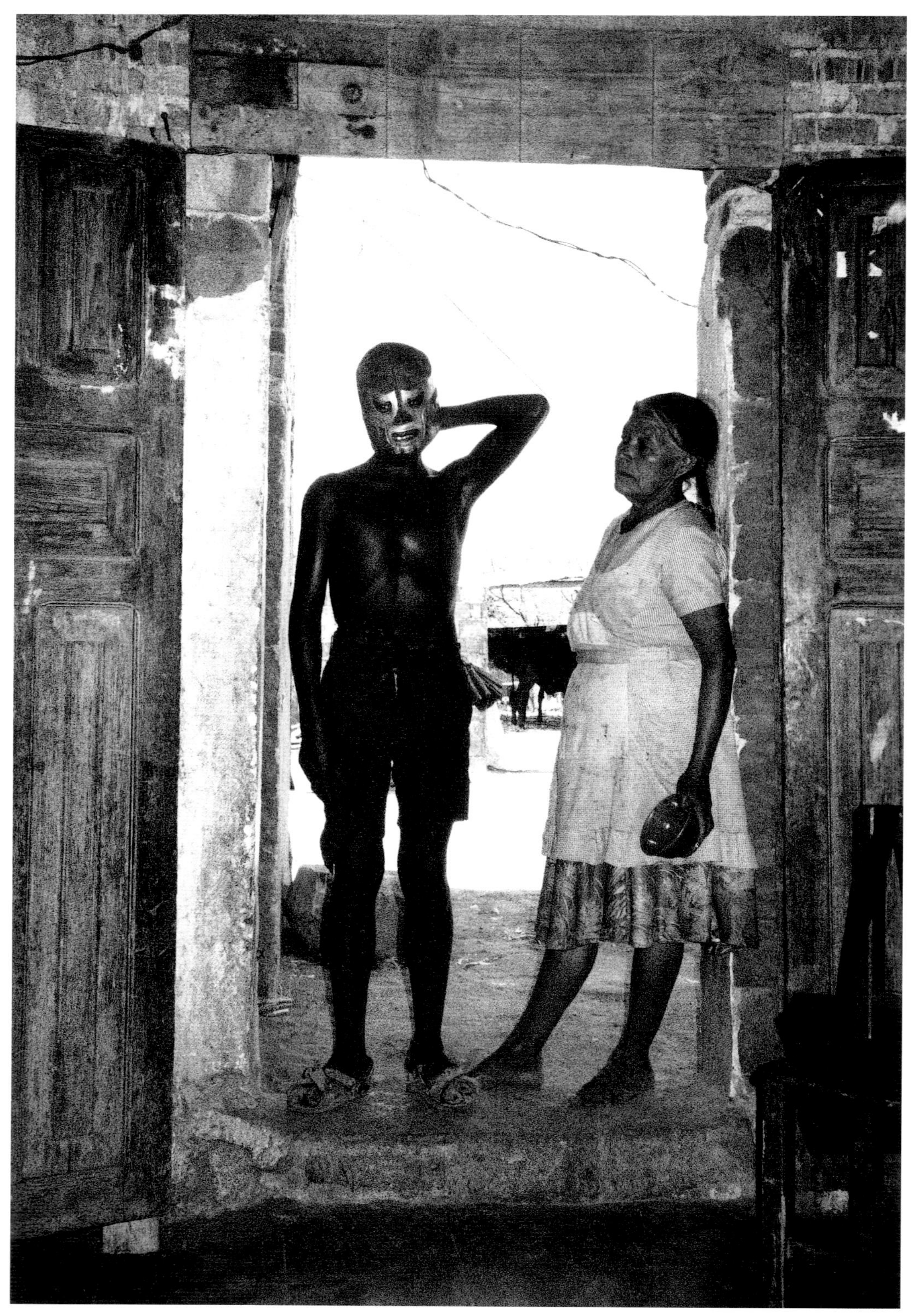

Margarito Melchor Jr. and his grandmother, Concepción Fuentes. San Martín. 1990.

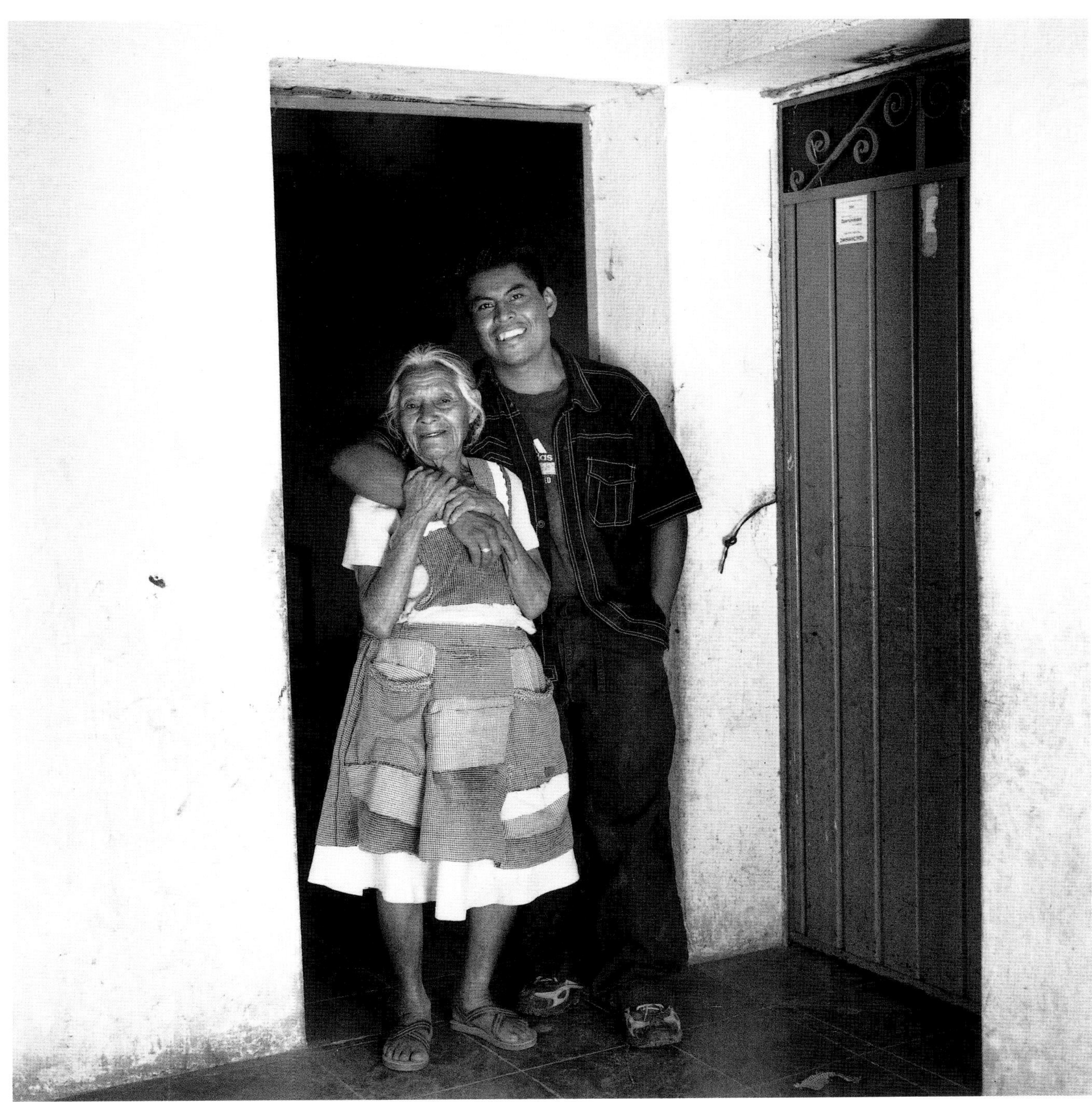

Margarito Melchor Jr. and his grandmother, Concepción Fuentes. San Martín. 2006.

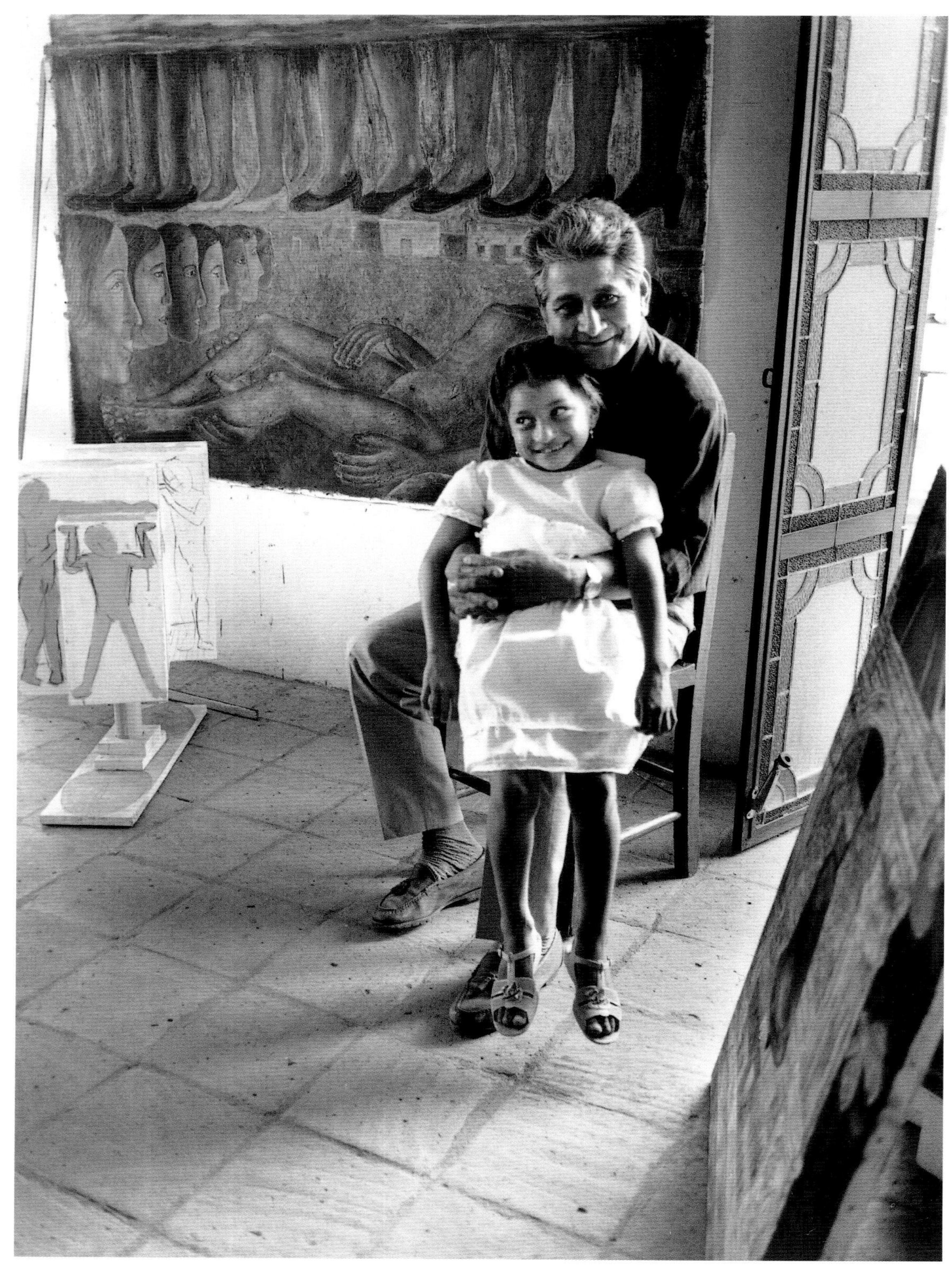

Isidoro Cruz and daughter Blanca. Ocotlán. 1990.

Isidoro Cruz
San Martín Tilcajete

When a craft made for export takes over a village, its origins can usually be traced to a single villager who for one reason or another enjoyed unusual access to a foreigner.

Isidoro Cruz brought wood carving to San Martín in the late 1960s, shortly after he landed a job at a government-owned store that sold folk art to tourists in Oaxaca. Like a lot of campesinos, Isidoro had made tops and toys as a boy and was handy with a machete, so he had little trouble teaching himself how to carve the sorts of figures he saw selling in the shop. But then, to his everlasting credit and San Martín's good fortune, he shared his connection with friends and family back home. He encouraged the peasants to carve, guaranteed them a market for their carvings, and, as things turned out, bound what had been a poor, isolated village to the U.S. economy in an enduring relationship that shapes the town to this day. Dozens of families in San Martín make wood carvings, both for tourists, who now come by the busload, and for shipment abroad.

Isidoro remains the most sophisticated craftsman in the village and the most learned about Oaxaca's artistic traditions. He makes colonial-style furniture for clients in northern California and devil masks for himself to wear at Carnaval back home. He has been invited by the Mexican government to show his work in Japan. He has a green card and goes to the United States several times a year, often staying for months at a time—sometimes with his son in New York, sometimes with friends in California.

He expresses an elder statesman's ambivalence about the current state of the carving business. He worries about quality and complains that the government all but wrecked the tradition by encouraging people to go into it just as demand in the States was declining. But he is also proud that his youngest daughter, Blanca, who had studied to become a preschool teacher but gave it up after discovering that teaching was a state-sponsored sinecure for the corrupt, has decided to brave the competition and be a carver instead.

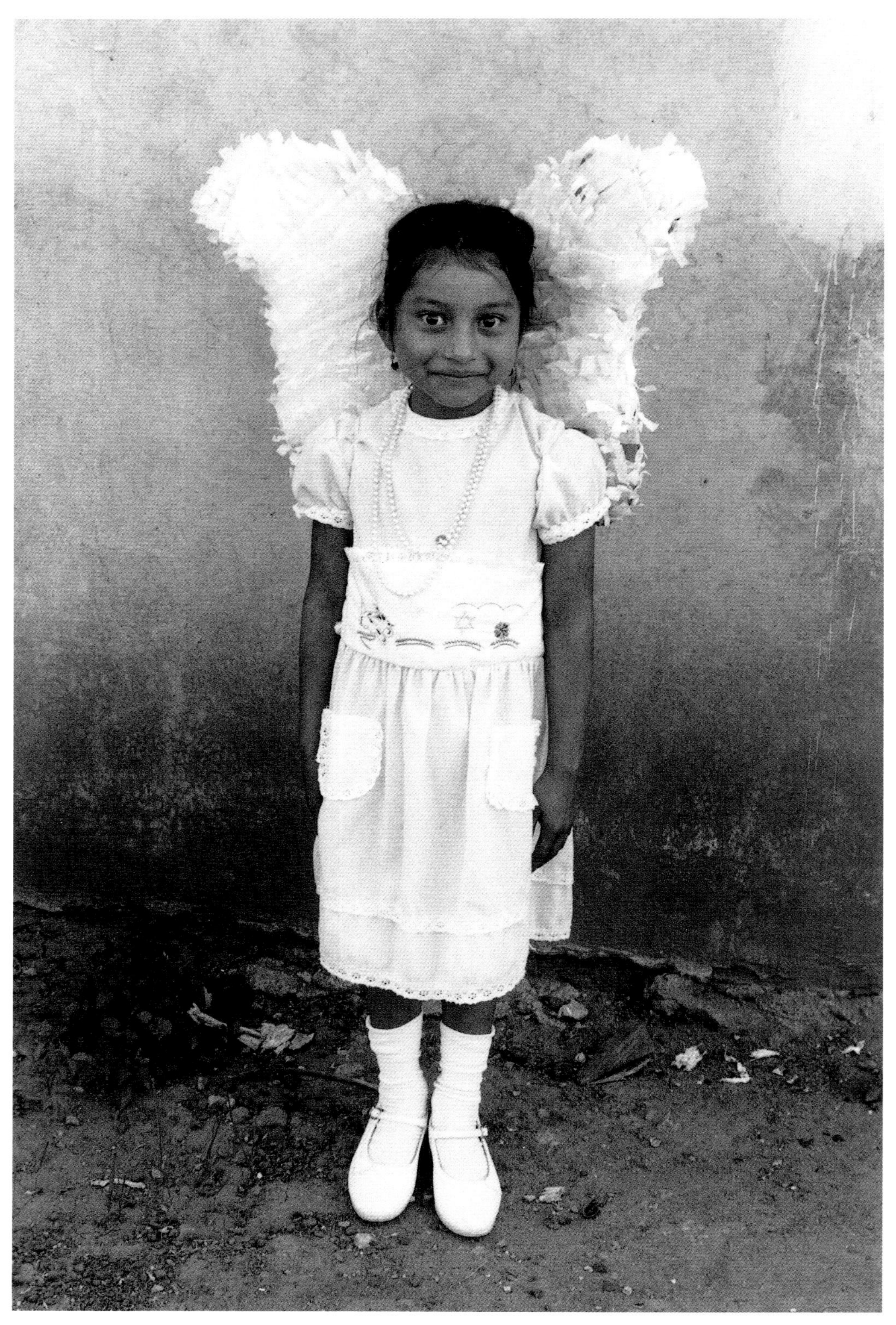

Blanca Cruz. San Martín. 1990.

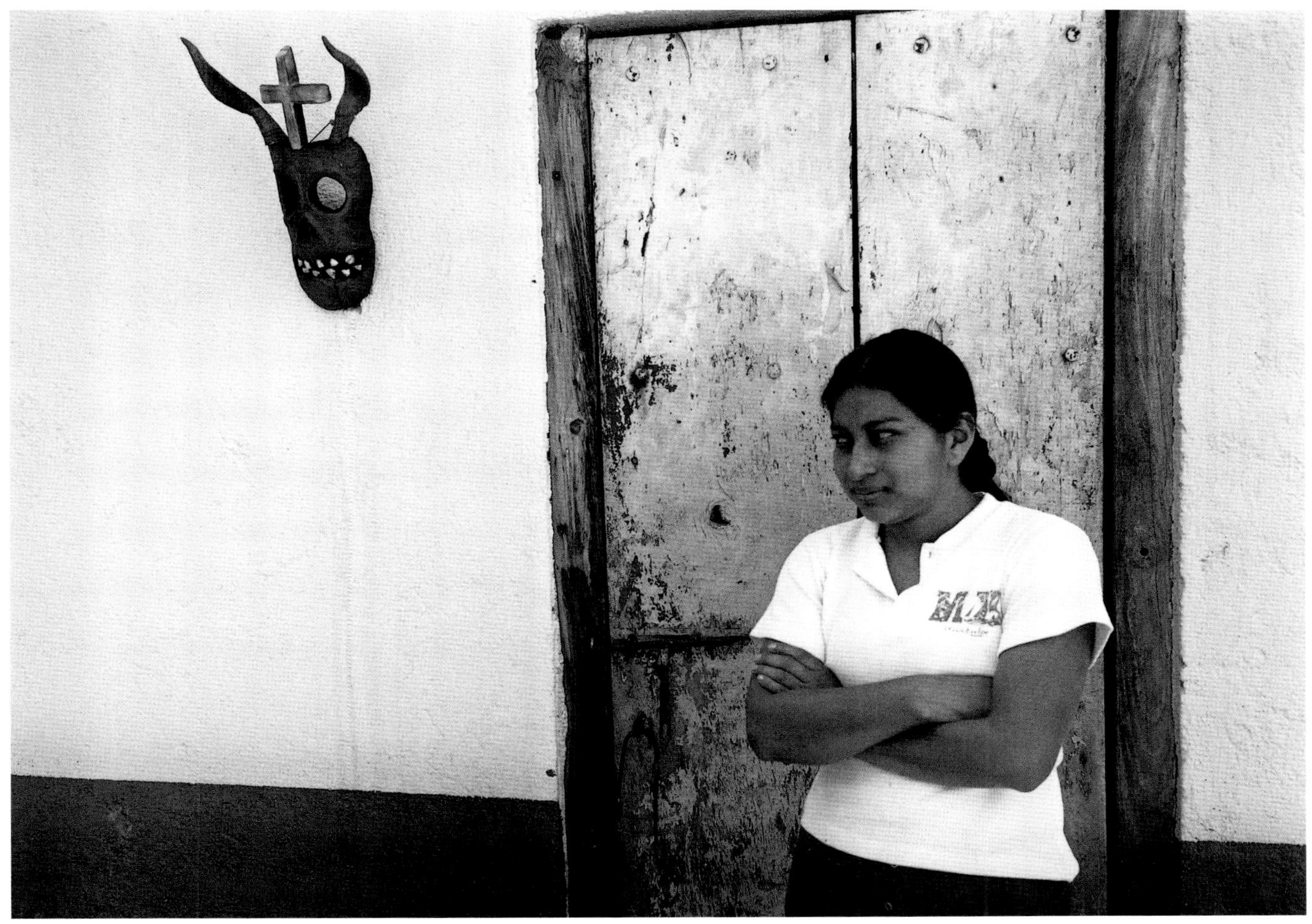

Blanca Cruz. San Martín. 2004.

Adrián Xuana
San Martín Tilcajete

Most people who knew Adrián Xuana in 1989 assumed he would be dead by now. Here is what I wrote about him back then:

> Adrián Xuana's friends describe his drinking skeletons as self-portraits. He is slowly drinking himself to death. Thirty bottles of Dos Equis lager, the brand his skeletons drink, is a normal binge for him.
>
> Adrián says he drinks because he's nervous. Bored by San Martín, he sings and binges in the cantinas of Oaxaca, where he studies the singers closely and dreams of flying to the moon. Besides skeletons, Adrián carves drinking musicians. "People don't buy my work because it's good," he says, "they buy it because it's funny. And it's fun. I like merriment, so I make my pieces merry."

Bright, restless people sometimes die young in the villages. They get bored and go off on adventures. Adrián's older brother, Rufino, couldn't stand the tedium of tending their father's animals alone in the hills. Fleeing the heat of the desert sun, he would run off to a man-made lake to swim. One day, he dove in, caught himself in a tangle of branches, and drowned.

Adrián stopped drinking for eighteen months while he was in jail—convicted of sexual assault, although the version of events that dominates San Martín is that he had an affair with another man's wife and was framed when things ended badly. He stayed sober for a while after his release, married an older woman from the city, and relapsed soon after the couple moved back to the village. As of Christmas 2006 he was still carving and had a twelve-piece Nativity scene on display at a new museum in Oaxaca.

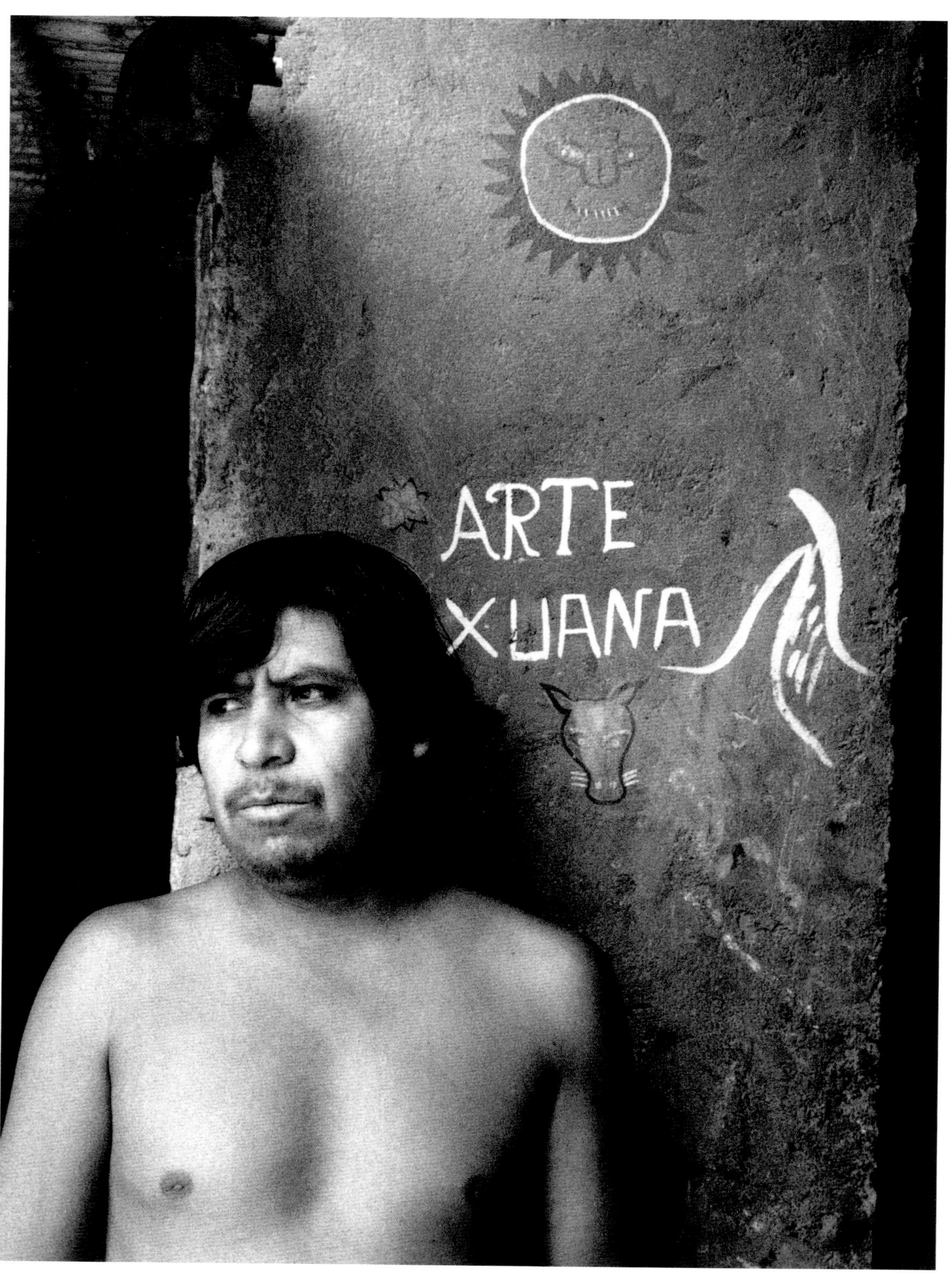

Adrián Xuana. San Martín. 1989.

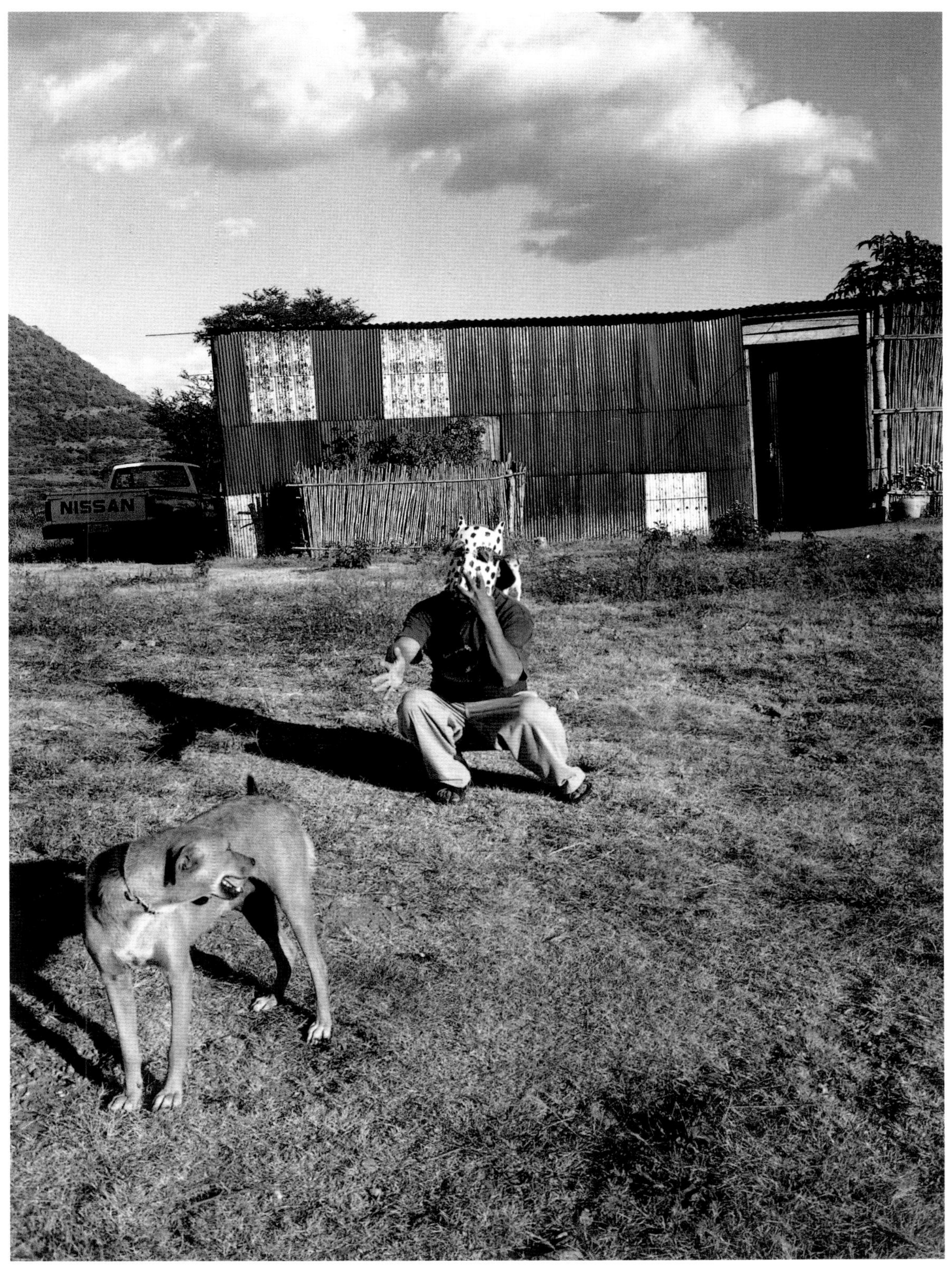

Adrián Xuana. San Martín. 2004.

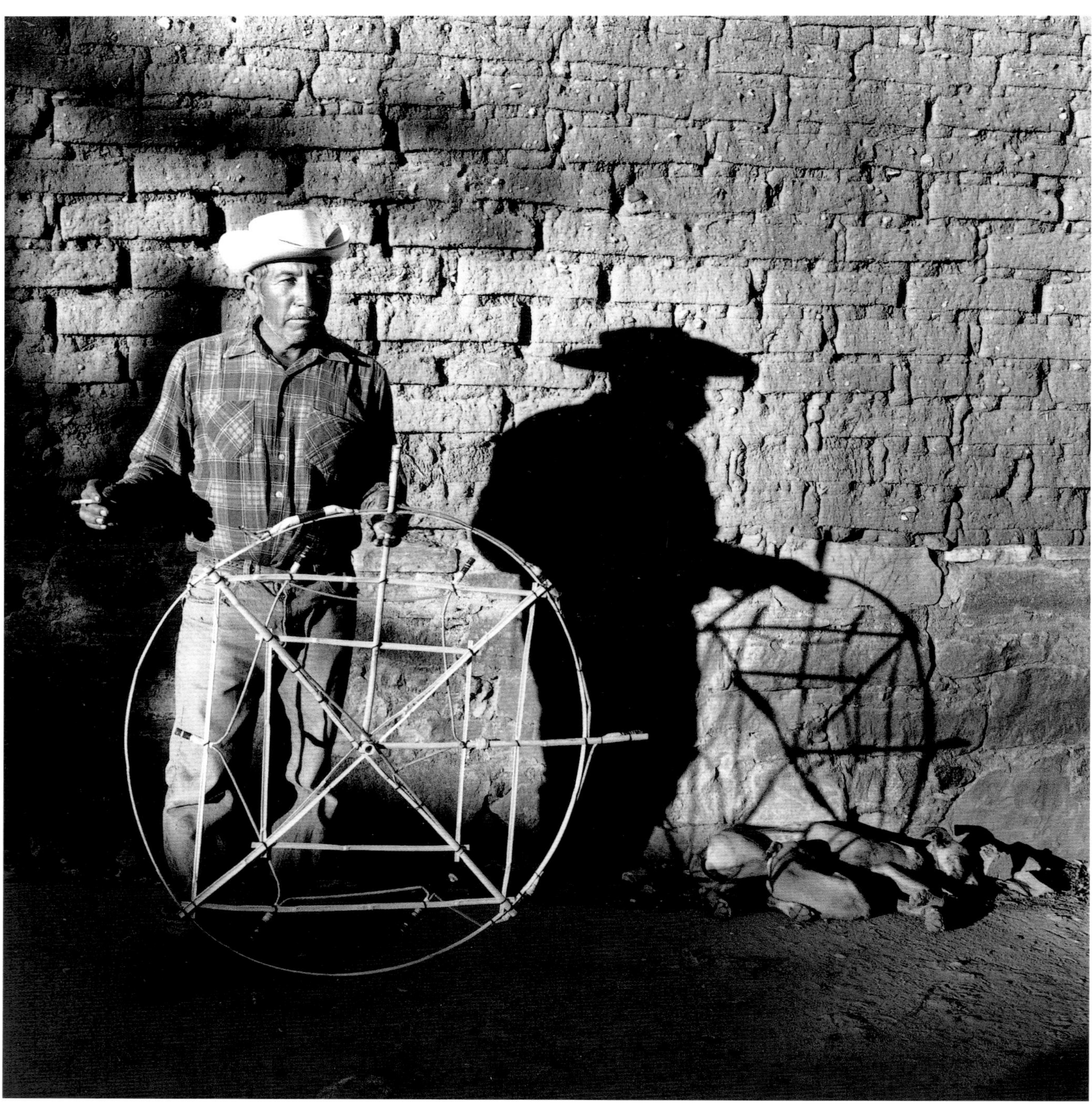

Ventura Fabián. San Martín. 1989.

Ventura Fabián

San Martín Tilcajete

Not long after Ventura Fabián was featured in our first book, he started signing his pieces "Ventura of San Martín." He hadn't really changed; he was simply accepting his notoriety. Even after a short film was made about his family and he was invited with his son, Norberto, to the premiere in Boston, he came home amazed— "We have two-story houses, you have two-story freeways!"—but still the same. His pieces have lost none of their rustic, eccentric charm, perhaps because unlike most carvers, whose goal is realism and whose work tends to lose its appeal as their technique carries them toward it, Ventura was never out just to capture nature, but something less visible and verifiable. He believed in witches before going to Boston, and he believes in them still.

What *has* changed is the village around him. "We used to mend our own huaraches," he says. "Now everyone has running shoes, and when they wear out we throw them into the fire. Kids are better dressed. Life is less pressured. We can go where we want. I work less and make more." He made more money in Boston than he made in a year back home. He spent most of it on Norberto's wedding—the important things don't change—but he also bought two pieces of land. He wants to start growing maguey, the cactus used to make mescal. The drink is selling better than the carvings these days.

Norberto, who paints his dad's figures, has little interest in farming and, like most sons, has little patience with the family's eccentricities. He would just as soon forget his days as a child when Ventura would clip his hair to make the family's paintbrushes. And he would rather not have been present when the old man balked at his first set of revolving doors in Boston. Still, the wedding was grand, the family business is good, and the newlyweds have their own room.

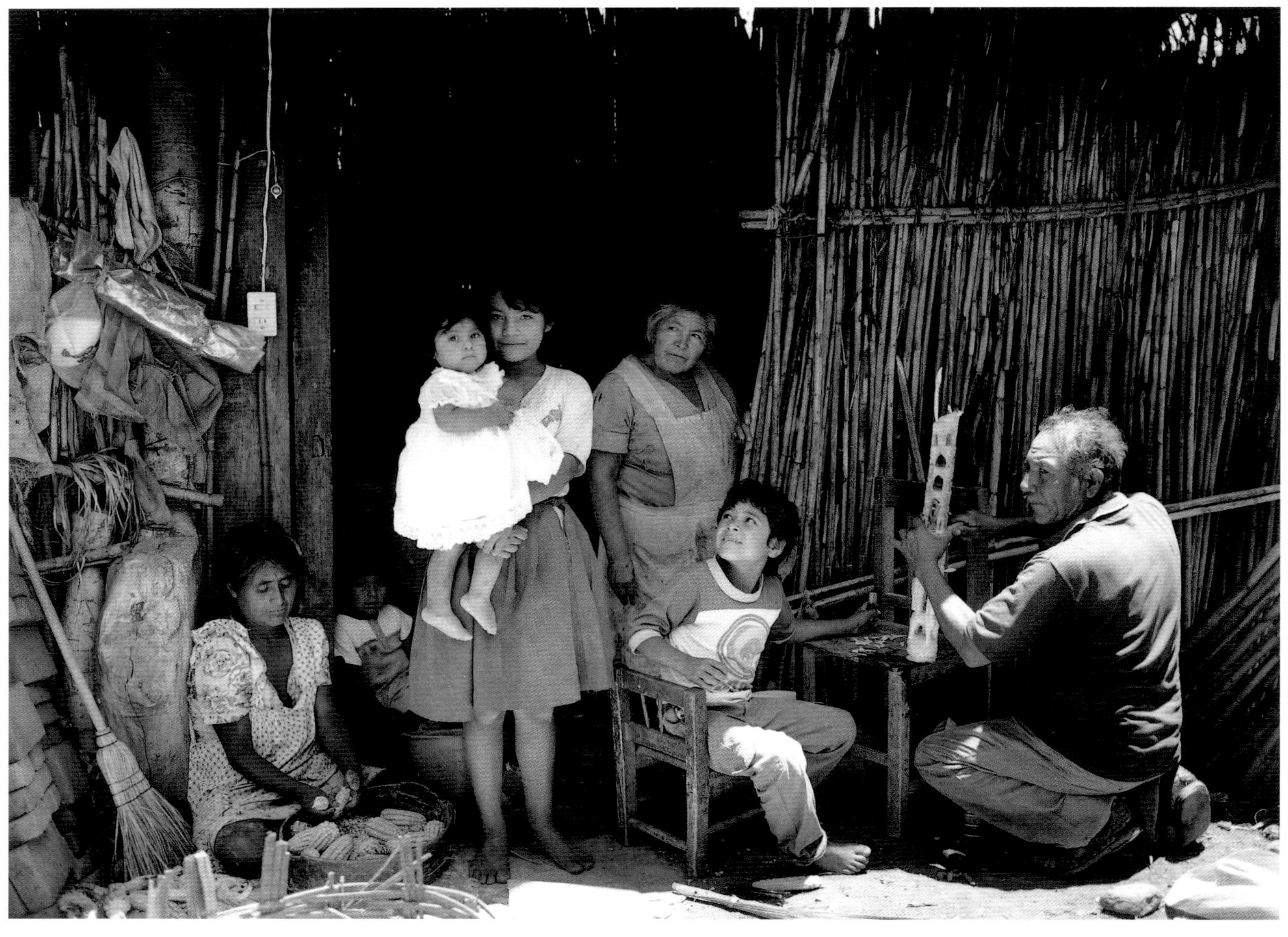

Family of Ventura Fabián (with son, Norberto, seated). San Martín. 1989.

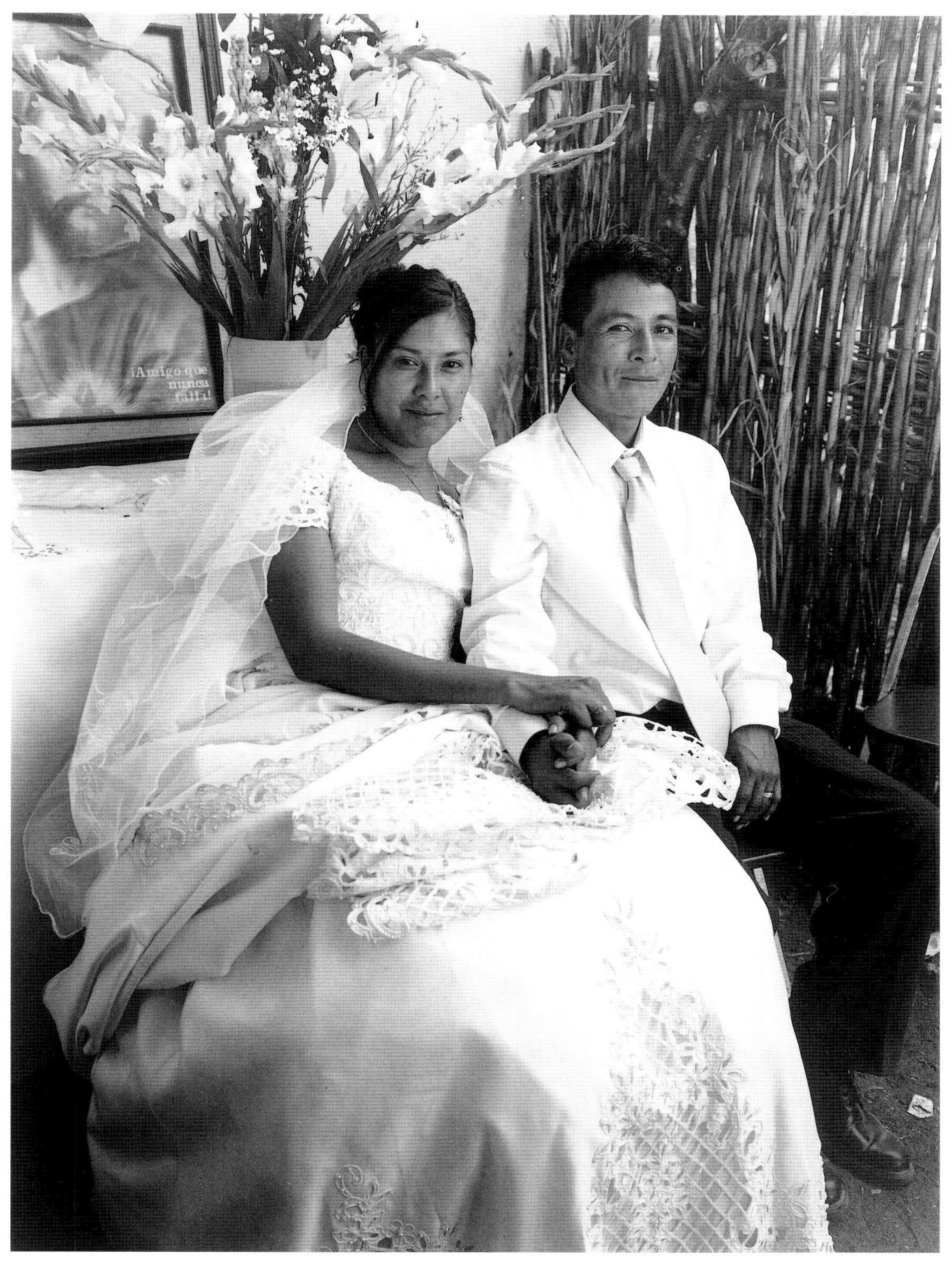

Blanca Melchor and Norberto Fabián. San Martín. 2004.

The Xuana Family

SO MANY GOOD THINGS have happened to the Xuana family over the years that one of their American buyers lapses into the language of the supernatural when he speaks about them. "They're witches," he says.

The Xuanas have the magic touch as both carvers and campesinos. Three of the siblings—Ana, Víctor, and René—are the finest miniaturists in the Oaxaca valley. Their dad, Abad, who taught them to carve, has an uncanny ability to grow things in Oaxaca's fickle, arid climate.

Abad typifies his generation of carvers, who despite their success as artisans remain attached to their five-acre plots, farm animals, and the unhurried routines of the peasant farmer. "He says he feels physically sick when he doesn't go into the fields," Ana says. The rhythms and demands of the seasons hold him as if spellbound. Loath to break the charm by doing anything that might take him too far from the land for very long, he rarely if ever accepts invitations for the family to mix with their buyers in Oaxaca. Better to risk losing clients than to jeopardize their fragile connection to nature.

The Xuanas grow corn and beans and keep cattle, goats, and turkeys. Using methods known only to themselves and which others dismiss as luck, they seem to know just when to plant so that their seeds and seedlings get just the right amount of rain, at just the right times. Tractors are deemed impractical for their purposes. "They don't cover the seed well, and the seed doesn't fall where it should, so it doesn't sprout as often," Ana explains. Or so Abad thinks. An embodiment of the stubborn, conservative farmer that the world is trying to enlighten, he continues to plow his tiny holdings the old way, with a team of bulls, and to grow enough year after year to feed the nine members of his extended family who live with him.

The Xuanas take good care of their animals, escorting them into the hills each day so they can eat well and sheltering them in their own special areas next to the house at night. As if to give thanks, when Xuana cows calve, they often calve twins—a fact that surprises no one in the family and that is explained as a natural response to the treatment the animals have received. Indeed for all the mystery of their good fortune, the Xuanas make clear their belief, as old as it is sensible, that luck is the residue of design, and that the fates can sometimes be controlled.

Like their dad, the Xuana children are resolved to make the most of their gifts. Though perhaps not as attached to the land as he is, they have refused to join the exodus of young people leaving San Martín and southern Mexico to work in the States. Ana in particular has defied the expectations of her sex: she carves, she controls her own finances, she is building her own home, and she is not rushing to marry. She and her brothers are good businesspeople—disciplined, prudent, hard-working. They command high prices and make pieces worth the price. René's turkeys are elegant, as are Víctor's fish. Ana's earrings are irresistible.

There is no magic, only time and patience. "There is my work," Ana says, pointing to the three-room brick house, still under construction, that has taken her sixteen years to build. Working as a wetback roofer in the States, her half brother Antonio Xuana earned enough to build his house in a year—but he also broke the law to do it and lived apart from his wife and children for eleven months. Ana expresses neither regret about her choices nor disapproval for his. She was glad to be home. She eagerly awaited the birth of her little brother's baby. Only Víctor's wife didn't just have a baby. Married to a Xuana, she had twins.

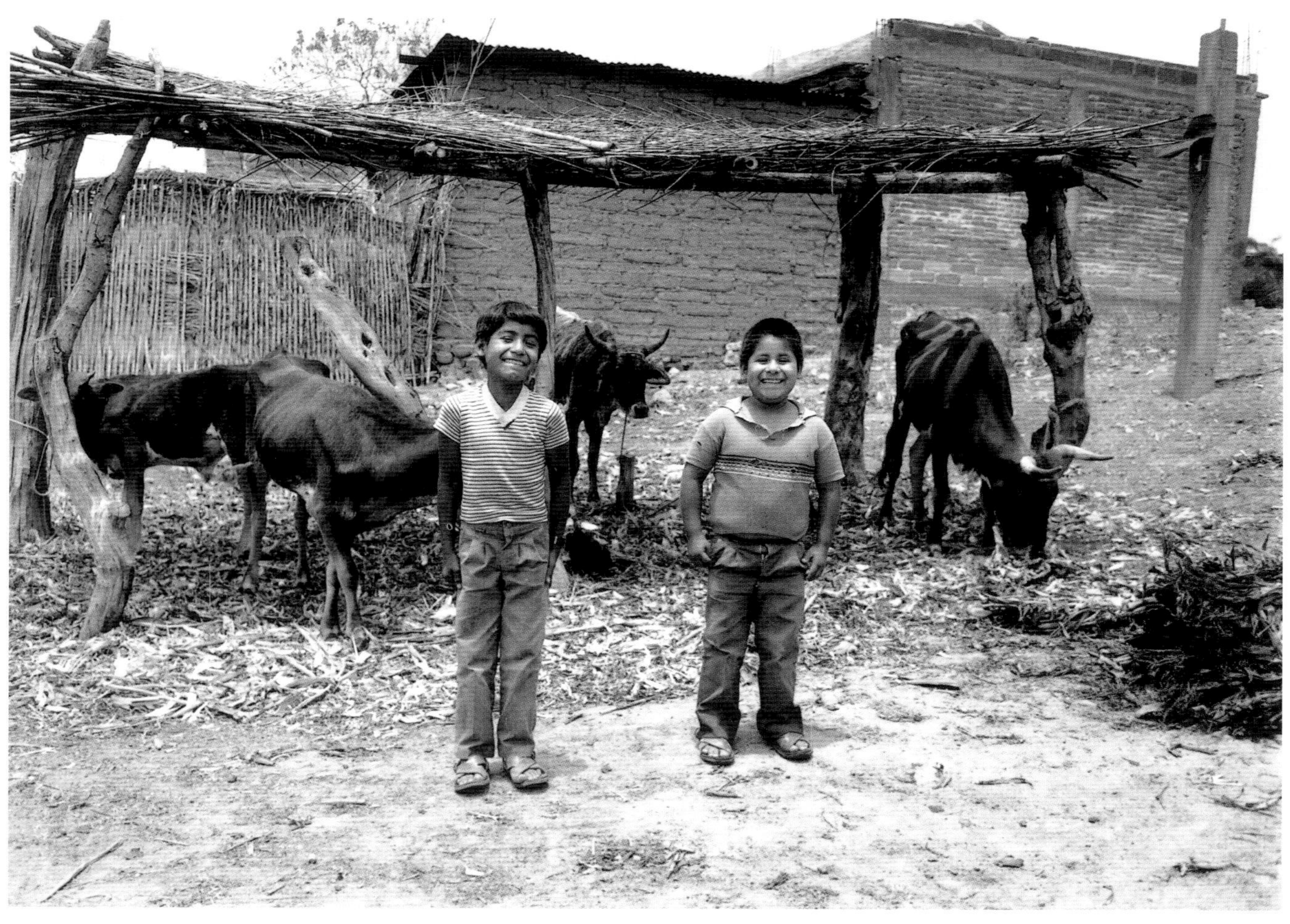

Víctor and René Xuana. San Martín. 1989.

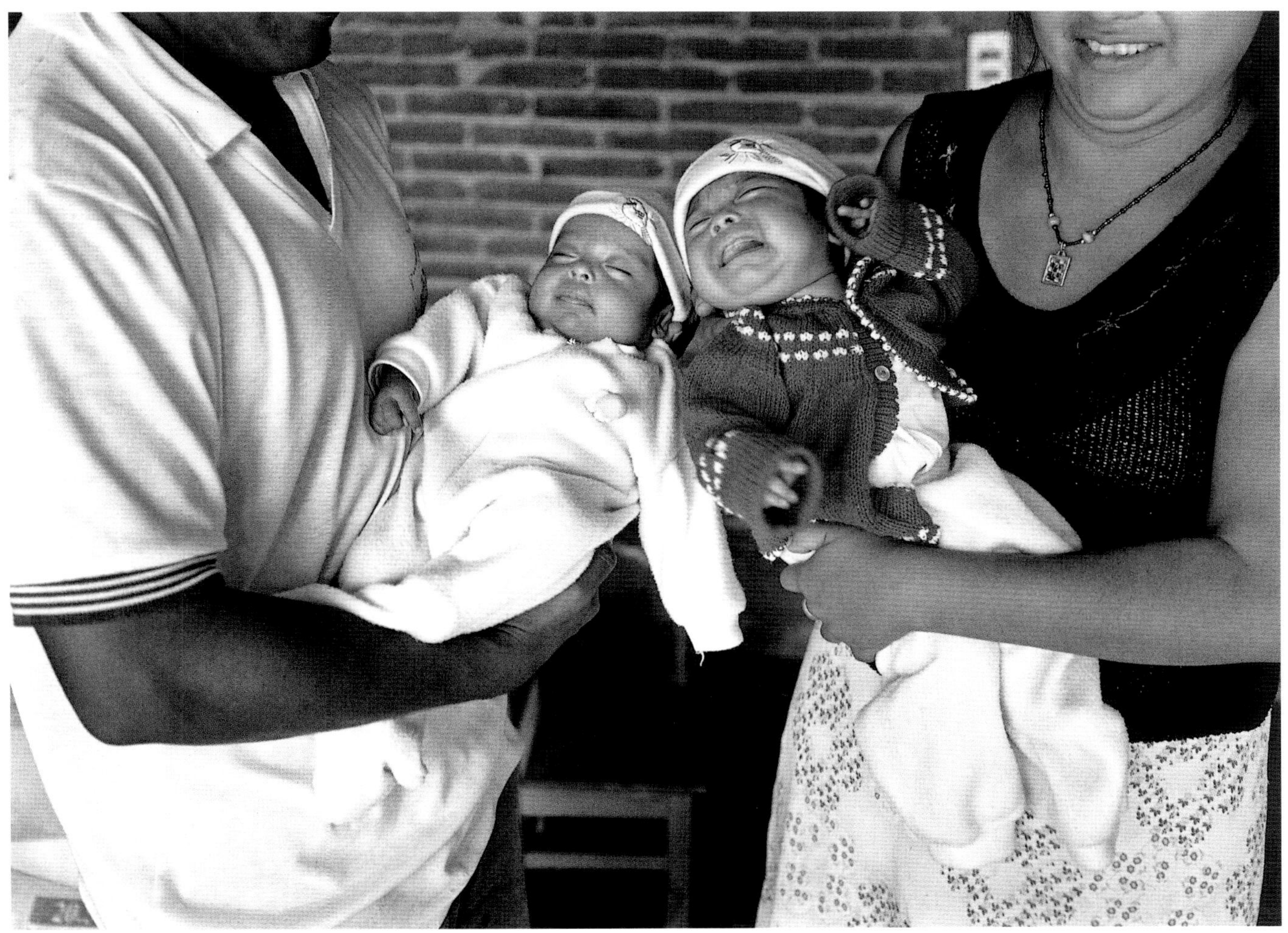

Víctor Xuana's twin daughters, Guadalupe and Andrea. San Martín. 2004.

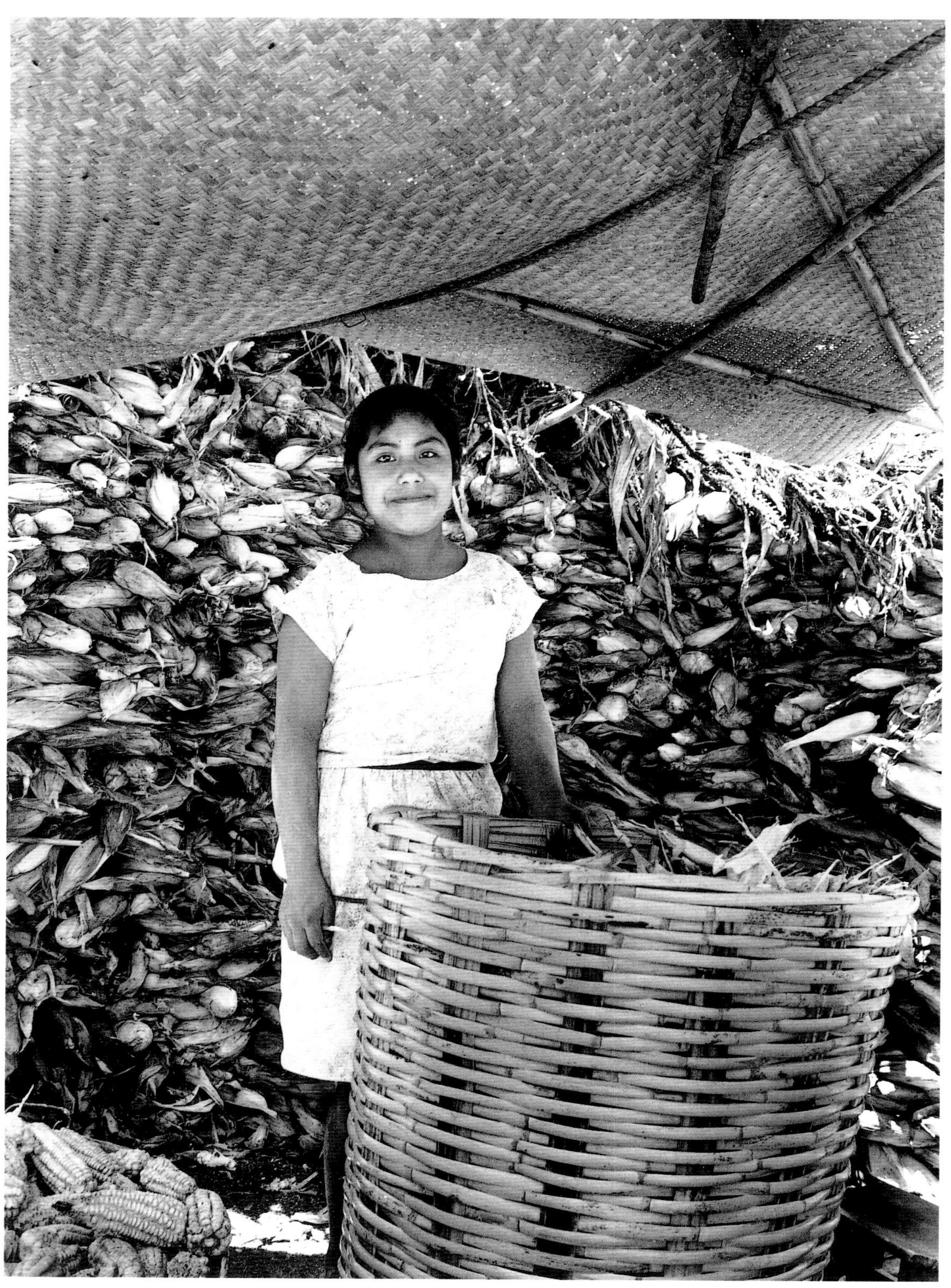

Ana Xuana. San Martín. 1990.

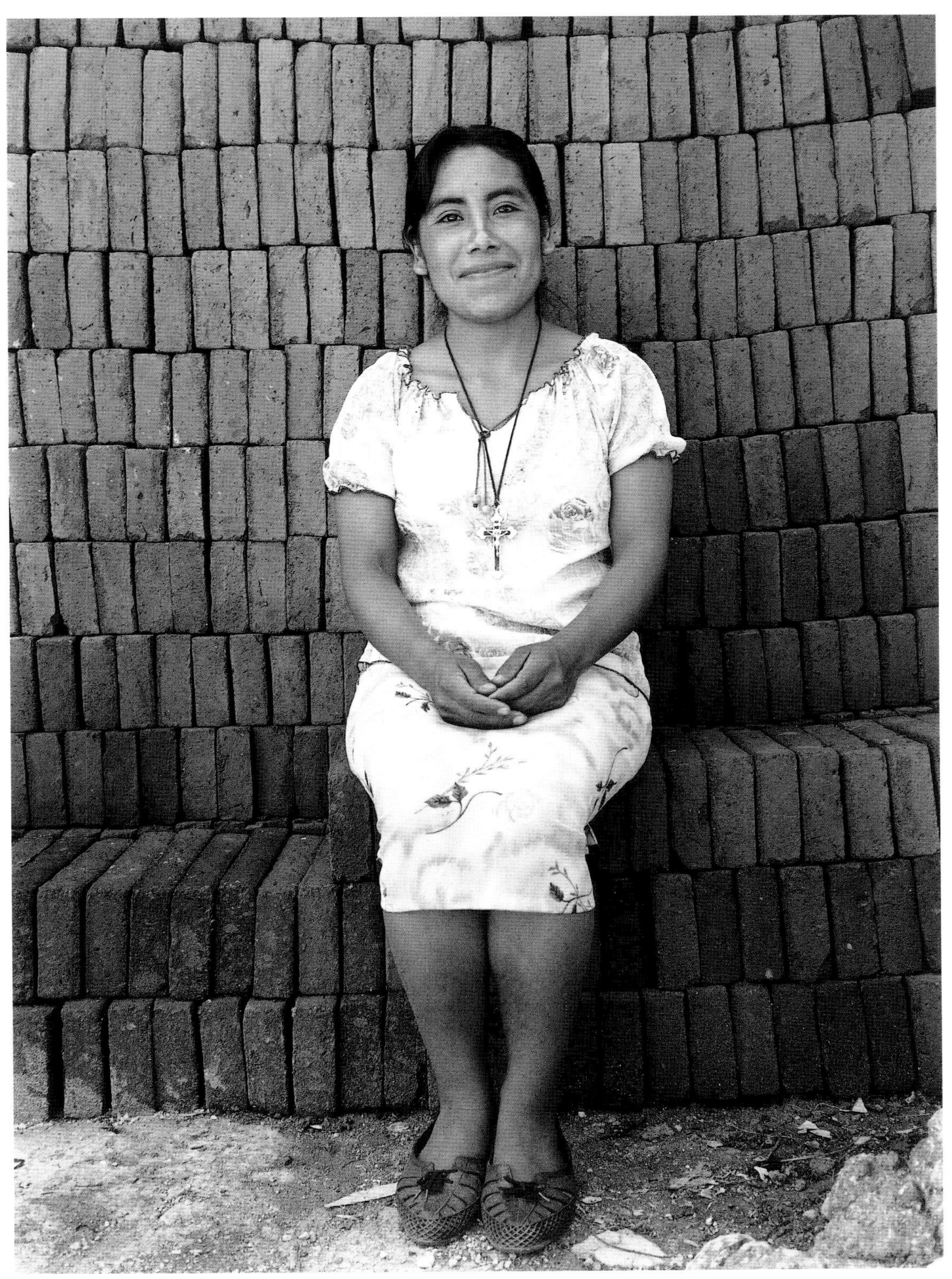

Ana Xuana. San Martín. 2004.

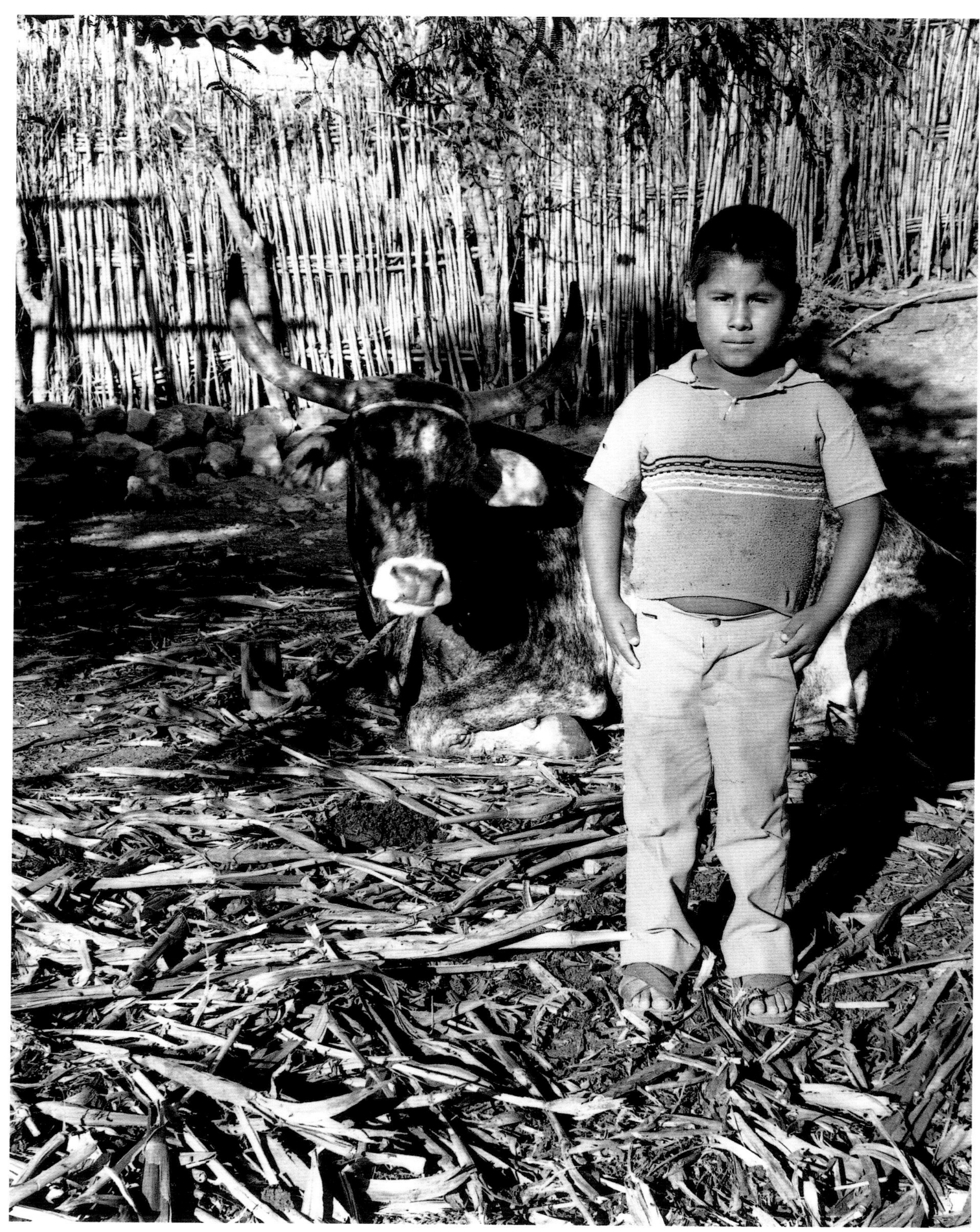

René Xuana. San Martín. 1990.

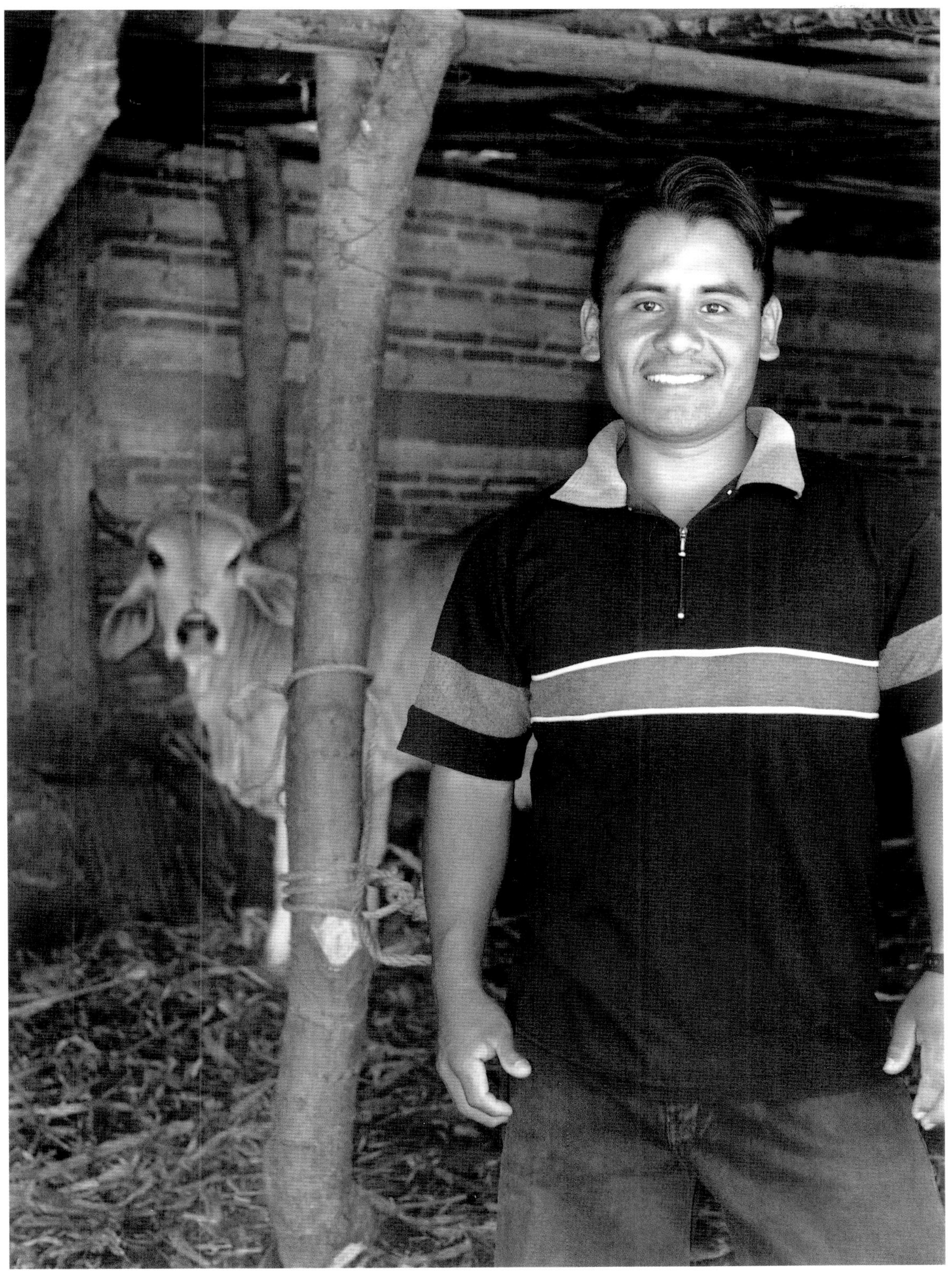

René Xuana. San Martín. 2004.

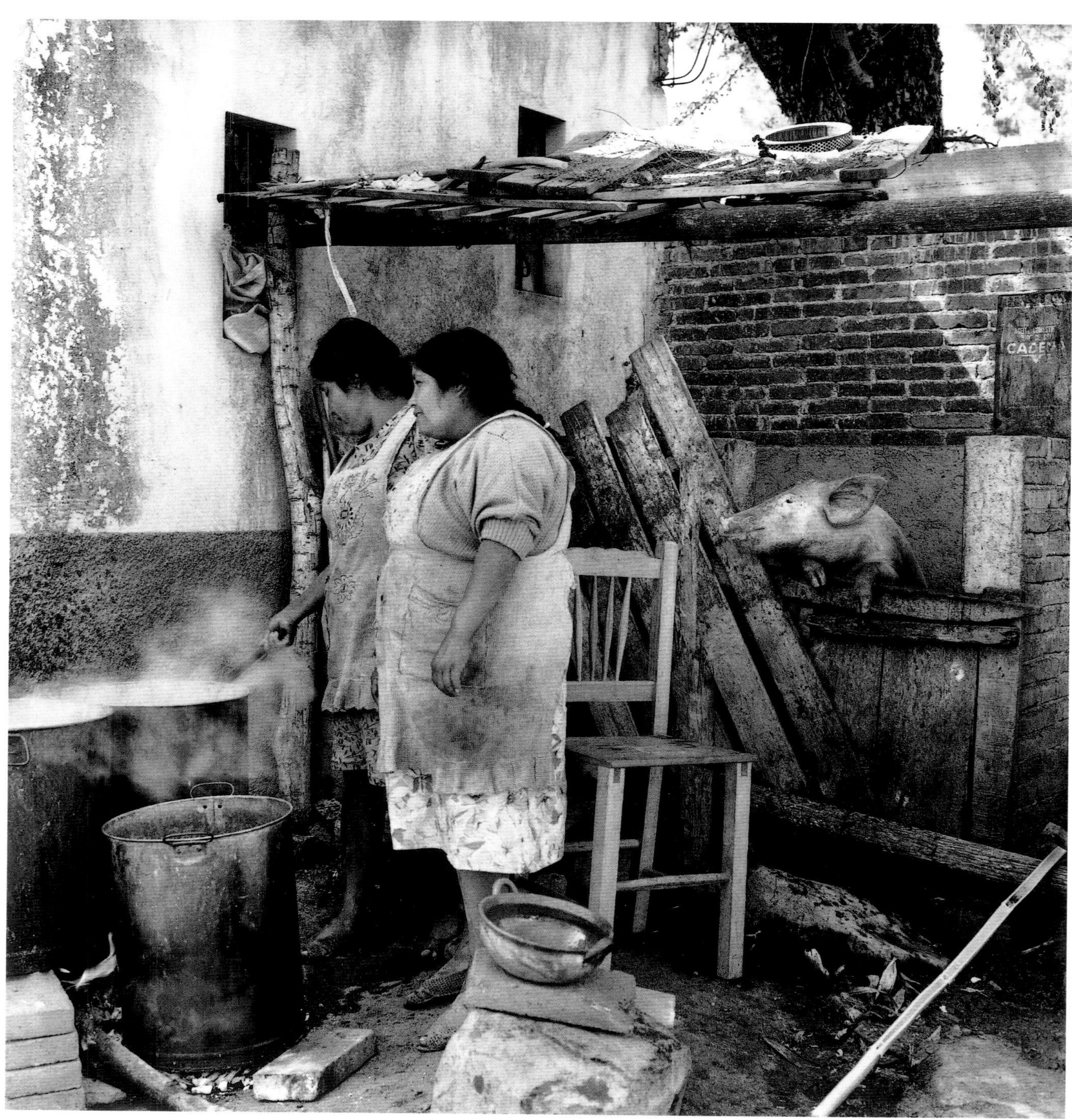

Christmas fiesta at the childhood home of Jacobo Ángeles. San Martín. 1987.

Jacobo Ángeles
San Martín Tilcajete

ONE OF THE MORE PLEASANT
EXPERIENCES to be had in San
Martín is to dine at Jacobo Ángeles's restaurant at the entrance to
the village. There, surrounded by
displays of Mexican crafts, visitors can enjoy generous portions
of chicken mole, green enchi-
ladas, roasted grasshoppers (in
season), and other Oaxacan specialties, prepared by a team of
cooks led by Jacobo's aunt and
served up by earnest, young wait-

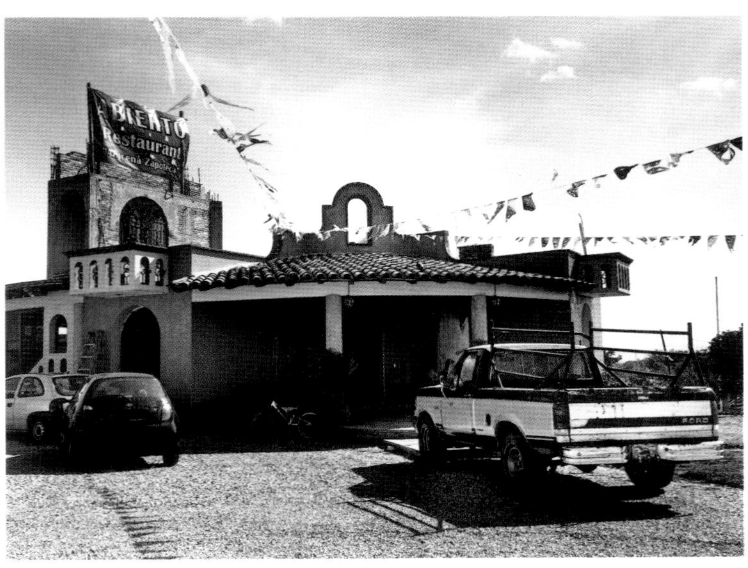

Azucenas Restaurant of Jacobo Ángeles. San Martín. 2004.

ers, the children of campesinos. The charming incongruity of the venture—there are
plans to offer rooftop dining—extends to the parking lot, an empty piece of desert
fastidiously spray-painted with parking spaces and planted with trees. Jacobo has
high hopes.

Behind every successful woodcarver is an American entrepreneur. Jacobo, the
top-selling carver in Oaxaca, says he owes his good fortune to his partner, "Gerónimo"—Jerry Boyd, an enterprising merchant who buys his carvings, sponsors his
trips to the States, and employs him as a local agent in Oaxaca. Between his restaurant and his carving business, Jacobo is the largest employer in San Martín. His rivals
dismiss him as a wheeler-dealer, but he has invested heavily in his village, promotes
its traditions, and even defends its antiquated form of government. His cousins, the
Jiménez siblings, say he takes their carvings in the off-season when no one else will.
The thirty other families he buys from in San Martín could say the same.

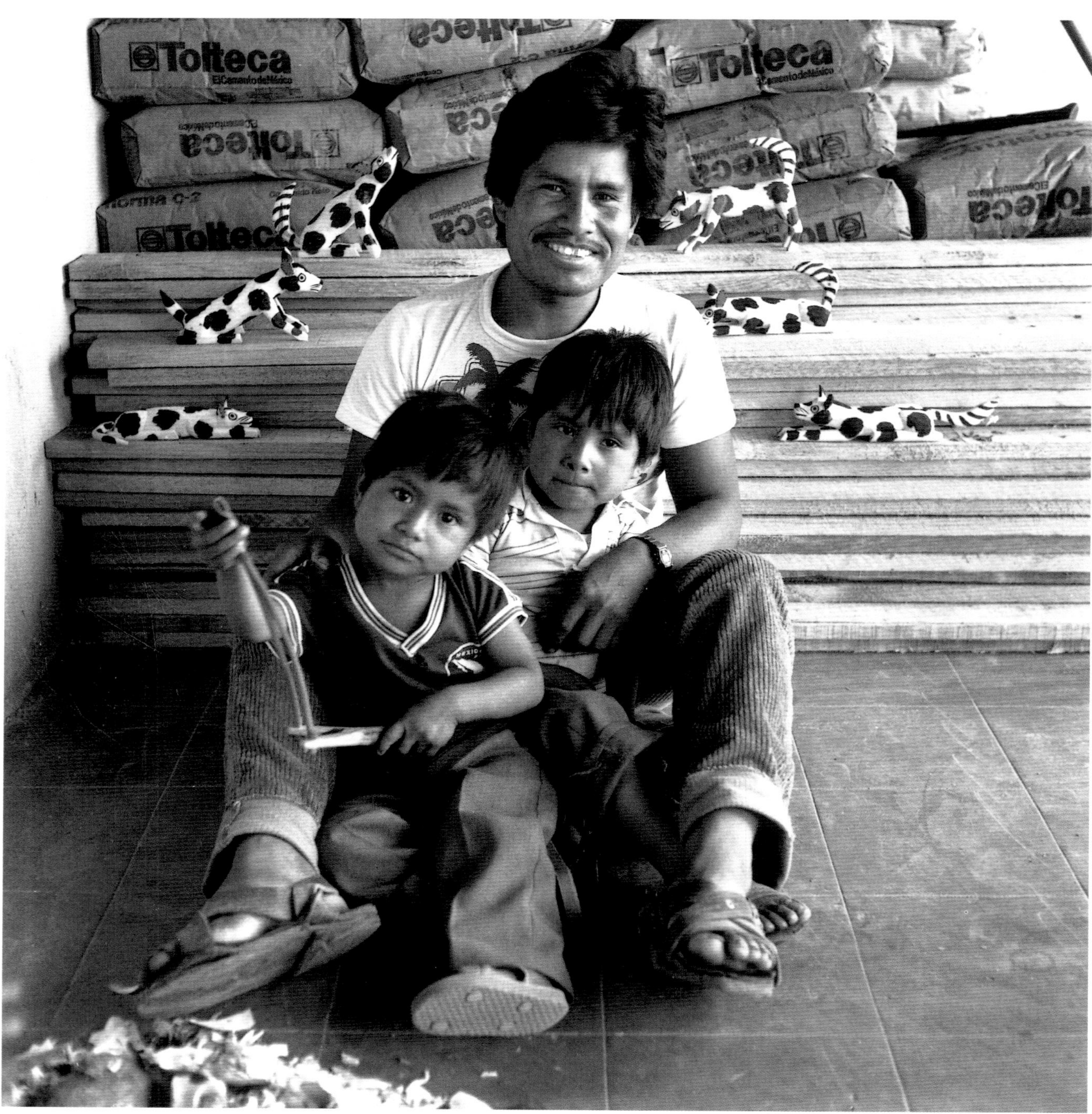

Jaime Santiago. La Unión. 1989.

Jaime Santiago
La Unión Tejalapan

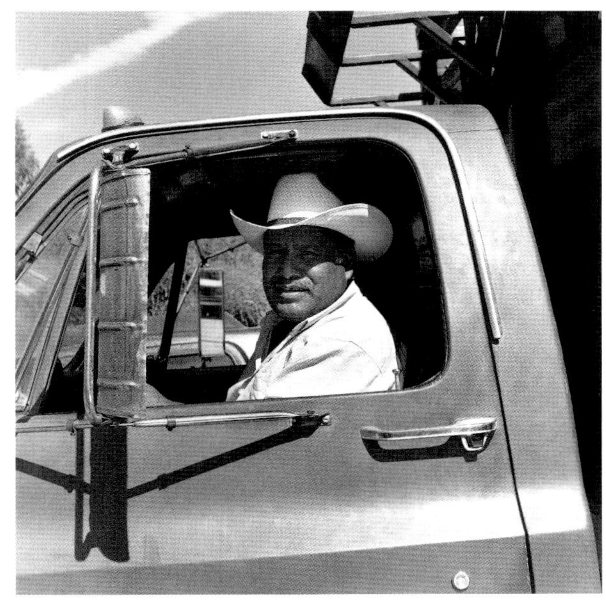

Jaime Santiago. La Unión. 2006.

A GENERATION AGO, Jaime Santiago was the top-selling carver in La Unión and one of the most gifted. He worked hard and efficiently—eight hours a day, six days a week, one hundred small figures a month. He made bucktoothed rabbits, sleeping and wild-eyed dogs, and exquisite fiesta scenes complete with masked dancers, devils, musicians, and bulls loaded with fireworks. Serious collectors loved him because his pieces affirmed their notions of what traditional Mexican folk art should be: they were simply carved, gracefully proportioned, painted plainly with aniline, and evocative of village life. In a word, they were "authentic." His dogs captured the essence of *dog*. Merchants loved him because his prices were reasonable and he finished his orders on time.

In 1990, in an act of astounding prodigality without precedent in his village, Jaime bought himself a truck. Impulse buys are not unknown among campesinos who come into money, but when the truck sat broken down and unused in front of his house for months, even his most loyal customers couldn't help adopting a bemused, patronizing air about the whims of peasants.

Jaime doesn't carve anymore and hasn't carved for years. He drives a three-ton Chevy. There's more money in it, and it gets him out of the house. The same paved roads that have made it easier for his former clients to reach his cousins and uncles who still carve have facilitated the flow of other goods even more traditional and authentic than his *alebrijes*. He hauls wood and corn during the week and bands of musicians (tropical and rock) on weekends. He supports a wife and four children and fulfills his communal obligations by maintaining La Unión's new water system. He could return to his craft at any time, but so long as there are more people in the market with machetes than with trucks, it perhaps would be whimsical for him to do so.

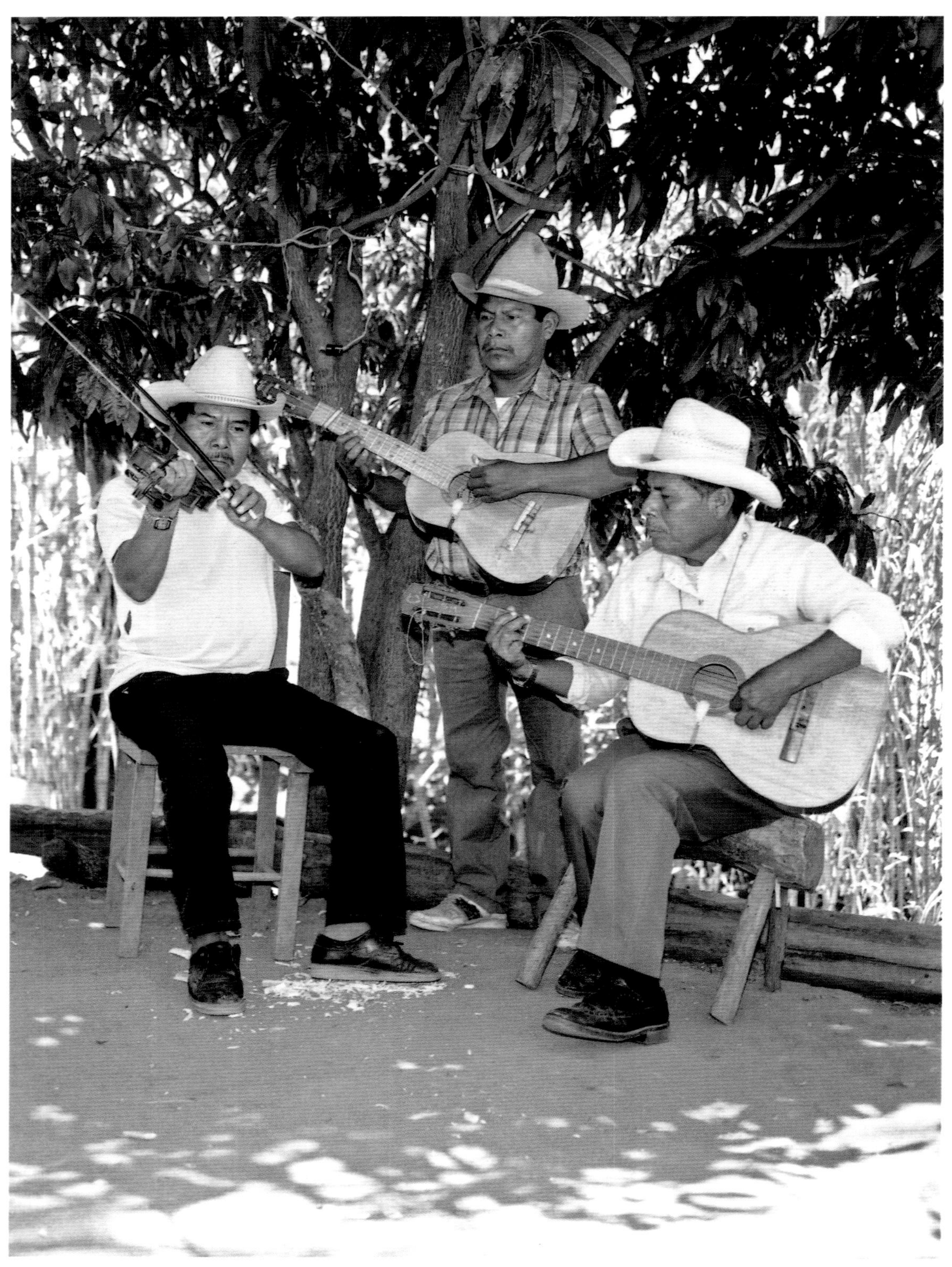

Santiago brothers: Quirino, Plácido, and Martín. La Unión. 1989.

The Santiago Brothers
La Unión Tejalapan

THE BEAUTIFUL STRAINS OF TRADITIONAL MEXICAN MUSIC are not dying away—they're being drowned out. Village bands and guitars still can be found at fiestas in Oaxaca, but they share the stage with deafening amplification systems that prop up the latest pop dirges, belted and pounded out by singers who can't sing and keyboardists who can't play, at prices no campesino should be able to afford. Flatbed trucks boasting "eighty tons of sound" wheel portable stages into courtyards emptied of cows and turkeys and (for many times the price of the village band) play away a host's savings by dance floors of wetted dirt.

The Santiago brothers—Quirino, Plácido, and Martín (Jaime's dad)—sang ballads at birthdays and weddings. They were never full-time professionals, but in a village whose diversions were limited, they enjoyed playing for their friends and they sang in tune. They were also the first family in La Unión to become woodcarvers. They still carve, but they haven't played together in years. With half the village's men gone to the States, fewer people would be around to hear them.

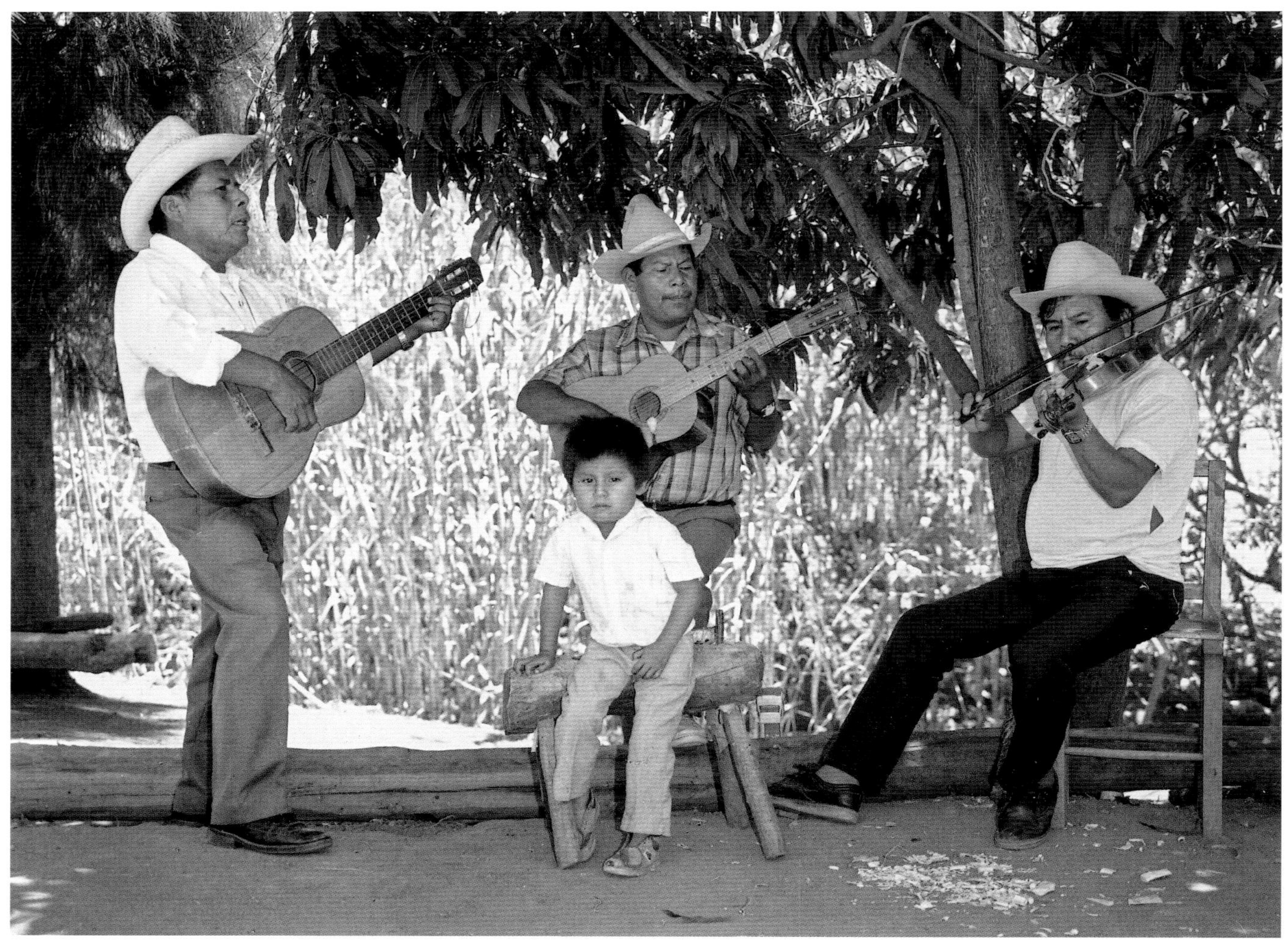

Santiago brothers: Martín, Plácido, and Quirino, with Plácido's son, Eloy, in front. La Unión. 1989.

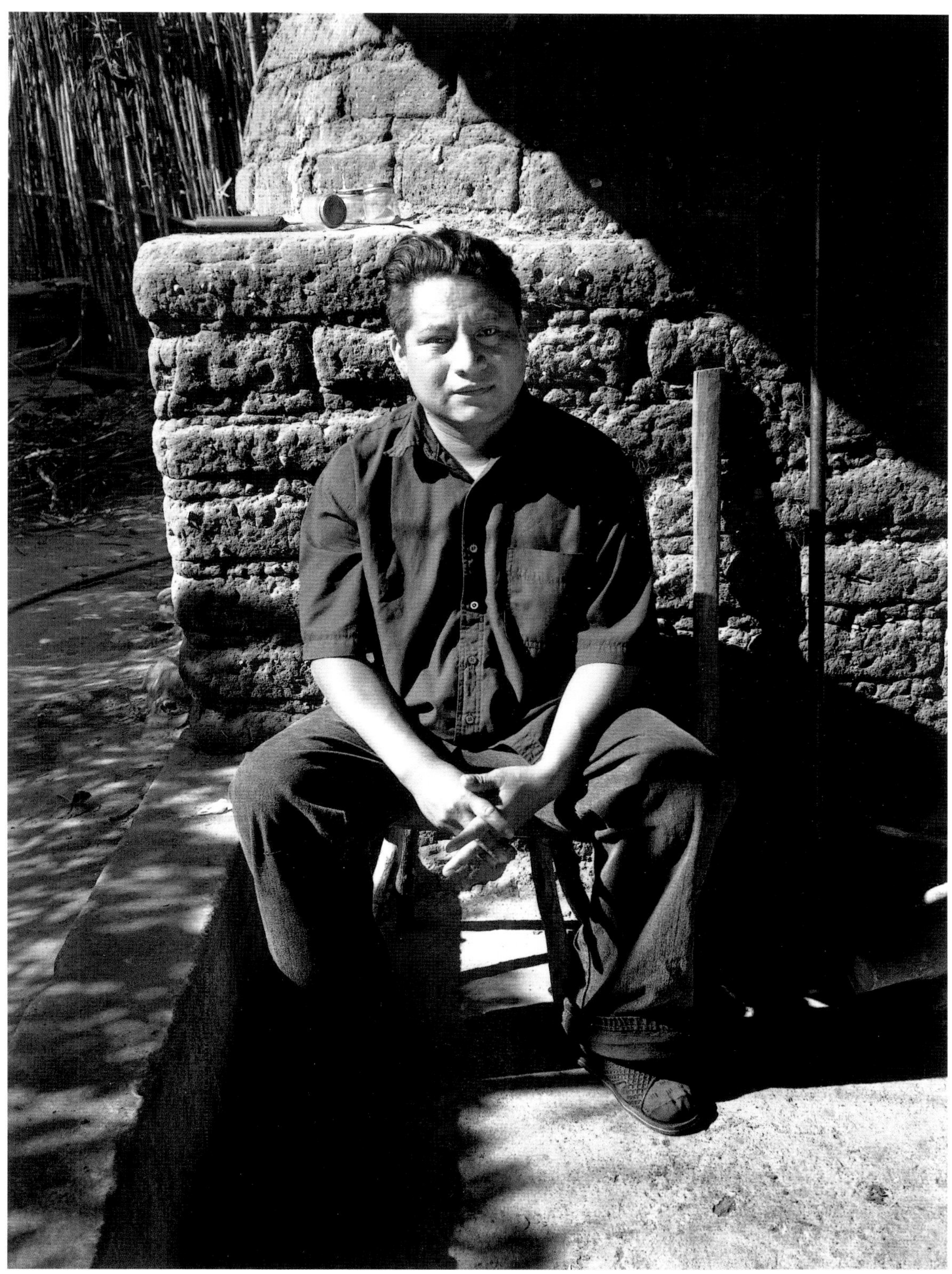

Eloy Santiago. La Unicń. 2006.

Pablo Vásquez
San Martín Tilcajete

OF THE DOZENS OF FIESTAS celebrated every year in San Martín, Carnaval is Pablo Vásquez's favorite. Boys coated in tractor grease dress up as devils and roam the streets for three days, shaking cowbells and brandishing staffs. A mock wedding is staged, with bride and bridesmaids in drag. Boys and, more recently, girls dress up as old people and dance to music from the village band. "Two years ago I was the groom, three years ago I was a girl in a short skirt," Pablo says.

Observing the holidays is part of being a good Catholic, and Pablo is in fact hardworking and religious. He leads a church youth group, the Divine Light of Angels, and works as a carpenter and electrician. He traveled to Mexico City to see the Pope on his last visit. He carves pyramids of skeletons, angels, and devils—theatrical allegories depicting the dilemma of man, poised between good and evil. He puts himself in his carvings. "I'm one of the skeletons," he says. His father, Inocencio, also makes skeletons—fifty per order—but the family's house is still known as "the house of the devils," in honor of Carnaval.

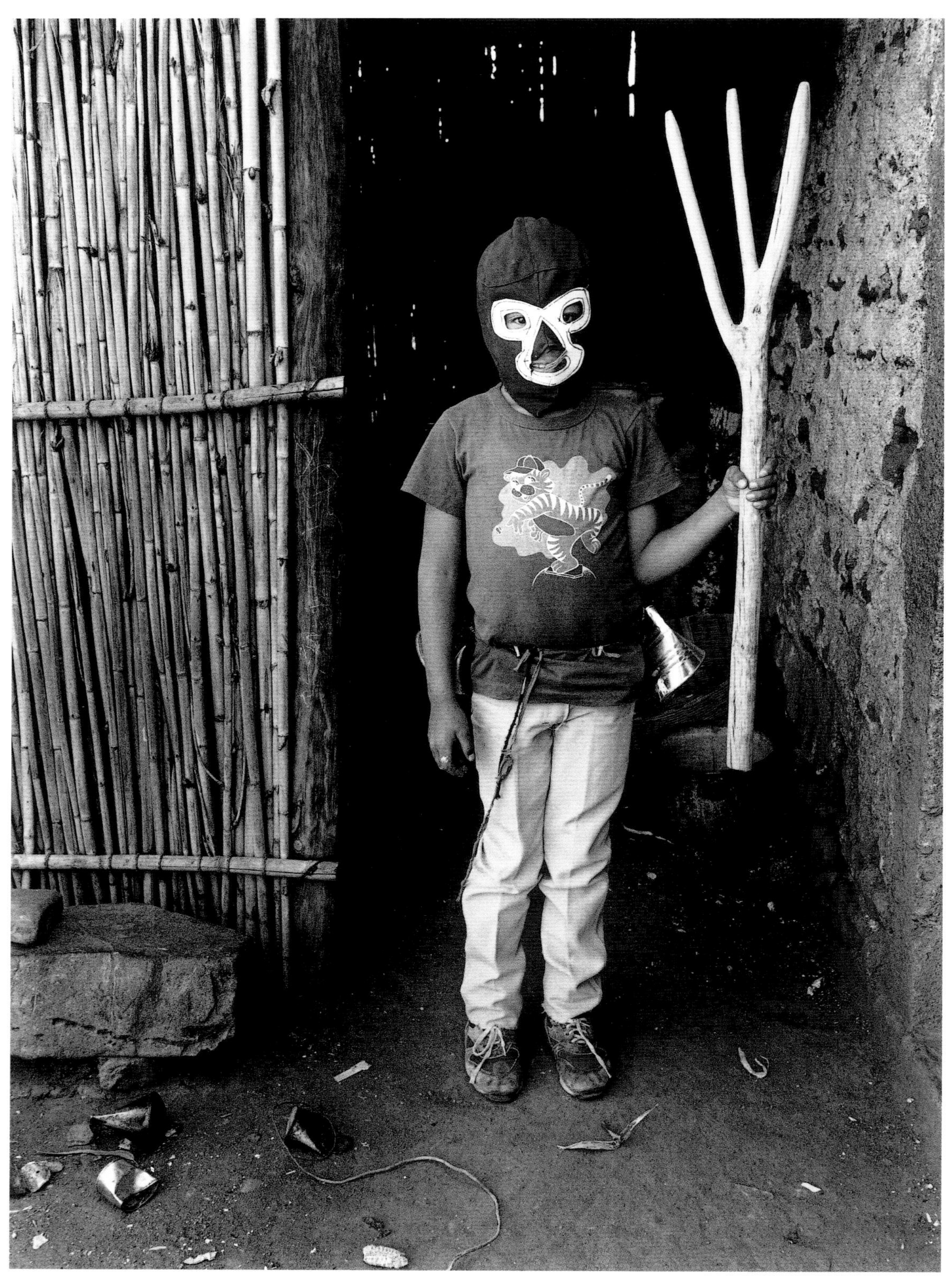

Pablo Vásquez. Carnaval. San Martín. 1990.

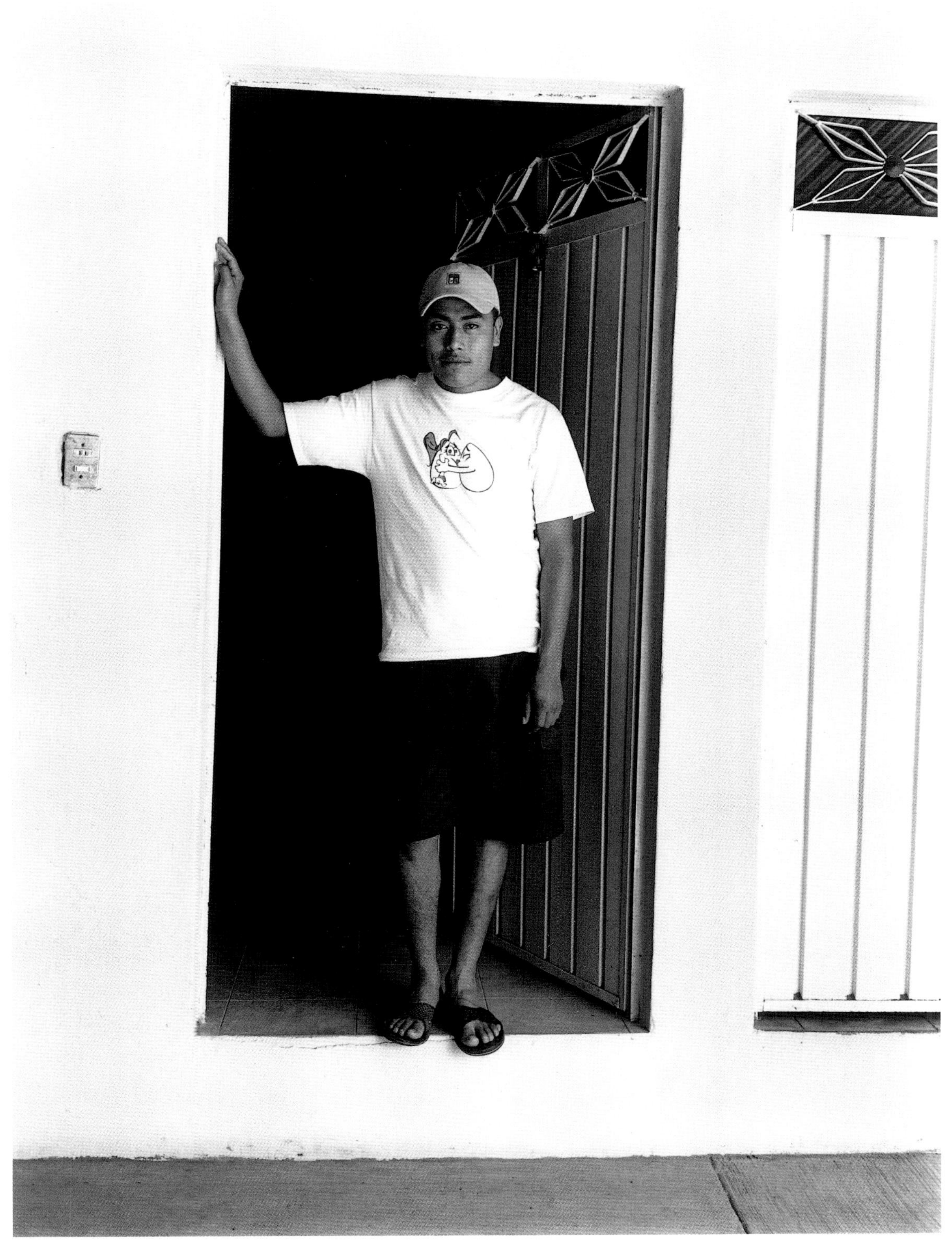

Pablo Vásquez. San Martín. 2004.

Fiestas in Oaxaca

People come to Oaxaca for the fiestas. Tourists may come to see ruins and *mojados* may sneak back to see friends and family, but these things are incidental. Americans looking for something different and campesinos longing for something familiar find what they're seeking at a Oaxacan fiesta.

Enduring all expectations, the fiesta is a kind of divinity, timeless and eternal—destined to survive free trade, political revolution, and the implacable forces of globalization that have caused so many other things to change. The pyramids of Monte Albán will crumble to dust before the fiesta disappears. As old as God, it seems certain to outlive Him: centuries-old Catholic churches stand empty and untended across the state, even as the celebrations honoring their saints and saviors grow and multiply each year.

Most tourists know all about the Day of the Dead in November, the Night of the Radishes in December, and the Guelaguetza dance pageant in July. That doesn't begin to cover it.

Hardly a week goes by in a village without some orgy of consumption. The list of fiestas is eye-popping. There is Christmas, Easter, Carnaval, Three King's Day, All Soul's Day, Independence Day, Constitution Day, Benito Juarez Day, and Worker's Day. There are days for the saints, days for the Virgin, days commemorating military victories, days commemorating defeats, days for teachers, masons, and mailmen, days for doctors, architects, and journalists. Finally, there are the rites of passage: an endless parade of weddings, baptisms, birthdays, confirmations, *quinceaños*, and so on, all cause for extended celebration.

I wrote that in 1990. The list has only grown since then. In San Martín, a group led by one of the carvers has built an amphitheater on a hill above the church so that the village can stage its own Guelaguetza. Another group organized by the priest has started a fiesta to commemorate Oaxaca's Indian martyrs, Jacinto de los Ángeles and Juan Bautista, defenders of the faith who were killed by idolaters in 1700 and beatified three centuries later.

Fiestas have also gotten bigger. Food, flowers, and fireworks—the high arts in Mexico—are everywhere more abundant. Creaky, dilapidated carnival rides and old video games—expelled hand-me-downs from the States—have found their way into the village square, where they stay busy far into the night. Government and residents foot the bill together—the former deriving much of its income from oil sales to the United States, the latter deriving much of their income from relatives *in* the States or tourists *from* the States. If the business of America is business, the business of the Oaxacan village, where business opportunities are few, is the fiesta.

Things are even wilder in the city. In hillside *colonias* where the acoustics are good, the sounds of bottle rockets and brass bands can be heard every night of the year, mingled with the responsive braying of donkeys and barking dogs. Each of the state's seventy-two hundred localities manifests its own variant of the nation's revelrous culture, and as people from these places have moved to the capital in search of jobs, their distinctive customs have been adapted and adopted by their new neighbors. Thus does the Vela of San Gerónimo, a fiesta honoring the saint who translated the Bible from Greek to Latin, get transplanted from the Isthmus and become the Vela Jiménez, a dance celebrating the high spirits and warm feelings of Mr. and Mrs. Jiménez. There are now a dozen such private balls held across the city each year. Somewhere in Oaxaca—at this very moment—a band is playing, people are dancing, and a fiesta is in full swing.

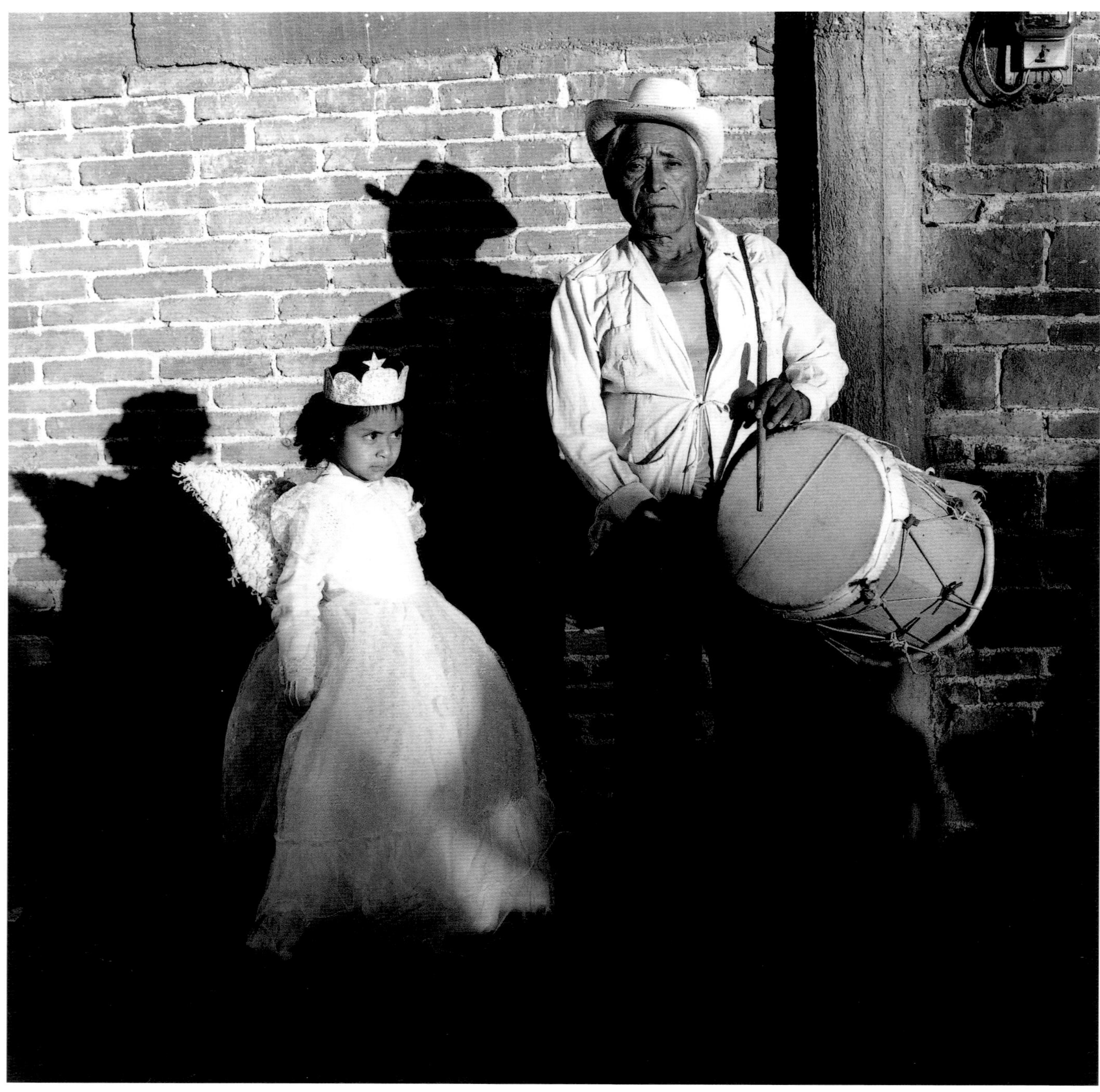

Fiesta honoring patron saint. San Martín. 1989.

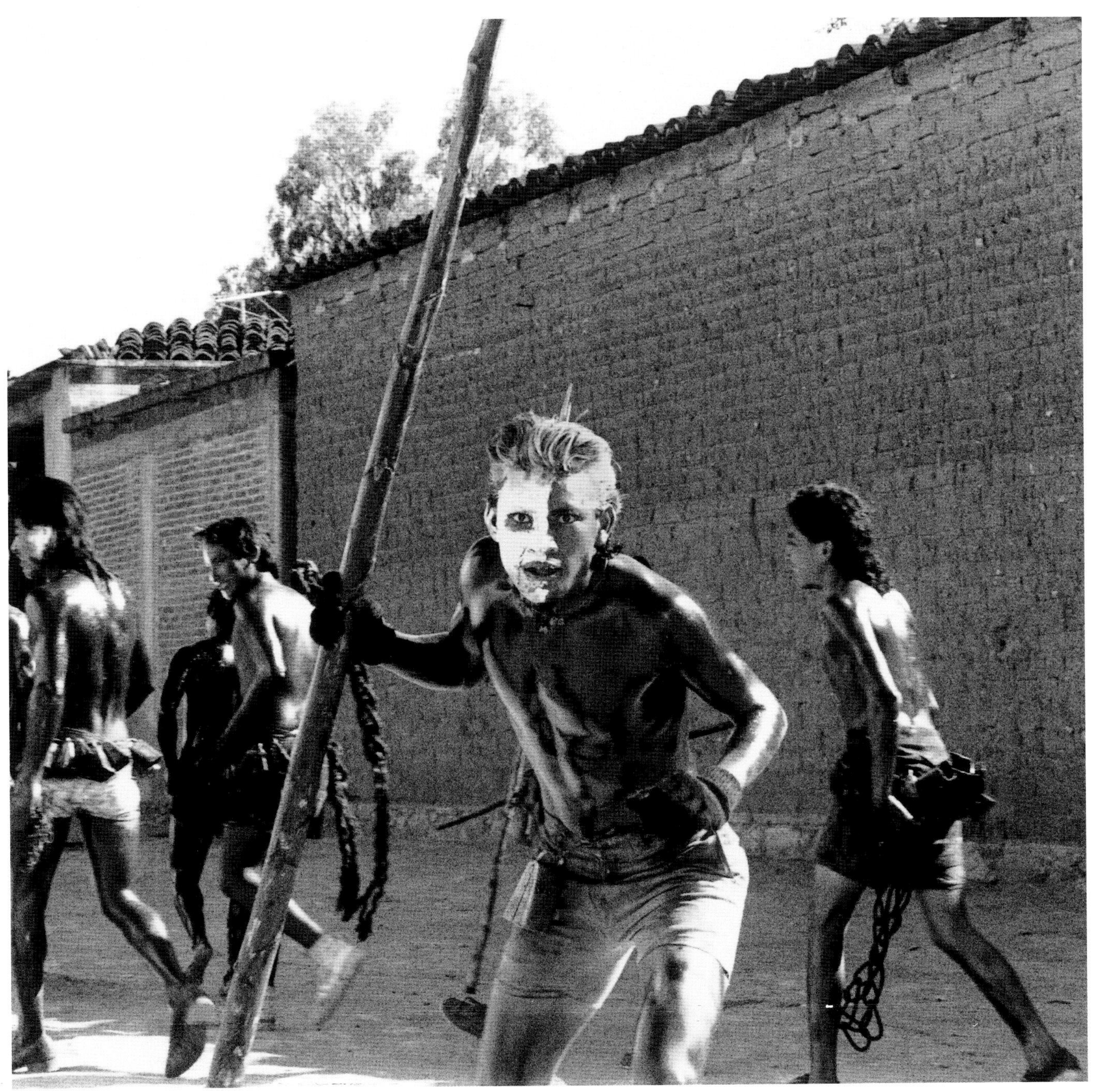

Carnaval. San Martín. 1990.

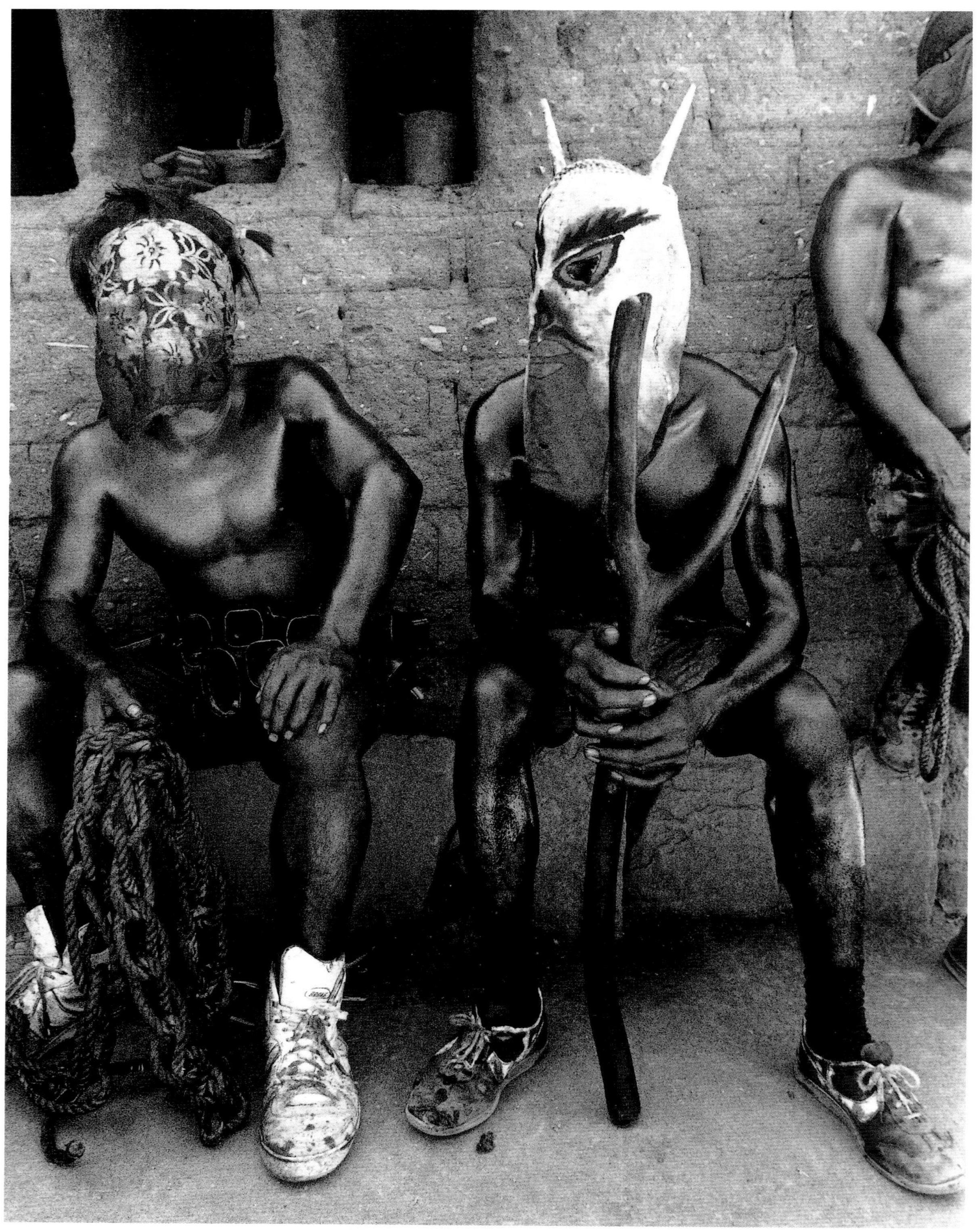

Carnaval. San Martín. 1990.

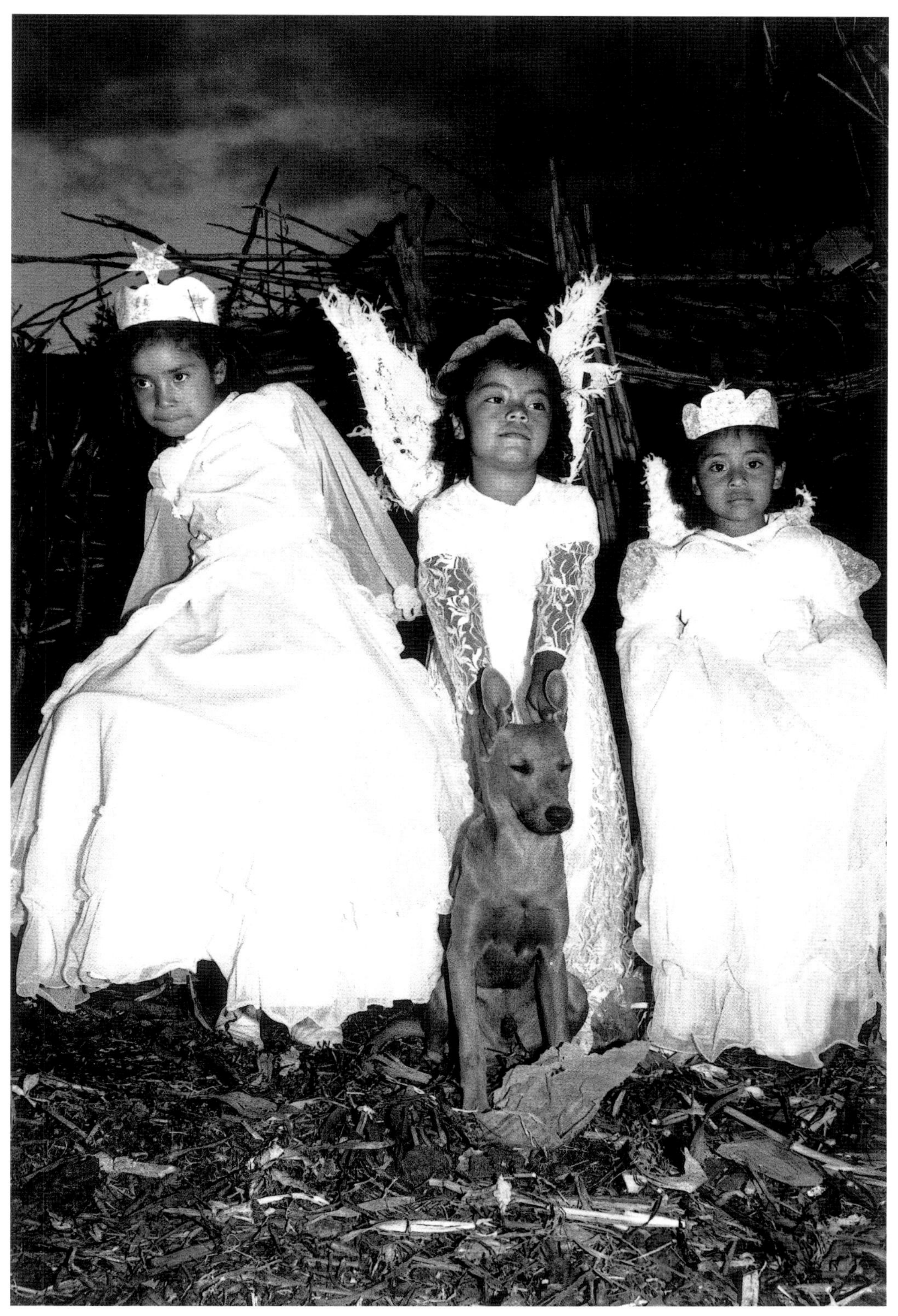

Fiesta honoring patron saint. San Martín. 1989.

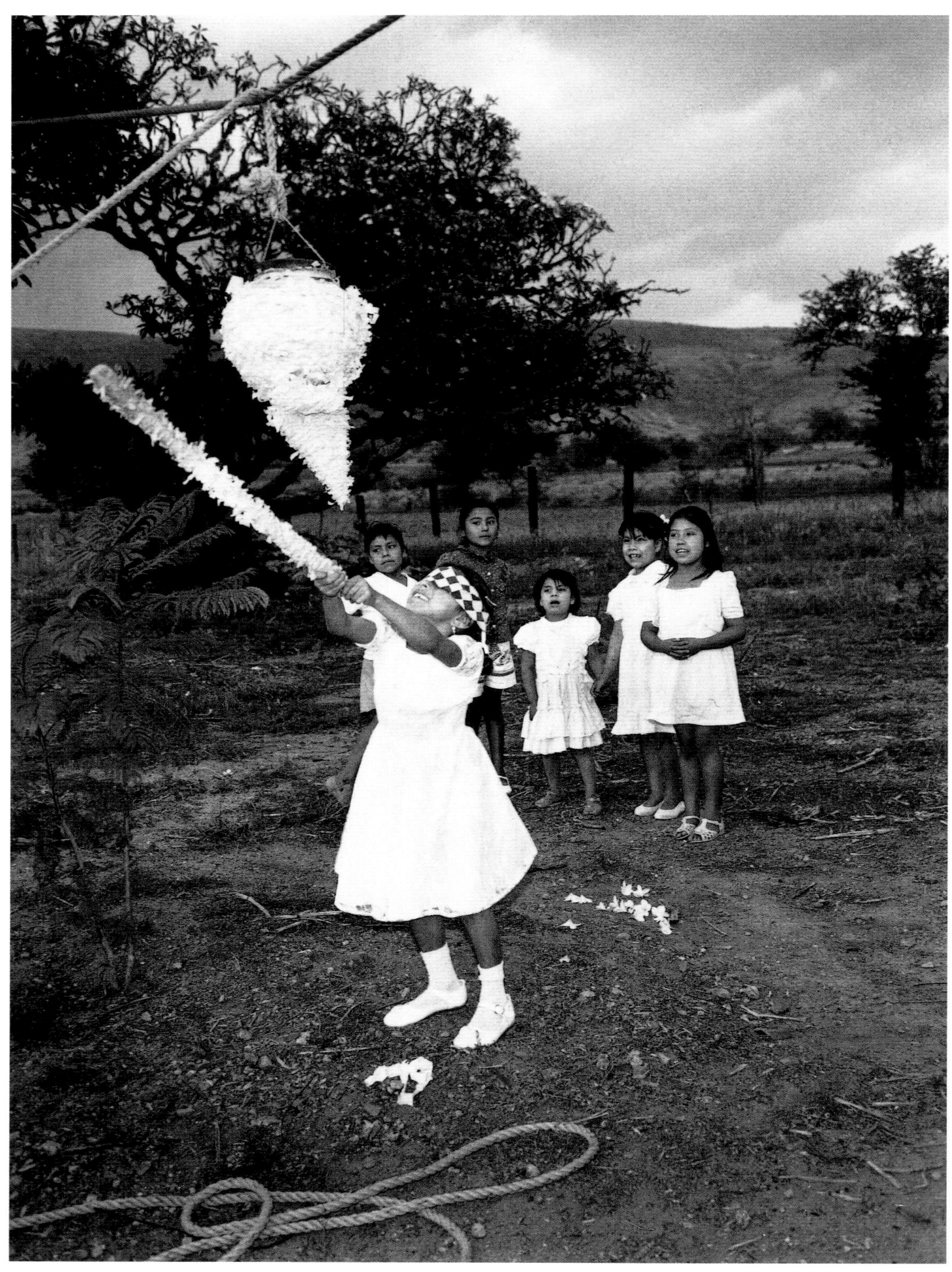

Blanca Cruz's birthday. San Martín. 1990.

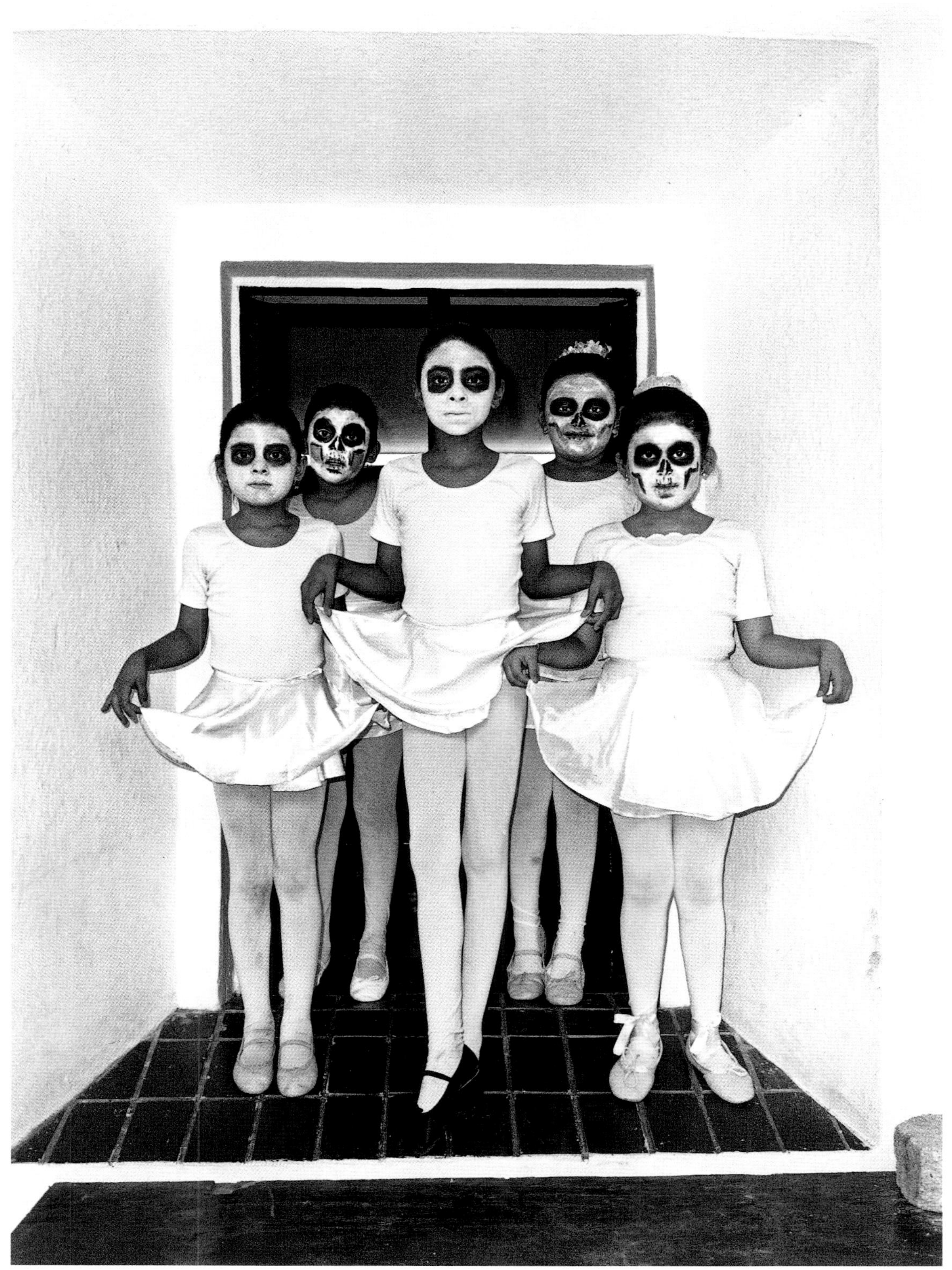

Day of the Dead. Oaxaca. 2004.

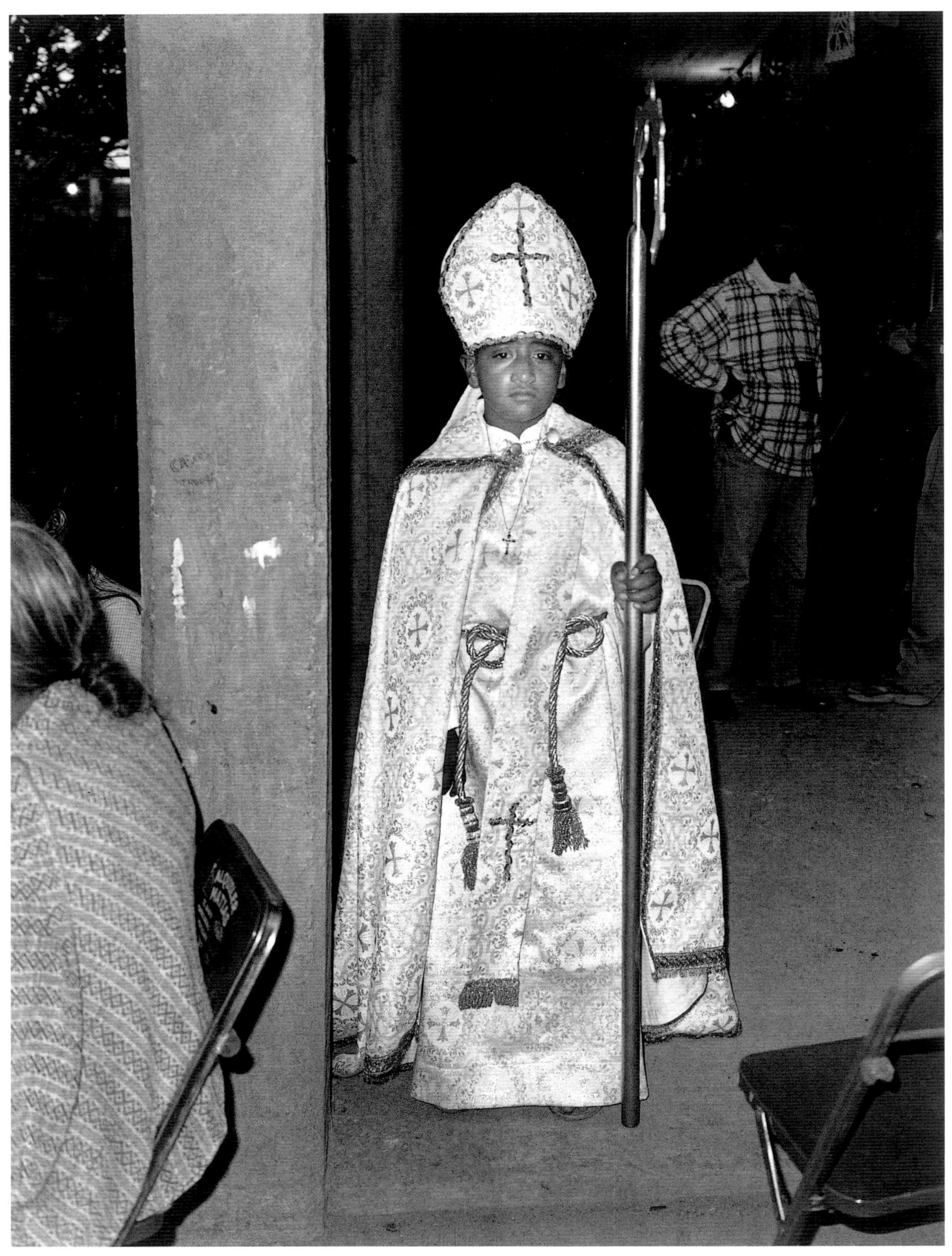

Fiesta honoring patron saint. San Martín. 2004.

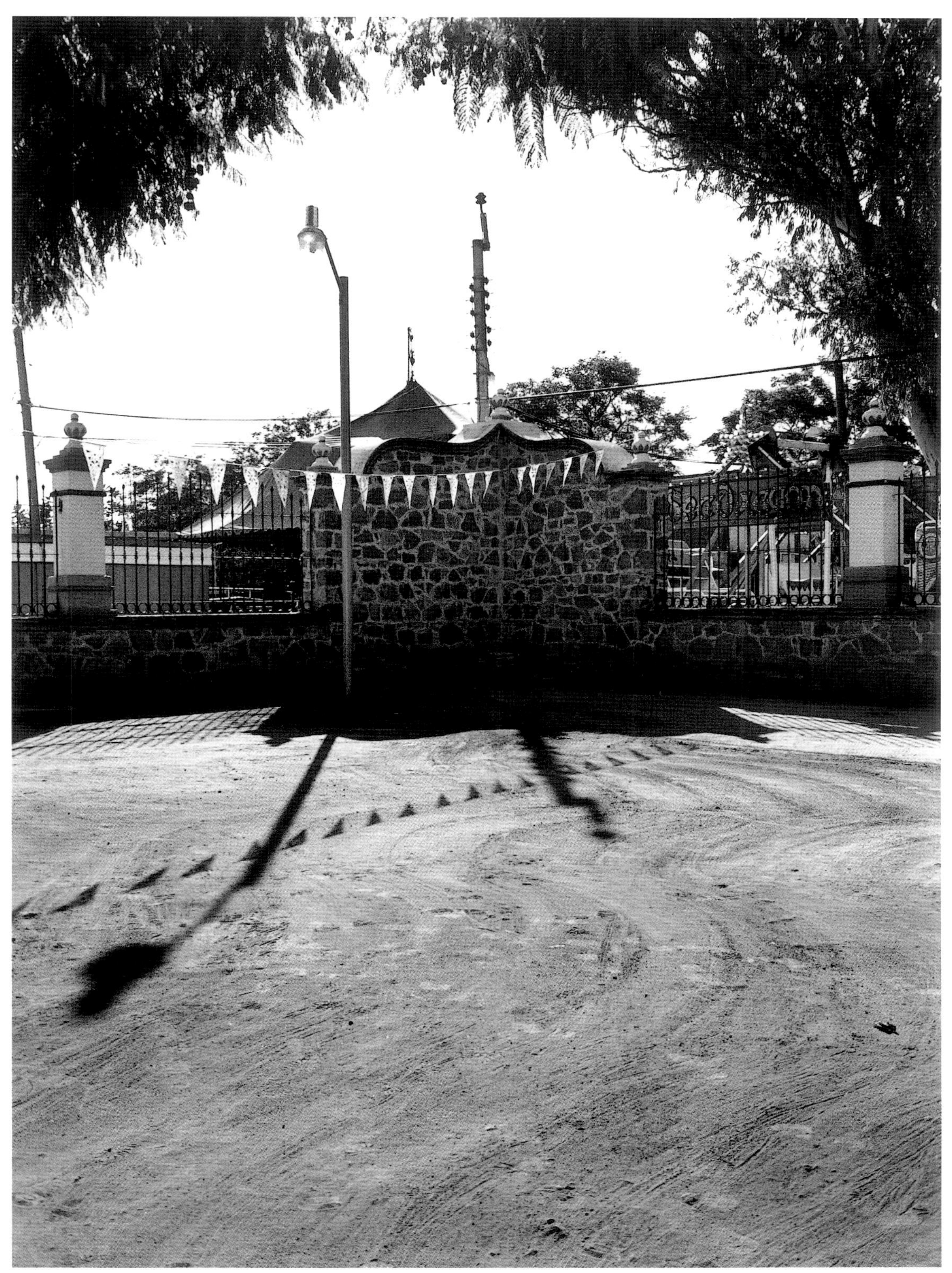

Churchyard. San Martín. 2004.

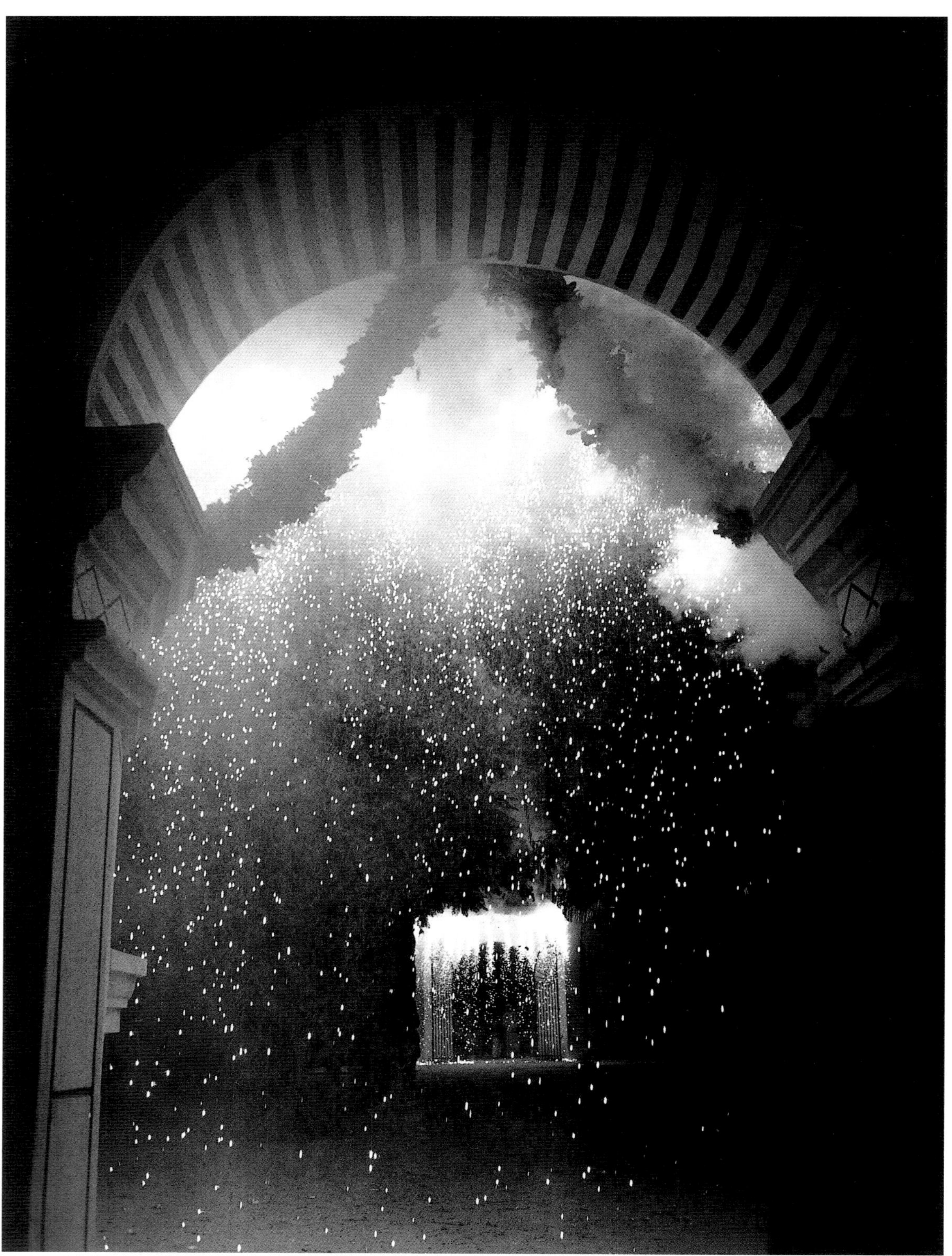

Fireworks under church arch at fiesta honoring patron saint. San Martín. 2004.

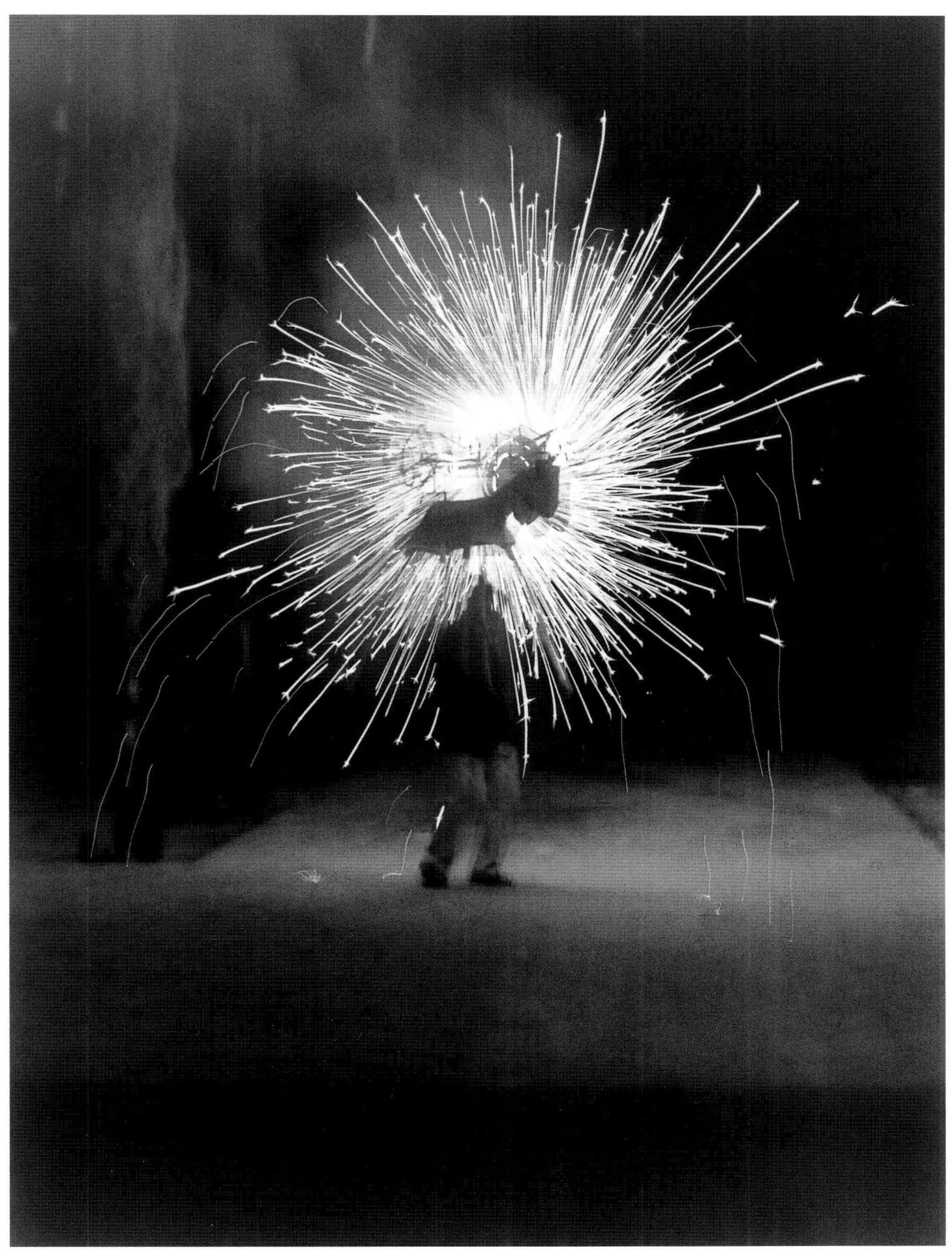

Fireworks in churchyard at fiesta honoring patron saint. San Martín. 2004.

Conclusion

Oaxaca has too many carvers. No one knows this better than the carvers themselves. Some of the most talented and successful among them would rather be doing other things. The state *needs* them to do other things. But the state is a failure in so many ways—its people so poorly prepared, their options so few, the hurdles to their prosperity so high and so many—that *alebrije*-making lives on as a popular calling long after it should have dissipated like a mirage. And so Blanca Cruz, who wanted to teach preschool, becomes a carver after discovering that Oaxaca's education system, though it consumes half the state's budget, is an almighty child abuser rotten to the core. Antonio Aragón's brother finds that neither his degree in administration nor his courses in computers and English are good enough to give him the skills or connections he needs to get a good job, so he paints carvings instead. Alejandrino Fuentes finds his degree in engineering to be worth less than his machete. For fifty years, the state has been made poorer by the artisans' inability to pursue their dreams. On a recent international test of student reading skills, Oaxaca's scores were the lowest of any state in Mexico—and Mexico's ranked thirty-seventh of the forty countries that took the test. I love my Blanca Cruz skeleton with its dyed-pink, maguey-fiber hair, but Blanca should be teaching! And yet in a system that fails to train its teachers, that pays and promotes its employees on the basis of how many protests they attend, that sells grades and extorts money from parents, that fails to get rid of criminals who beat and rape young students, that utterly fails to teach children the most basic skills of literacy and numeracy—in such a system, who can blame an earnest village girl for feeling like a good horse on a sloppy track?

"They put up with anything!" our son marveled after a week in Oaxaca. All the snags and depravations that the *mojado* flees fall like blinding snow on the people who stay behind. For our son it begins with the lack of drinkable tap water, but he could have started anywhere. Forty percent of the state's population live in extreme poverty. More than two thousand villages lack running water or schools. Job growth is slow, and purchasing power weak. There is little consumer credit. Houses are paid for in cash. Few people have bank accounts because few save or have savings and because the country's banks failed in 1994 so people don't trust them. Business credit is also tight. (NAFTA may have opened the borders to trade, but try getting a loan on a warehouse to take advantage of it.) Banks are afraid to lend because default rates are high and the law makes asset recovery difficult. There are no real capital markets, so sustaining growth is difficult; entrepreneurs like farmer Miguel Jiménez go as far as their individual efforts take them. Assembling land to farm or build housing is hard because villages that have controlled their land collectively for centuries do not like selling it to the outsiders that a free market inevitably brings.

Risk management is hard in a cash-poor society. Most carvers are one misfortune away from ruin—or being forced to leave everything to prevent ruin. Without health insurance, fathers often become *mojados* when their children get sick.

Initiative is strangled by the state, which owns too much of the economy and meddles with the rest where it can. Entrepreneurs brave or foolish enough to follow the rules for starting a business are tortured and killed off by a thousand pinpricks of regulation, irrationality, and delay. A Canadian company spent $41 million seeking approvals to do business in Mexico before giving up and going home; the federal water authority went for a year without processing a single permit; the former mayor of Oaxaca had to fight for months with the electricity monopoly to correct a billing error that was costing his business thousands of dollars per month. Everyone has a story.

Most people who make a living avoid the government entirely. Oaxaca has among the lowest tax-collection rates in the Western Hemisphere. "You see more money, you see more liberty, you see progress—what's disappearing is the state," the former mayor of Oaxaca says. "The disorder you see is the lack of a state. Millions of people have renounced it."

A casual lawlessness pervades, veiling and choking life's dealings large and small. Corruption in government is matched by a smiling duplicity and disregard outside it. We have lost thousands of dollars to good-natured carvers who failed to fill their orders or keep their promises, and we know dealers who have lost much more. The courts are clogged with suits alleging breach of contract. Bribery is expected. Intellectual property rights are neither respected nor understood: videos in most villagers' homes are blurry copies. Political violence is not uncommon and is usually blamed on the government, but the truth is there are many likely perpetrators—drug traffickers, rival politicians or businessmen, religious factions, neighbors fighting over land.

The everyday chaos caused by inept or absent government and a rebellious people is nowhere more vivid than on the road. Driving is the most frightening and frustrating thing about Oaxaca—the thing that makes you feel like you have indeed come to a Third World country. Navigating the city is like being inside a video game. Lanes and stop signs are not respected. Drivers run red lights with impunity in front of police. City buses on four-lane highways make left turns from the right-hand lane. Traffic is almost always bad on a certain bridge crossing the Atoyac River because the stoplight on one side is controlled by the city and the stoplight on the other side is controlled by the state, and the two are out of sync. Pollution is bad and hard to control because the aging vehicles that emit most of it are not registered. Hit-and-run accidents are not uncommon—it happened to us—and are not simply an expression of the *desmadroso* character but a rational response to a justice system that is not always just. (The parents of our son's best friend in Oaxaca had their life savings wiped out and went deep into debt after the dad got into a car accident and was outmaneuvered by well-connected lawyers and a crooked judge.) The advice an American gave us us about driving outside the city was never drive alone, never drive at night, and never stick around if you hit someone. That was in 1986. There are a lot more cars now and a lot more accidents.

The carvers, who enjoy their cars, recoil more at the degeneracy of government than at the disorder its absence creates. The arrival of democracy seems not to have brightened their attitude about politics nor made them any better at it. Voter turnout, like the tax-collection rate, is low. Unrest is high. Protests like those that paralyzed the state in 2006 reflect the growing competition for political power and the continued failure of the people to produce better leaders and govern themselves effectively.

The problems of the state are the problems of the village. Two years before the standoff between the teachers union and the governor, the entire volunteer police force in San Martín walked off the job when the village's top judicial officer freed his ne'er-do-well nephew from jail after a fracas. Other municipal officials did unauthorized work on the junior high school and incurred a huge fine from the state. A computer library was opened at great expense and closed the following year by a new president with other priorities. The village lost several hundred acres to neighboring Zimatlán in a land dispute that many say was mishandled.

Complaints about kickbacks and embezzlement have become more common as villages have been given more money to manage. Transparency and accountability remain elusive goals. It is hard to know whom to trust or what to believe. Interests and motives are masked, wealth and power lie hidden, and events rarely go down as reported. The real authors of mayhem often are not exposed. Media accounts are as untrustworthy as the outlets that produce them and the sources they depend on. (Reader be warned.) Money for serious research is scarce and data often unreliable. Gossip, rumor, superstition, and misunderstanding hold campesinos in thrall to stories that are not easy to sort out or verify. "Little village, big hell," Zeny Fuentes says, repeating a popular saying.

Smart people are fooled by the most basic things. Wealth, for instance: no one really knows how well or how poorly Oaxacans are doing because most of their business (70 percent and growing, by some estimates) is done off the books. Analysts at Sam's Club looked at their data and concluded that there were not enough people with enough money to justify opening a store. They changed their minds only after checking (at the urging of a state official) the zip codes of Sam's members at its store three hours away in Puebla and discovering how many were in fact from Oaxaca. To their amazement, the new store, far from the downtown tourist district, in 2005 ranked second in sales among Sam's stores in Mexico. Most purchases are paid for in cash and resold through the region's informal economy of family-run shops, eateries, and street vendors. Down the road from Sam's, the McDonald's Oaxacan franchise in 2005 also ranked number two in the country in sales. Domino's Pizza is doing well, too. All this in a state that gets more welfare money than any state in Mexico.

Indians in braids next to businessmen in suits, waiting on the checkout line at Sam's; girls on motorbikes, delivering pizza to buildings hundreds of years old; lines of residents half-a-mile long, waiting for their welfare checks on payday—Oaxacans are walking the uneven path to modernity that others have walked before them. As they do, they are falling farther behind the rest of Mexico, which is moving faster, and still farther behind the United States, which is moving faster still. If the daughters of campesino carvers now come to check out the tourist shops in Oaxaca, the fad among their better-off countrymen is to come check out the Oaxacans with their curious crafts and fiestas. The carvers have become exotic, even to their fellow citizens. Thus are new markets created and traditions sustained.

The irony that beauty should be created by people who in happier circumstances might be doing other things makes Oaxaca a bittersweet place, particularly for those without a *desmadroso* streak—but is it really that much more so than anywhere else? Is it really so much worse to have too many carvers than too many lawyers? Is it really so rare to do your work for people you may not understand and who may not understand you? Art born of hunger and fed by a foreign Muse is art nonetheless. And even if 99.9 percent of the carvings *aren't* art, even if they're just curios for the tourist or worse—still they are bound to outlast oil and anything else Mexicans might extract from the ground to meet the world's needs. Like fireworks at a fiesta, there will always be carvers who find magic in the trees to charm those who would be charmed.

Last night a possum got into our basement and damaged several carvings. There was a time when this would have mattered more, but this morning I find myself worrying instead about the carvers—whether this one has gotten over her dengue fever or that one is going blind with cataracts, whether the carver who serenaded me on my birthday is coming to the States anytime soon, whether his daughter whom we have always liked might like our son. The happiest by-products of commerce are the friendships it kindles between otherwise distant people—relations that endure long after the spark of interest that started them has gone out. It took some time to appreciate the fact, but the carvers have always meant more to us than their work.

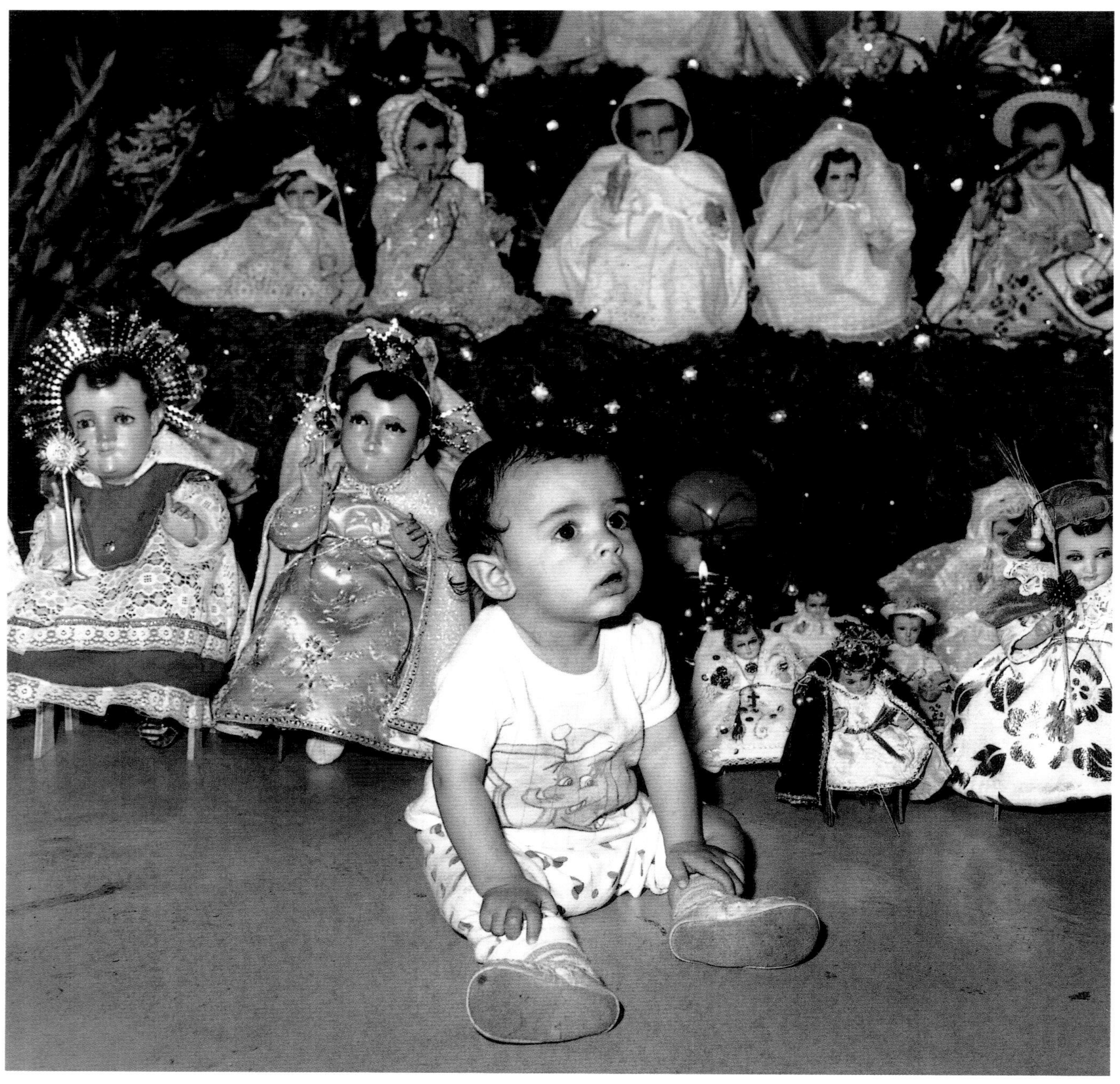

Edwin Ragan Barbash. Oaxaca, 1990.

"Pastor, I have some photos to show you," Inocencio "Chencho" Vásquez said, calling me by the name the carvers call me (a Spanish translation of my real name, which is hard for them to pronounce). We hadn't seen Chencho or his family for six years and had dropped by without warning to catch up. We learned that his little sister had gotten married, that business was good (it was November, the onset of tourist season), and that his wife was laid up with a kidney stone. We reminisced about the time I dressed as a priest and officiated at the mock wedding at Carnaval. This reminded Chencho of the snapshots my wife had given him of the event, back in 1989, and he retrieved them from an inner room to show me.

Seeing the images of the hectic scene, I was unexpectedly moved. There I was—fifteen years younger, with the thick dark beard I no longer have and the toddler, my son, who is now a man. On the back of one of the photos, someone had written: "Un recuerdo del Gringo Pastor"—a memory (or perhaps memento) of the Gringo Pastor.

"Do you want it?" Chencho asked, breaking my reverie.

My wife, who knows better than I what photos mean to people and what this one meant to Chencho, shook her head for me in answer.

"That's okay," I said after a pause. "We have our pictures, too."

Dedicated with love to Murray and Lillian Barbash

Project director: Mary Wachs
Manuscript editing: Karla Eoff
Art director: David Skolkin
Manufactured in Singapore
10 9 8 7 6 5 4 3 2 1

Library of Congress Cataloging-in-Publication Data
Barbash, Shepard, 1957-
   Changing dreams : a generation of Oaxaca's woodcarvers / photographs by Vicki Ragan ;
Text by Shepard Barbash.
      p. cm.
   ISBN 978-0-89013-505-1 (clothbound : alk. paper) 1. Wood-carvers—Mexico—Oaxaca. 2.
Wood-carving—Mexico—Oaxaca. 3. Folk art—Mexico—Oaxaca. I. Ragan, Vicki, 1951- II.
Title.

   TT199.7.B35 2007
   736'.4097274—dc22

                    2007019535

Museum of New Mexico Press
Post Office Box 2087
Santa Fe, New Mexico 87504
www.mnmpress.org